# *RACHEL WILSON*

## *and her Quaker Mission in 18th Century America*

*The Story of her Religious Visit to America*
*1768 – 69*

*as contained in the pages of her journal, transcribed by her daughter, and set in the context of contemporary American Quaker history*

**Front cover** *©The British Library Board. Map ref. *71490.(150.)*

"A New and Correct Map of the United States of North America" by Abel Buell, a silversmith in New Haven, claiming to be "the first ever published, engraved and finished by one man, and an American", published in 1784, eight years after the Declaration of American Independence but only one year after the cessation of hostilities with the British. Rushed out to appeal to a new, patriotic market, it ignores the western claims of the Native American Indians, the Spanish and the French and adopts a new meridian through Philadelphia, while several parts of it were obsolescent, dating back to the time of Rachel Wilson's visit or earlier.

## RACHEL WILSON

"having a fine figure, and striking presence, ... gifted with a clear, distinct voice, and all the pathos of pure, unstudied eloquence"

"prizing the privileges she enjoyed, and the drawings of divine wisdom in her soul, she was much led into solitude and secret retirement before the Lord, only choosing such company as might be profitable to her; and carefully dwelling under the forming hand, she witnessed a growth in virtue and piety, and became fitted for the work of the ministry, into which she was called about the 18th year of her age. She experienced a growth and increase in heavenly wisdom."

Her ministry "was remarkably interesting and eloquent" and those not in profession with Friends flocked to hear her. "She was eminently qualified for that service, explaining the way of life and salvation in a manner that reached the witness in the hearts of the hearers, whereby many were brought to the acknowledgement of the truth."

# RACHEL WILSON

## AND HER QUAKER MISSION IN 18TH CENTURY AMERICA

by

GEOFFREY BRAITHWAITE

ISBN 978-1-85072-412-4



Published and Printed by
Sessions Books
York, England

# CONTENTS

**Dedicated to my wife, Molly**

## Acknowledgements

I give my sincere thanks to the Librarian and staff at Friends House Library, London; to the National Archives, Kew; to the British Library; to Rachel's 'literary' descendants for their writings – Deborah Braithwaite (daughter), John Somervell, Anna Lloyd Braithwaite Thomas, Elizabeth Braithwaite Emmott and William Charles Braithwaite (great, great grandchildren) and Janet Whitney (great, great, great granddaughter); to Thomas O'Brien Baker and Gerald Drewett for reading and commenting on the draft text and most of all to my wife, Molly, not only for much constructive comment and proof-reading but also for expanding my life's horizons and inspiring me to discover my Quaker ancestors, most notably Rachel.

Net proceeds from the sale of this book will be donated to Quaker charities, including The Quaker Tapestry, Kendal, UK; Quaker Voluntary Action and Friends International Center, Ramallah.

THE WILSON FAMILY

Those living at the time of Rachel's visit to America (Aug 1768 - Dec 1769) are shown in bold type.

**Isaac Wilson** 1715-1785 m.1741 to **Rachel Wilson** 1720-1775

Children & *grandchildren*

**Dorothy (Doly)** 1741-1774 m.1765 to John Whitwell 1735-1782
*__Isaac__ b.1765; Hannah & Rachel (twins b. and d. Jul 1768);*
*__Hannah__ b.May 1769; John b.1773 d.1775; Rachel b.Jul 1774*
**Deborah (Deby)** 1743-1821 m.1767 to George Braithwaite 1746-1812
*__Rachel__ b.Jul 1768; Alice b.1770 & Sarah b.1772 (both d. young);*
*Deborah b.1775; George b.1777; Isaac b.1781; Dorothy b.1783*
**Rachel** b.1746 m. to Joseph Smith – *no children*
**John** 1748-1801 m.1779 to Sarah Dillworth
*Isaac b.1780 (d. young); Esther b.1756; Rachel b.1783;*
*Isaac b.1784; William b.1786; Dillworth b.1788 (d. young)*
**Anthony** 1750-1768 (Sept)
**Elizabeth (Betty)** 1753-1821 m.1786 to Josiah Messer
*3 sons and 4 daughters b.1787-1796*
**Mary (Molly)** 1755-1836 m.1781 to George Stacey
*2 sons and 4 daughters b.1783-1793*
Isaac b.1757 d. after 4 months
**Sarah (Sally)** b.1759 m. to John Abbott – *no children*
**Margaret (Peggy)** 1761-1840 m.1790 to Hadwen Bragg
*3 sons and 3 daughters b.1791-1801*

*Later Braithwaite (B.) and Wilson (W.) connections (see acknowledgements):*

*G'son, Isaac B. (as above) 1781-1861 m.Anna Lloyd 7 sons, 2 daughters*
*Gt g'son, Joseph Bevan B. 1818-1905 m.Martha Gillett 3 sons, 6 daughters*
*Gt gt g'children, Anna Lloyd B.Thomas 1854-1947;Mary Caroline B. 1857-1935 m. Willis Norton Whitney; Elizabeth B. 1858-1946 m. George Henry Emmott; William Charles B. 1862-1922*
*Gt gt gt g'daughter, Janet Whitney b.1894*

*G'son, William W. (as above) 1786-1840 m.Hannah Jowitt 7 sons, 3 daughters*
*Gt g'daughter, Rachel W. 1823-1889 m.John Somervell 2 sons, 2 daughters*
*Gt gt g'son, John Somervell 1857-1943*

The Wilsons' family residence and shearman dyer business, Kendal

*(From an early engraving held at Friends House Library, London)*

# RACHEL WILSON

(1720-1775)

## AND HER QUAKER MISSION IN 18TH CENTURY AMERICA

### Prologue

### JOURNAL OF MY GREAT GREAT GREAT GREAT GRANDMOTHER

I can trace my Quaker ancestry back to the earliest years of the Society of Friends and to the birthplace of Quakerism in '1652 country' in the north of England: two Quaker parents, four Quaker grandparents, eight Quaker great grandparents ... and predominantly Quaker intermarrying all the way back before that. In following my father's line, a George Braithwaite married a Deborah Wilson in 1767 – both from long-standing Quaker families in Kendal, Westmoreland. George's ancestor, another George, had become a Friend in 1655. Deborah's mother was Rachel Wilson – my great, great, great, great grandmother – who had married Isaac Wilson in 1741. Rachel was born in 1720 – the year when her 109 years old great grandfather, William Wilson, had died "by falling from a haystack". He was in his forties and fifties at the height of Quaker persecution in England and had been on a Quaker missionary visit to Germany.

A Friends' school was founded in Kendal in 1698. It progressed to the point where, in 1785, it passed to Quaker brothers Jonathan and John Dalton, the latter subsequently becoming famous as a scientist. They took over from the retiring headmaster who had originally set up his own writing school in Kendal, attended by Wilson children.

Rachel, having completed her education, became a Quaker 'minister' in 1738 at the age of 18. (Both her mother and, later, one of her daughters also were ministers.) When she was only 24 years old (and the mother of two small daughters), Rachel 'travelled in the ministry' for ten months, accompanied by another local Quaker, Jane Crosfield (or Rowlandson as she was then). They went to Liverpool, Warrington, Manchester, Chester, Matlock, Derby, Burton, Birmingham, Stourbridge, Worcester, Shrewsbury, Dolobran (home of the Quaker Lloyds), through Wales to Carmarthen and Swansea, then Bristol, Bath, Bridgewater, Taunton, Minehead, Launceston, Penzance, Lands End, Plymouth, Totnes, Exeter, Poole, Southampton, Godalming, Guildford, London, Chelmsford, Colchester, Ipswich, Woodbridge, Norwich, Spalding and finally made a hurried return home, almost certainly in response to news of the southward advance of Prince Charlie's troops in the Jacobite rebellion of 1745.[1] 6,000 reached Kendal in November and the Wilson family residence was commandeered to quarter army officers – a change from the usual Quaker travellers.

For the whole of her adult life, Rachel was frequently away from home on 'religious visits'. In a book of family memoirs published in 1909, we read that she paid such a visit to the American colonies in 1768 and 1769, a little prior to the Revolutionary War.[2] These memoirs reveal the incredible nature of her travels in America – the subject of this book. In it we read:

"This journey was performed almost entirely on horseback. It covered many thousand miles through districts very imperfectly cleared, in Pennsylvania, New Jersey, Virginia, North and South Carolina, New York and New England. Her simple narrative (still preserved amongst the family records) gives a vivid picture of the toil and occasional peril then encountered. It is contained in three tiny books which have every appearance of having been written during the journey, often under difficulty.

"One extract must suffice –

'Wm. Paine sett us to ye [the] River Don 12 miles which we ferried over without much danger, tho' ye water high and ye current Rapid. We could not cross hogin's Creek at ye usual place, ye water was so high yt [that] we went a By path yt night 15 miles in ye woods with some difficulty and Lodged with a friendly man a Presbeterian; his son was remarkably kind & wished it had bin in his power to have done better for us; he gave up his own bed for my companion & me & spread Skins upon ye ground for Samuel & Micajah so that we put on tolerable well. In ye morning he helped us over hogins Creek, swam our horsis & we went over on a Log tho' not without fear, our saddles & Bags Being first borne over.'"

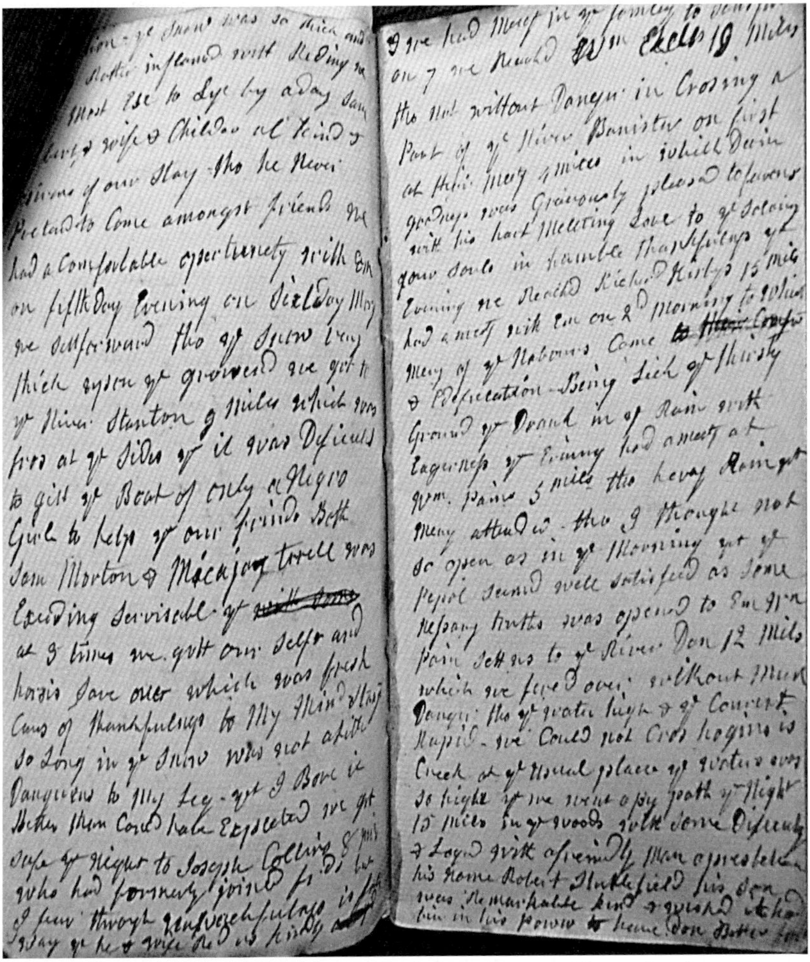

Page from original journal *at Friends House Library,London*

In 2008 I held these three little notebooks – priceless family treasures – in my hands. It was a deeply moving moment as I absorbed their extraordinary power. They transported me through the unbroken line of my Quaker ancestry – seven generations back to Rachel Wilson and, indeed, the three generations before her to the original Wilson and Braithwaite Quakers. This precious moment sowed the seed which germinated and grew into my resolve to discover the full account of Rachel's mission and, one day, to go to America and search out some of the places that she journeyed through (especially 'hogins Creek') and present day Quaker meetings that had their roots in the American colonies of 1768 and 1769. Her old-fashioned handwriting, compressed into these tiny pages and using the archaic language of her time, would have presented a daunting task, but, in beautiful writing, her daughter, Deborah Braithwaite, "carefully transcribed" the whole manuscript "for the Information and Benefit of her Children and near Relations". It is in a bound notebook that has also survived and is what I have used for my account now.

Rachel left at home her husband and children – seven daughters (three by now married) and two sons. Five were still under 20, including the invalid Anthony, aged 18, who had "scarce a day's health in ten years". Rachel's and Isaac's other child, Isaac, had died when only four months old in 1758. In an early letter home, Rachel is very mindful of the domestic burden falling on Isaac during her absence and on John (20) and Elizabeth (15) "both Capbale [capable] & willing to do their part."

Isaac has been described as a father who was one of a thousand in the tender care of their children. He wholeheartedly supported Rachel as she responded to God's callings to make religious visits, never more so than this one to America. Their love for each other and how keenly they felt their long separation shines through in their letters. A testimony to Isaac in the minutes of Middletown, Pennsylvania, Monthly Meeting reads: "His wife was much engaged from Home in the Cause of Truth, and though separation was a close Trial to them, yet he was always willing to give her up to the Service, frequently accompanying her to the neighbouring Meetings, and at all times strengthening and encouraging her to follow the pointings of Duty; being sensible that Obedience to Divine Requirings brings Peace." [3]

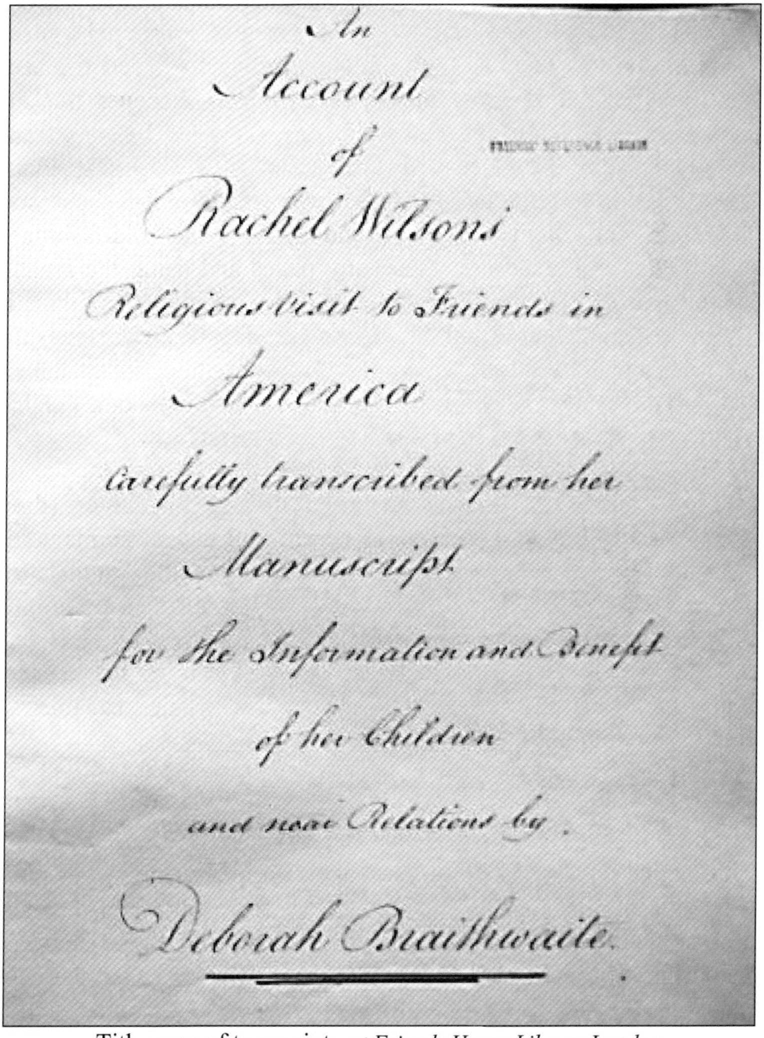

An
Account
of
Rachel Wilsons
Religious Visit to Friends in
America
carefully transcribed from her
Manuscript
for the Information and Benefit
of her Children
and near Relations by
Deborah Braithwaite

Title page of transcript *at Friends House Library,London*

We are looking at 1768 and well into the so-called 'quietist period' in the history of the Society of Friends – "the lull which followed the forty years' storm of bitter persecution [when] the Quakers settled down into a quiet, peaceable and respectable sect ... and there was very little revival of spiritual life. There were, however, many faithful men and women whose loving and devoted lives were true to the ideals of the early days of Quakerism".[4] Rachel was one of these women, knowing God as did the early Quakers, experiencing the same 'openings' and making every personal sacrifice that God called her to. As I read her journal and travelled beside her in spirit, my prayer was to experience these 'openings' myself.

I had been expecting the real interest to start after her arrival in America, but in fact her journal makes gripping reading even from Day 1 when she travelled by stagecoaches – in the state of the art 'flying machines' of the time – from the family home in Kendal to London.

After only a few pages I felt turned inside out. My prime object had been to recount an epic journey of two and a half centuries ago. Instead, I found myself accompanying my ancestor – this wonderful Quaker woman – soaking up her ministry as each day proceeded. The physical side became incidental to the spiritual. The past became the present. Rachel's words placed me in the 18th century. It was as if I had been there. I felt blessed.

Chapter 1

# QUAKER MINISTRY IN THE 18$^{TH}$ CENTURY

In old Quaker meeting houses up and down the country, both in Britain and in America, there is often a narrow raised platform with a row of seating, behind a waist-high partition or handrail, in the otherwise level meeting area. This was the 'ministers and elders gallery' and was where the Quaker ministers and elders sat, facing the rest of the meeting.

Ministers' gallery, Hertford Meeting House, England

Built in 1670 at a cost of £243, Hertford is the oldest purpose-built Quaker meeting house still standing in Britain. It was closed for two years from 1684 to 1686, because of damage by the authorities, but has been in continuous use as a meeting house ever since. John Woolman attended Quarterly Meeting at Hertford on 15$^{th}$ of 6$^{th}$ month, 1772.

In a meeting for worship the gathered worshippers wait in silence to experience God's presence in their midst and, if any of them is moved to do so in response to a calling from God, he or she will speak God's word – will 'minister' – to the rest of the meeting. The basic tenet of Quakerism has always been the individual's direct experience of God without the intervening offices of a priest, whether paid ('hireling') or otherwise. The silent waiting was and is the bedrock of meeting for worship and completely silent meetings were and still are common. At first sight, therefore, affording some kind of status to individual Quaker ministers may seem out of keeping. But some Quakers became regular preachers who were clearly gifted to voice God's message; they were recognised by their Meeting's elders as possessing this gift and were formally recorded as 'ministers'. In fact the gallery was no more than a practical expedient to enable these ministers to be better heard and, indeed, there was one occasion during Rachel's American visit when she climbed up on to a table for this purpose.

Quaker ministers travelled mostly on horseback, both at home and abroad, on religious visits, sponsored by their local or national Friends' meetings, who provided them, on each occasion, with a certificate of recommendation to those whom they were visiting in fulfilling their 'gospel ministry'. The certificates usually contained specific geographical limits, almost like a modern work visa, which the minister had to observe, partly because of being funded by their Meeting and sometimes because of other ministers travelling at the same time in adjoining areas. Normally, but not always, ministers had a Quaker companion travelling with them. These religious visits were a vital part of the continued existence of the Society of Friends and the older generation trained up the younger.

Quakers realised the benefits of ministry and, during this period in their history, actively encouraged it. The important distinction then (as now) between Quaker ministry and that of any other church was that the Quaker, whether as a recognised minister or otherwise, spoke only in response to a direct calling from God and had no prepared message or sermon. In fact, there are numerous examples of ministers not being moved to speak and of the people present feeling disappointment if they came away from meeting without having received the ministry that they had been expecting.

Just as the North American colonies at the time still came under English rule, so the Religious Society of Friends in America still came under the aegis of London Yearly Meeting of the Society. Peripatetic ministers, both English and American, played a key role in maintaining and furthering Quakerism in the colonies. They were commonplace and there were routine meetings of ministers and elders. As they were unpaid, their travelling expenses were usually covered by their sponsoring meetings and their accommodation was provided freely by Quaker hosts. They made their visits in direct response to their individual, inner callings from God to undertake particular ministry or to visit specific groups of Friends both at home and overseas. God's calling to Rachel to visit America had been gaining strength within her for more than two years before she applied to her Meeting for the necessary certificate.

In America, the importance of these travelling ministers is especially relevant in the context of the spiritual decline of Quakerism that took place during the first half of the 18th century, arising in part from the paucity of local ministry and the dependence on ministers from abroad. By then, Friends had come to view ministry "as something wholly in the inscrutable will of God, who conferred or withheld His gifts as He would. This ignoring of the human element was one of the most costly blunders which Friends made and there is no question that the sporadic character of the ministry was a forbidding aspect to most persons outside the membership." [5] Spiritual decline also manifested itself in such things as departure from simple living by amassing personal wealth and luxuries; yielding to worldly temptations and pleasures; lax application of Quaker 'discipline'; 'marrying out' and the general tendency for Friends to be less than 'convinced' of the truth or to be less than committed, many having merely inherited their Quakerism through birthright membership.

However, in 1755, Philadelphia Yearly Meeting – the principal Quaker authority in America – initiated a conscious process of reform, resulting in a significant return to Quaker principles (and a consequential increase in disownment of Friends who refused correction). In 1768, Rachel made her visit against this positive background. On the other hand, Quaker principles had been severely tested (and to some degree compromised) because of the war between England and France (1755-63) which had given rise to armed conflict along English-French borders in America where Quakers, until then, had held the balance of political power and had desisted from preparing for war.

Records show that, in the 84 years before 1768, there were 84 religious visits by English and Irish Friends, 21 of them as pairs (or in one case a trio), but the remainder as single Friends. This made a total of 106 Friends; 30 of them were women, of whom 19 had left England unaccompanied.[6] (Jane Crosfield, Rachel's travelling companion in England in 1744/45, had visited America in 1760.) Rachel felt 'called' to visit the whole extent of Quakerism in the American colonies, from Charleston in South Carolina to Casco Bay, New England. Her passage to America had to be arranged and likewise the provision of horses for her entire journey of some 4,500 miles, this being the only practical mode of transport. As a much travelled Quaker minister, she was an experienced horse-rider. Three Quaker men accompanied her on her voyage where she was the only woman on board though, as she wrote in one of her letters to Isaac, "great decorum was observed and an agreeable delicacy presided". Once in America, a female companion had to be organised as well as any male accompaniers, these Friends changing at different stages of the journey.

Local Friends' experience, built up over more than 80 years, meant that there were tried and tested arrangements for providing horses and for finding companions and Quaker hosts for visiting ministers. Nonetheless, there were still plenty of gaps to be filled on the spot, such as overnight stops at inns, or obtaining the services of a complete stranger to act as guide when local Quakers were not available, or in response to unforeseen delays.

By now there were well defined routes for travelling Friends to follow from meeting to meeting, but most of these ministers made a point also of visiting as many individual Friends as possible – especially those who lived in remote places, well away from any meeting. Rachel set her sights firmly on reaching the furthermost outposts of Quakers in all the colonies. In common with the practice of fellow ministers, she had a basic outline for her journey but then took each day as it came, following wherever God – her "inner guide" – led her.

Notwithstanding that these religious visits between England and America were quite frequent, so that there were already effective lines of communication, one should remember that a mail packet ship would take 6-8 weeks for each voyage. Rachel wrote home several times before finally leaving England but then had to wait 9 weeks until she arrived in America before she could write again followed by another long interval during the section of her journey preceding Charleston when there was no opportunity to write. The first letter she received from home was when she reached Charleston, five and a half months after leaving England.

The colonies were still at a very early stage in their development. Especially in those south of Pennsylvania, Quaker meetings existed at many of the obscure creeks along the coast and the main rivers, from which roots colonial penetration of the hinterland gradually spread. Overland travel from one creek settlement to the next involved crossing much inhospitable terrain, including rivers and, in places, uncertainty about the correct track to follow. At one stage, it took Rachel 42 days between leaving the only sizeable place recognisable on a modern state road map at one location and arriving at the next (Winchester, Virginia to Hillsborough, North Carolina). Many physical difficulties and emergencies awaited her (like Hogins Creek quoted above) and who could tell what other risks there might be, such as encountering robbers en route or hostile people, or even piracy while on the high seas?

For the most part, Rachel 'dined' (mid-day meal) and took supper and 'lodged' with local Quakers but in some places she had no alternative but to lodge at inns. Her visits were widely publicised, both throughout the Quaker network and publicly. This resulted in large meetings, consisting not only of local and visiting Quakers but also of local inhabitants. Frequently, the Quaker meeting houses were filled to overflowing or it became necessary to hire the local court house or to borrow premises from the neighbouring Baptists or Presbyterians. All of this involved much forward planning as well as spontaneous arrangements on location.

The whole of her religious visit was paid for by the main administrative body of the Society of Friends in England – Meeting for Sufferings. Just the passage, one way, between England and America typically cost £63 per person, equivalent to about £8,000 in today's money.

Rachel starts her story in England, carrying her 'certificate' from her local Westmoreland meeting to London for approval at the highest level within the Society of Friends, making final preparations for her voyage and ministering tirelessly at every opportunity before finally setting sail.

Chapter 2

# PREPARATION AND DEPARTURE

Quotations from Rachel's journal (as transcribed by her daughter, Deborah) are given in *italics.* Quotations from her letters home are in ***bold italics.*** Quotations from other sources are placed in quotation marks in the usual way as are single words and short phrases from the transcript when forming part of the narrative.

Within Quakerism in Rachel's time, the practice of replacing the pagan names of days of the week and of months with a numeric system was universal. Sunday was 'first day' through to Saturday which was 'seventh day'; January was 'first month'; December was 'twelfth month'.

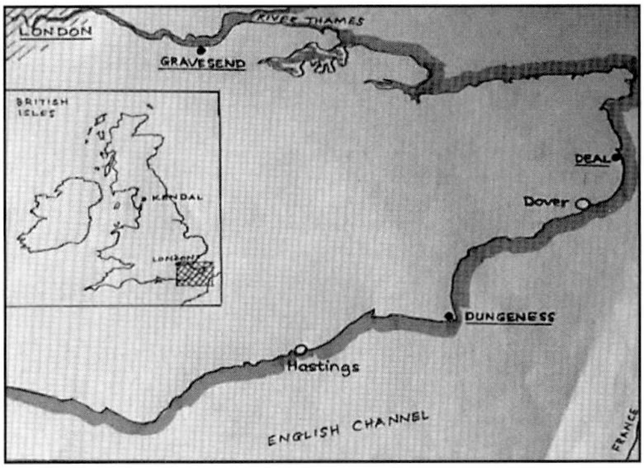


*I left home the 25 of the 7th month 1768 my dear husband accompanying me to Lancaster; about 4 o'clock next morning set out in the Coach for London. We were six passengers to Warrington where we dined ... and got to Middlewich that night ... went in the Coach on fifth day the 26 at 3 in the morning, breakfasted at Talkothill* [Audley, Staffordshire], *dined at Litchfield lodged at Coventry. Was in the Coach on 6 day a little past one a dark dull*

*morning with thunder and fire, we breakfasted at Stow* [probably Stowe, near Daventry], *dined at Dunstable, got to London about 7.*

Four years later, in 1772, the American Quaker, John Woolman, prominent not only in his opposition to slavery but also in upholding the Quaker principles of simplicity and of respect for creation, paid a religious visit to England.

He provides a harrowing description of the new stagecoach services; he was so appalled at the practices employed that he refused to travel in them and instead walked all the way from London to York.[7] Stagecoaches had been introduced in the early 1760's and covered up to 100 miles in a day, depending on the state of the roads and the terrain. Long hours, loose stony surfaces, deep ruts and wet weather made life difficult for all concerned – the six horses, post boys, coachmen and the passengers themselves. The boys riding the two leading horses had little rest. They arrived stiff with cold at the staging inns (where the horses were changed with pit-stop precision) and were sick with fatigue and poor food, made worse by their having been selected for their youth or slight physical build. The coachmen rode outside on the roof, controlling the other four horses. The horses were driven to extremes, under the whip, their eyes bulging with the strain and many went blind or died as a result. Even the passengers had much to endure with the rough roads and rigorous timings.

Rachel's journey was followed by eleven days of doing the rounds of Meetings in and near London, in each case attending meeting for worship: Gracechurch Street (five times); Devonshire House; Bromley; Park; Tottenham; Plaistow; Peel; Wandsworth Weekday Meeting and Women's Two Weeks Meeting. As a Quaker minister with her specific concern to visit Friends in America in this capacity, Rachel wanted these London Meetings to hear from her at first hand and to ensure their support. Specifically, she wanted from Morning Meeting a 'travelling minute' or 'certificate' to endorse the one she had brought with her from Kendal. In her journal she recorded those who ministered in meeting – those who 'appeared' – and her own ministry.

One may smile at her language of the time and even more so at some of the situations she describes but one is inspired and humbled by her closeness to God, her energy and the power of her ministry. This is the strong current that flows through the whole of her journal. In the company of the Friends with whom she stayed and whom she met one finds the same spirit, for example: *I dined at Thomas Wagstaffs with my old Landlady where we had a melting season together at table...* She uses this expression 'melting season' in several places, meaning the spiritual blending of the hearts and minds of those gathered together.

At Morning Meeting (also called 'Second Day Meeting', responsible for supervising all travelling ministers):

*2nd day* [Monday] *morning the 1st of 8 mo. I laid my concern before Friends at London at which time Divine goodness broke in upon our minds into the baptizing our Spirits into a new Union with each other, and some had to open their mouths incouragingly – Robert Bell and Timothy Bevin were desired to draw up a few lines to be signed at the next Morning Meeting.*

[Timothy Bevin may be incorrect – see William Smith, below.]

A week later:

*I lodged with Zacha. Cockfield who brought me in his Chariot to Morning Meeting in which my spirit was deeply humbled in a sense of Divine good, and had a few words in the fore part of the Meeting, after which the Minute of last Meeting was read, and the Friends appointed to draw up a few lines on my account produced and read them, which greatly disturbed my mind as I viewed them – having no sense or feeling of the weighty concern I was under but went intirely upon my former Certificate without mentioning their own feelings. Several remarks were made upon it, and two words added with which it passed tho' greatly to my uneasiness.*

These minutes read:

Morning Meeting the 1st of 8th mo. 1768

"Our Friend Rachel Wilson of Kendal in Westmorland, having signified to this Meeting that she hath had a Concern on her Mind to pay a religious Visit to Friends in America, laid before this Meeting a Certificate from the Monthly Meeting of Kendal and Quarterly Meeting of Westmorland, signifying their Concurrence with her Concern therein. William Smith & Robert Bell desired to draw up a few Lines by way of Certificate & bring back to next Meeting to be signed."

And: "Rachel Wilson having informed this Meeting she is about to embark on a religious Visit to Friends in America, the Meeting for Sufferings are desired to provide for her Passage and Accommodation. Robert Bell is desired to carry a Copy of this Minute to Meeting for Sufferings."

Morning Meeting the 8th of 8th mo. 1768

"Robert Bell & William Smith, agreeable to a Minute of last Meeting, brought in a Certificate, on account of our Friend Rachel Wilson's Concern to pay a religious Visit to Friends in America, signifying the Concurrence of this Meeting therewith, which was read & signed in this Meeting."

The day after reaching London, Rachel briefly visited the packet boat and the captain who were to take her to America. It was the normal practice of 'travelling' Friends, engaged in long voyages, to spend some time sitting in – to 'feel out' – the ships available to them so that they could feel inwardly led to choose the right one for their service to God or one that would sail protected under the divine hand of Providence.[8] If their ship arrived ahead of a more obvious alternative, then they were meant to have that extra time at their destination for Quaker service. If their ship was blown off course and delayed by calm or storms, then they had the opportunity while on the voyage to relay to those on board – both crew and passengers – that it was all part of God's purpose. If they let an otherwise obvious choice of ship go and it subsequently perished at sea, then it was some form of divine guidance that held them back from going on it. Every situation that arose, therefore, was God's handiwork: the system was foolproof!

As far as one knows, there were no instances of any Quakers having being 'led' into a doomed vessel. But there were examples of ships carrying Quakers being boarded by hostile forces, for example: Quakers losing their possessions to enemy forces, such as to the French during the war with France, and Quakers being taken as slaves by Barbary pirates and released only on payment of redemption monies, typically raised by Meeting for Sufferings.

On the other hand, there were examples of ships carrying Quakers enjoying providential deliverances from pirates and from dangerous weather conditions where the captain sought and followed the divine leadings of his Quaker passengers. (George Fox was one example; Rachel, en route to Nantucket Island, was another, notwithstanding that they had no nautical experience.)

Rachel records: ... *went on board the Pensilvania Pacquett ... Capt. Faulkner* [Falconer] *with which I was very easy and thankful in my mind to find such agreeable accommodation, which appeared a great favour for so long a voyage as was like to be my Lot in that Vessel.*

To Isaac she wrote:

> ***The Captain looks to be a good natured active little man; the Cabin and State Room rather elegant and that if I had been never so generous I suppose could not have had more agreable accommodation.***

Other Quaker ministers before her had travelled on this ship. 'Packet' ships of this period were quite small, built for speed so that, as well as the commercial benefits, they could usually outrun pirate ships and manage with only minimal arms (or be unarmed). A lot of effort went into looking after the passengers and making their voyage comfortable, even if the cabin (apart from the captain's) was communal. Passengers always had to bring their own food, drink and mattresses. In her last letter home from England Rachel mentioned the "rather eloquent" provisions carried for the voyage (described later in this chapter).

By contrast, life for the sailors in the steerage was the opposite: cramped, airless, sweaty bodies, soaking wet clothes getting mixed up with the dry, shifts changing every four hours, swearing and hard-driven labour. John Woolman, on his voyage to England, refused the luxury of the passenger cabin and, true to his Quaker testimony to equality, insisted on travelling in the steerage with the sailors.

The *Pennsylvania Pacquet* was owned by the Fisher family who were Quakers in America (like a great many other Quaker shipowners) and, indeed, one of them – Samuel Fisher – was to be one of Rachel's travelling companions on the voyage and for the first part of her religious visit.

On 4$^{th}$ of 8$^{th}$ month, Rachel had replied to a letter from home:

> ***Conveying ye*** [the] ***accounts of all your well fare and Daughter Debys Safe Delivery*** [Rachel Braithwaite born 30$^{th}$ 7$^{th}$ mo. 1768] ***which I could not but be a little anxious about – all Contributed to make My Stay their Comfortable.***

On 11$^{th}$ of 8$^{th}$ month she sent her personal effects and provisions on board and on 13$^{th}$ went by "chariot" to Gravesend, only to find that the ship had been delayed. She had been very poorly on 3$^{rd}$ *when I had a fresh attack of my old complaint in my breast, which affected me a good deal* and again on 11$^{th}$/12$^{th}$, so it could have been a good opportunity for a little rest.

Instead:

*I found an engagement to have a meeting and Friends falling in with it a proper place was inquired after and the Town Hall pitched upon which the Magistrate readily granted – there were about forty friends; the Meeting began at ten, to which a great number of the Inhabitants came, amongst whom I found great openness to preach the Gospel; the Meeting concluded in prayer and praises ... and as there was no prospect of going on board that day we had another Meeting appointed at five which was much crowded and many more than could get in ... the people were reached many of whom came to bid me farewell and wish me a prosperous Voyage with Jesus.*

One of the inhabitants was a poor woman (another account says "rude") who could not be persuaded to sit still and be quiet but kept getting up and standing on the seat. The seat gave way and she broke her leg much to the consternation of all Friends present, who immediately collected five and a half guineas among themselves which they gave to one of the magistrates for the woman's use.

Having received another letter from home, Rachel replied:

> ***A Little while ago Read thine of ye 8 which afected me a good deal as it was Lick*** [like] ***to be thy Last on this Side of ye great occeane ... My mind is not in a situation to write much More at Present. Is in yt*** [that] ***Love yt Many Waters Cannot quench nor Distance of Miles Erase – so I dearly salute thee my dear husband with all our Dear Childer & Family & bid you farewell.***

The ship arrived on 15th. On the evening of 16th, Rachel was poorly, brought on because of *the leaving my friends and the thought of so long a Voyage, with the humbling View of my own Usefulness for such an Undertaking, but merciful Goodness was pleased to interpose for my help, and broke in upon our minds to the tendering our Spirits that we were favoured with a Solemn parting.*

She boarded on the morning of 17th of 8th month for a voyage that would last until 16th of 10th month.

In addition to the three Friends, William Coleman, Samuel Fisher and James Buck who were to accompany her on her voyage, a few of the men Friends and her landlady accompanied her on board to The Downs (Deal) where the ship anchored on 18th and remained there for a week until the wind was favourable on 25th. At one stage a "smart gale" made her and others seasick; indeed, for most of that week she and her visitors on board, while in port, felt ill because of the high winds.

She said good bye to various Friends the *parting more affecting, which was in great Love and near Sympathy with each other.* She also went ashore during this time, visited an elderly Friend who could not get to meeting and wrote:

*... a Mill purchased by Robert Chester, whose Son and Daughter was then there, with whom we sat a while, having to point out to them the necessity there was to be upon their guard, their situation exposing them to many temptations, which I earnestly desired they might be enabled carefully to withstand.*

Although recalled to the ship on 7th day (20th of the month) because of the possibility of favourable weather, the wind died and she was able to go to meeting in Deal on 1st day (1st week of voyage). The meeting house was "small and close" and was overcrowded, so arrangements were hurriedly made to use the town hall for the afternoon meeting. Despite being large, it was still not big enough for the great crowd who attended and meeting was not as quiet as she could have wished *yet Merciful Goodness graciously favoured in opening the way of Life and Salvation to the people to the humbling and baptizing our Spirits together that our prayers were ardently put up to the God and Father of all our Mercies on their account with living praises and thanksgiving for his unmerited favours both past and present.*

They then returned to the boat.

*The weather being mild that evening I found an inclination with the Captain's permission to sit with our little family* [the Friends accompanying her] *which was readily agreed to, and the Sailors came down into the Cabin, where I had to lay before them the great advantage that attended an humble waiting upon God whereby we might know our strength in him to be renewed, and that his fear might be before our eyes that would keep from every evil way; as well as the inconsistency of swearing with the Command of our Dear Lord and Blessed Saviour – after which I was engaged in supplication on their Account, as also that we might be preserved in Christian Patience, & not murmur or repine at what might be permitted to attend us now, when on the unstable Ocean, for our refinement, and the trials of our faith, that it might not stand in words but in Power to the purifying of our hearts by Love. I lay down that night in great peace.*

*Third day the wind increasing, I was sick and obliged to lay down ... 4th day the 24 of the 8 month being mild and pleasant I was able to walk upon Deck and write a little; before we dined my mind was overwhelmed with Divine Good that at Table I found a necessity to acknowledge the goodness of God and his wonderful mercy in dealing with us, for the advancement of his own Glory and our Comfort, tho' at times hid from us, and as our Voyage had been retarded by his Infinite Wisdom, I had ardently to beg if consistent with his Blessed Will he would cause the North Wind to blow that our Voyage might be prosperous – after which I was quiet and a peaceful calm covered my mind for some time till reasoning a little got in, by which I was tossed by the Enemy of all our happiness* [i.e. the Devil], *but his power was limited and I had a secret hope raised that the Petition would be granted, as it was not put up in my own will, but I trust in the Will of Him at whose commands the Winds and Seas obey.*

Next day, the wind was favourable and they set sail.

They cast anchor at Dungeness that night, giving Rachel the chance to write home from England just once more and to report "our provisions are Rather Eloquent when our appetite can take Em – but James [Buck] & I have not always been in a Condition to Relish food – ye wind being mostly Brisk."

There is a family description of these “rather eloquent” provisions: [9]

“The large stores provided for Friends crossing to America in the old days have often been the subject of comment, but were doubtless not the gauge of a large appetite, but something in the nature of insurance against starvation, should the voyage be greatly prolonged, through the ship being driven far out of her course ... Such a case is recorded where Friends and crew were reduced to eating rats and drinking the water they could collect on deck. It is also understood that the captain and ship’s officers expected to share the provisions of their passengers – alcohol especially ... in those days considered as a necessary food.

“Stores for our Friend, R Wilson provided by MA:

30 fowles; 12 ducks; 4 hams; 2 doz Madeira wine; 2 bottles Jamaica spirit; keg WI rum; 4 bottles brandy; 2 bottles vinegar; 6lbs rusks; 2lbs maple biscuits; 3lbs ginger bread; 8lbs raisons; ½lb Singlo tea; 2lbs ground coffee; 2lbs chocolate; 1 loaf D refined sugar; 1 loaf M refined sugar; 14lbs musco. Sugar; peck [2 gallons] cranberries; 2 quarts oatmeal; 6lbs rice; 5 bushels [40 gallons] Indian corn; 100 eggs.”

At last they could settle down to a voyage, now into its second week, that was to take them to the very heartland of the first American Quakers. How much did Rachel and British Quakers in general know about their fellow Americans and what to expect in what, in effect, was London Yearly Meeting’s distant protectorate? Probably, their knowledge was extensive and well informed through the frequent religious visits, through Quaker international trade and through the communications passed up and down between London Yearly Meeting (as the ultimate authority) and yearly meetings in America – primarily Philadelphia – in the form of their epistles to each other, matters of Quaker discipline and other business. At this point, therefore, it is perhaps interesting to take a quick look at the history of early American Quakerism.

## Chapter 3

# AMERICAN QUAKERISM IN 1768 – PREHISTORY & HISTORY

### *American Quaker Prehistory*

North American colonisation only really got underway in the first part of the 17th century. Large tracts of unseen and unknown land in the New World were granted to the English nobility, often as rewards for military successes, such as in the wars with the Dutch or as repayment of money lent to the Crown. But these owners ("proprietors") had to establish ways of managing and making money from their new lands. They needed capable, reliable settlers. The prospect of huge personal prosperity in a vast, new continent, with abundant natural resources, was still an insufficient incentive for most people to pull up their native roots and to risk a completely new start in distant, untried and vaguely defined foreign territory.

A system of 'quit rents' to persuade people to quit the land that they rented in England in exchange for a small annual rent in the colonies was only partially successful. The landowning nobility needed something more to entice people away from their secure and productive livings in their homeland. Cynically, they found the solution in the religious persecution of the time. As conformists, they wanted to preserve the status quo – they wanted to be rid of non-conformists – so they offered religious liberty in their far-flung territories in exchange for these rents, whether in cash or in kind. Their ruse worked quite well. Moreover, if the rents did not come up to expectations, they also made money by selling parts of their lands to people (like John Woolman's English grandfather) who sold everything they had in England and bought their land entirely on paper, not really knowing what they had purchased until they reached the other side of the ocean.[10]

Elizabeth I was Queen of England from 1558 to 1603. During this time, through religious and political upheaval, marked by persecution and wars, Europe had emerged divided between Roman Catholicism and Protestantism. The Dutch United Provinces were an exception, however, enjoying religious tolerance, civic freedom and provincial independence well beyond that in any other part of Europe.

In England, the Church had already become autonomous when Henry VIII (Elizabeth's father) proclaimed himself head of the Church and disowned the authority of Rome. The nature of the English institutions that developed had characteristics that appeared similar to the religious and civic freedoms of the Dutch but, in fact, England was neither truly Protestant nor tolerant. It continued the basic Catholic doctrine, but this was achieved through Royal Supremacy approved by Parliament; it progressively strengthened the State's legislative authority to the point where limitation of privilege and individual freedoms was more severe than in the rest of Europe.

Puritanism in England – the movement from the 1560's onwards to 'purify' the Church by purging it of unscriptural hierarchies and ceremonies – gained growing support from sections of both the clergy and the gentry and became a driving force during Elizabethan times and into the 17$^{th}$ century.

Instead of holding fast to absolute Calvinism as in Scotland, namely the rejection of everything that could not be established by scripture, its ultimate form was characteristically English in that it retained everything that scripture did not disprove. True Calvinism was a totally authoritative institution – "a logical scheme of Divine truth which satisfied the intellect, compelled the enthusiastic acceptance of multitudes, and, if circumstances served, would not hesitate to claim for itself universal obedience." Two struggles ensued: firstly, the supremacy of the Crown versus the Pope and, secondly, the Divine right of Bishops and Kings versus that of a theocratic Presbytery.[11]

"The practical sagacity and untheological temper of Elizabeth had at first enabled her to keep within the Episcopal establishment of many Puritan-minded clergy ... but the doctrine taught by the most earnest of her clergy was the doctrine of Calvin ... [and] the zeal and bigotry of Thomas Cartwright, English champion of the Calvinist system alarmed Elizabeth, especially his fanatical advocacy of Presbyterian church government, to the absolute exclusion of the State." [12] She responded by requiring acceptance of Royal Supremacy and other 'articles'; thereafter, religion became the springboard for eroding the Crown's authority. Cartwright "taught that the ministers ... were to wield full spiritual power and jurisdiction. Their weapon was excommunication, and they were responsible for its use only to Christ. The civil power was 'to see their decrees executed, and to punish the contemners of them'. Other forms of faith – Papal, Episcopalian, or Sectarian – should be ruthlessly suppressed, and all heresy should be punishable with death." [13] This was Puritanism at its most extreme, but gives the clue to its underlying nature.

At the start of his reign, James I (reg. 1603-25) had a golden opportunity to win over moderates within the Puritan clergy when he denounced the Church's service as "an evil-said Mass in English" and declared the Presbyterian's church as the "purest in the world". But he threw away the opportunity so that he could force these Church reformers instead to conform to the existing structures and doctrines controlled by the Crown or else be deprived of their livings.[14]

There were many who became Independents and of these, a large number from the newly formed Congregational Church had fled to Holland in 1608. In 1620, having by then become disenchanted with life in Holland, it was a company of them who became the so-called Pilgrim Fathers. After serious setbacks brought about by the obstructive tactics of opponents and malevolent opportunists, they sailed from Plymouth, England in *The Mayflower* to establish a colony in the New World. They dreamt of a land where religion and liberty could find a safe and lasting home. They arrived in Provincetown Harbour, Cape Cod and chose Plymouth Harbour across the bay for a landing for their new colony. (The 'Plymouth' colony was absorbed into Massachusetts in 1691.) The legend of their near idyllic alliance with the Native Americans, who taught them how to fish and to plant corn, is the 'nostalgic concoction' of subsequent generations of New Englanders in their annual Thanksgiving Day celebrations.[15]

After the original 200, a further 1,500 came over in the first year and the number grew to unprecedented levels, peaking at 3,000 in a single year and totalling over 20,000, brought across in some 200 ships, in the space of 10 years.[16] In 1629, the charter establishing the colony of Massachusetts Bay was granted just as Charles I (reg. 1625-49) was resolving to govern without Parliament. When religious intolerance gripped this colony, the colony of Rhode Island was established in 1636 on the principles of absolute religious freedom.

In time, Charles so divided his subjects over constitutional and religious supremacy that his reign ended with the civil war between Royalists and Parliamentarians from 1642 to 1649. The Petition of Right in 1628, addressed by Parliament to Charles, had sought to reaffirm old statutes and to secure the benefit of them for individuals, but Charles had refused to allow any dilution of the royal prerogative. In the event, it contained a recital of statutes alleged to have been broken and of grievances against the Crown for which redress was required. This was the start of the Puritan Revolution which lasted until 1660 and whilst it succeeded in assuring the supremacy of Parliament it was less successful in achieving the full aims of Puritanism.[17]

The attempt by the Church under Archbishop Laud, with Charles' support, to impose an anti-Calvinist policy on the whole of England had the effect of uniting Puritans and Parliamentarians as they both strove to satisfy their respective agendas: for one an exclusive Presbyterian religion and for the other a popularly elected government. Charles used his powers arbitrarily in 1634 to raise funds for the country's defence, knowing that Parliament would have refused to support him. The confrontation between King and people reached a climax in 1641, under the terms of the Grand Remonstrance which was for reform of the Church on Puritan lines to be combined with a continuance of Parliamentary governance. In 1642, Charles went to war with Parliament.[18]

With its army facing defeat, Parliament enlisted the support of the Scots in return for which it undertook to preserve the reformed religion of Scotland and to reform that of England and Ireland along compatible lines, effectively imposing Presbyterianism on England. This, in turn, caused a division in Parliament and drew the more enlightened Puritan leaders towards the Independents whose system better suited the Puritanism of England and had produced a degree of religious liberty. [19]

After being captured by the Scots and handed over to Parliament in 1647, Charles escaped and tried to exploit the division by entering into an 'engagement' with the Scots for military aid in return for establishing Presbyterianism in England for three years. The Civil War ended in 1649 with the overthrow and execution of Charles for "treason against the people of England".[20]

This resulted in England's only ever republic (1649-1660) – the Commonwealth under Oliver Cromwell who, himself, had been alarmed at the prospect of an imposed, rigid Presbyterianism and who now sought to govern through Parliament without creating an intolerant Protestantism. (Constitutional power struggles actually resulted in a break from 1653 to 1659 during which there was a Protectorate, rather than the Commonwealth, with Cromwell as Lord Protector.)

In 1660, the monarchy, under Charles II (reg. 1660-85), was restored. As well as a general amnesty and equitable land settlement, Charles sought "liberty to tender consciences",[21] but Parliament flagrantly disregarded this liberty such that religious persecution in England reached its most intense level during this period, abating only after the Toleration Act of 1689 two reigns later: James II (reg. 1685-88); William and Mary (reg. 1689-1702).

In this climate of the first half of the 17th century, an astonishing array of new sects and debates sprang up, threatening the whole religious fabric of the country. Most prominent were the Baptists who made full liberty of conscience a central tenet from 1614 and who rejected the Calvinist dogmas of original sin and predestination. Several other of their tenets were mirrored later in Quakerism, such as lay preachers, including women, itinerant "messengers", opposition to both tithes and "hireling ministry" (i.e. paid clergy) and there was even a preacher advocating the doctrine of the Inner Light.

George Fox – the founder of Quakerism – emerged at this time. He left home in 1643 at the age of 19 and travelled through England on a long, often despairing spiritual quest, searching out all manner of priests, "professors" (i.e. those professing Christ in words only), dissenters and others to provide him with the answers he so urgently sought. Three years later, he tells of the moment in his life that was the central experience out of which the Quaker message sprang: "When all my hopes … was gone, so that I had nothing outwardly to help me, nor could tell what to do, then, O then, I heard a voice which said, 'There is one, Christ Jesus, that can speak to thy condition,' and when I heard it, my heart did leap for joy." [22]

For Fox and his followers, the most significant of the contemporary sects were the Familists and the Seekers, the two sometimes being classed together. Here one can see the makings of the meeting for worship that was to become the lifeblood of Quakerism: waiting in silence for a direct, inward spiritual experience of God's presence. It was to these people, in the north of England in 1652 (the popular birthdate of Quakerism), that Fox brought his message. They became the new-born "Children of the Light" and "Friends in the Truth" or "Friends" as they came to call themselves where all are disciples of Christ. Elizabeth Hooton (see also p.123) – a Baptist – in 1648 had, in fact, become Fox's first follower, thus pre-dating the point when Quakerism can be identified as a new movement.

### *The arrival of Quakerism in America*

In 1655-56, the first Quaker "Publishers of the Truth" reached the New World. The initial trickle became a flood, realising Fox's exhortation to Friends:

"Be patterns, be examples in all countries, places, islands, nations, wherever you come that your carriage and life may preach among all sorts of people and to them; then you will come to walk cheerfully over the world, answering that of God in everyone."

Elizabeth Harris brought the Quaker message to the Chesapeake region of Virginia and Maryland; Anne Austin and Mary Fisher brought it to Boston, Massachusetts and others soon followed. (Barbados already had a strong Quaker presence with five Quaker meetings.) In 1657, eleven Friends, including four women, arrived in the famous *Woodhouse* that was far too small for a transatlantic crossing, but succeeded, against all the odds, in landing on the shores of Long Island. Their absolute trust in Divine guidance continues as the most compelling explanation of how this extraordinary voyage ever came to be completed. Five Friends went to "the Dutch plantation called New Amsterdam" (later New York) – in those days a very inaccessible region – while the rest went to Rhode Island, the home of religious liberty.

Fox himself went to the New World in 1671-73: firstly Barbados and Jamaica and then Virginia, Maryland, New Jersey, Long Island, New England, Rhode Island, Delaware and Carolina, following arduous routes that took him and his party through several uncharted areas. A striking feature of these and other early Quaker missions is how, by living out their inward experience of God, where all people are equal, Quakers were accepted into the indigenous Indian communities that they encountered on their travels.

### *Quaker colonies & Quakers in government*

Even though so many shiploads of non-conformist settlers had arrived, many of them Quakers, seeking freedom to worship according to their persuasion, driven by the lack of religious toleration back home, this process was still too slow for the proprietors. In 1674, Lord Berkeley, who had been given half of the province of New Jersey, offered this for 1,000 pounds sterling. Through association with the well-connected Quaker, William Penn, he preferred to sell it to

Quakers who snapped it up. Quakers now had the opportunity to create their own ideal community – no oaths, no compulsory church, no tithes or 'hireling priests'. The principal Quaker purchaser went bankrupt and Penn became trustee for the creditors, giving him control of the territory.[23]

Despite Lord Berkeley having sold his half of the province, it had never been delineated, since none of the people concerned had ever actually been there. A line was now drawn from Little Egg Harbour up to the northernmost bend of the Delaware River, the Quaker trustees taking the land to the west, while the owner of the other half took the land to the east of the line, including the settlements of Elizabeth and New Ark. When this owner died, four years later, Penn and eleven other Quakers bought East New Jersey from the owner's widow. The whole province thus became united under one government – a province that had originated as New Netherland under Dutch rule until it fell as a prize to England in 1664 at the close of the Dutch wars, thus giving the English (the Duke of York, later to be King James II) the great province lying between the Hudson and Delaware Rivers.[24]

Then, in 1681, in redemption of an unpaid debt owed by Charles II to Penn's late father for successful military exploits, Penn had received a private grant from the Crown of a much larger and richer province of his own – that which became Pennsylvania. To this he now devoted his attentions but not before he had helped organise a company of shareholders, partners and a board of control and had drawn up a charter of government for the equitable allotment and settlement of lands in New Jersey ("Concessions and Agreements") which can be seen as the foundation of democracy in America.[25] Under this charter, some three thousand Quakers arrived in West New Jersey over a period of just four years, well equipped for permanent settlement.

A good example of Penn's far-sightedness was manifested in his realisation that access to river frontages was vital to the well-being of communities who depended on the rivers for their prime means of transport. Accordingly, land occupation was granted in very narrow strips extending from the water into the hinterland. For instance, the Woolman's water frontage was a mere 250 yards, but their land went back about 2 miles.[26]

The original planting of Quakerism in America took hold so firmly and so rapidly "it seemed as though Quakerism might well become the prevailing religion. It was solidly entrenched everywhere, and white-hot with convictions and enthusiasm. The meek were, apparently, really going to inherit the earth. This was undoubtedly what Fox and Penn expected." [27] (Even in England, at this time, it was the third largest religious group.) It was not universal, however. Marked variations between the colonies existed deriving from their denominational origins, both those of their proprietors and those of their settlers. For example, under Puritanism in the New England colonies, with the exception of Rhode Island, religious persecution of Quakers was extreme.

These early years are captured in the following thumbnail sketch:
"... some English Friends ... went to New England about the year 1656 to preach Truth there. Although suffering, and in some cases death, befel them, their message reached many hearts and quite a number became Friends. In Rhode Island they found a safe shelter from persecution, and here the Society increased fast, and soon became very influential. In 1672, the Governor, Deputy-Governor and magistrates were Friends, and in 1675, under this Quaker leadership, the Colony refused to join with other New England Colonies in preparations for a war with the Indians.

"Maryland was another place of refuge for persecuted Friends, especially for those from Virginia. [George Fox came here in 1672 and, from a contemporary account] 'did wonderfully open the service thereof unto Friends, and they with gladness of heart received advice in such necessary things'. This was the beginning of what was afterwards known as Baltimore Yearly Meeting. In 1681, a Yearly

Meeting was 'set up' at Burlington in New Jersey. Philadelphia Yearly Meeting ... was established in 1683, and increased in numbers so rapidly that as early as 1684 ... 'there were about 800 persons in regular attendance on First and week-days at Friends' meetings in Philadelphia'. By the close of the seventeenth century, Yearly Meetings of Friends had been established in all the British North American colonies." [28]

As already mentioned, the attraction of America can be attributed not only to the zeal of Quakers to spread their message worldwide but also to their desire to escape the severe new wave of religious persecution in England that followed the restoration of the monarchy under Charles II in 1660 – the most severe in the history of British Quakerism. Many Quakers who remained in England suffered imprisonment and/or extensive deprivation of property, while some 320 died for their beliefs. This persecution stemmed from the activities of a group, known as the Fifth Monarchists, who held that military revolt was required of them to establish Christ's rule on earth and were thus a direct threat to the monarchy. This group was an extreme Puritan sect which believed that the last of five universal monarchies, as foretold by the prophet Daniel, was at hand: Christ after a second coming – supposed to have been in 1656 – would reign on earth with his saints for 1,000 years and end the Roman monarchy. This was the fourth, the previous ones having been the Assyrian, Persian and Greek monarchies.

Anything less like Quakerism is hard to imagine. Nonetheless, Quakers, because of being non-conformist and because of their confrontational stands against the established authorities were accused of treason. For convenience, they were tried and convicted for their refusal to take the oath of allegiance to the Crown (since their allegiance was only to God) and for refusing to observe 'hat honour' (taking off of one's hat to acknowledge another person as being superior), making them easy targets of the oppressive regime of the time. This was despite their pacifism and their formal declaration of their peaceful principles and practices as delivered to the King in 1660 in their well-known written testimony against all wars.

In America, as already noted, several colonies became Quaker strongholds. Others were settled predominantly by Puritans in most of the New England colonies and by Episcopalians in colonies like Virginia and the Carolinas. In the 17th century, hostility towards the early Quakers was prevalent in Virginia and was particularly harsh in Puritan colonies. Before the arrival of the Quakers, a small party of Baptists had, in 1638, founded the colony of Rhode Island and, in due course, spread through all the colonies. In 1663, two of their founders, John Clarke and Roger Williams, secured a charter from Charles II guaranteeing civil and religious freedom in Rhode Island which provided a refuge in later years for persecuted Quakers, driven from neighbouring colonies, where they were able to prepare themselves for re-entering hostile territory in answer to their inner callings to spread the Quaker message.

Baptists at this time were characterised by being largely scattered, autonomous congregations, not becoming organised as a main denomination until much later, whereas the Quakers were highly organised from the outset. Like the Quakers, the Baptists were at pains to recognise the human rights and dignity of the American Indians and to make friends with them. Moreover, they had a special appeal to the African slave population by virtue of their belief in conversion experiences. At the other extreme, Puritans in power were so zealous that they rigorously denied people religious freedom and persecuted, imprisoned and banished dissenters, employing practices every bit as cruel as those they themselves had escaped from.

The colonies were owned by their English proprietors, but, by the early 18th century, democracy in one form or another had evolved in all of them, comprising a body of elected representatives – an assembly – that spoke for its inhabitants to a royal governor appointed from London.

In Rhode Island, Quaker governors held office for 36 successive terms while, in New Jersey, many Quakers served as governors, assemblymen and councillors. In North Carolina they were the only organised religious body until 1701. They controlled Pennsylvania until 1756. Up to 1740, the largest group migration from Britain to America was that of the Quakers. For the first half of the century, Quakers were the highest proportion of the American population, attaining their greatest secular power in the colonies and reaching as much as 50% in Pennsylvania, before the ever-increasing number of immigrants of other persuasions changed the demographics.

## *Penn's "Holy Experiment": rise and fall*

The Quakers' friendship with the Indians grew out of the "Holy Experiment" as lived out by William Penn in his creation and leadership of Pennsylvania from 1681.

His constitution for his province gave considerable power to the people, total religious toleration to all to worship God according to their own consciences and only limited authority to the Governor. "I propose" Penn had written "to leave myself and successors no power of doing mischief, that the will of one man may not hinder the good of a whole country".[29]

Before arriving in his new possession, Penn had instructed his agent to buy lands from the Indians in the same way that white men bought from one another and to explain to them that, among other things, the new governor was unarmed. Penn also had a clear vision for his new city, Philadelphia – the City of Brotherly Love. Building friendship with the Indians became a very proactive process. His agent walked with them, joined their feasts, learned their language and got to know their chiefs intimately. It culminated in a summit meeting, headed by Penn and the chosen principal chief, when the Indian warriors all threw down their arms and Penn addressed the gathered company in their own tongue on the treaty he now laid before them. He embraced their 'Great Spirit' in the same context as the 'One' in which he believed, and went through the treaty sentence by sentence: the children of the Indians and the children of Onas (their word for 'pen') should live as brothers.[30]

If this is Quakers' 'nostalgic concoction' of their own American origins (cp. the reference above to the *Mayflower*), "There is probably more or less truth in all of [the many traditions of Penn's life in America]".[31]

Even though Penn had "purchased" the Indians' lands, he wanted them to remain and for both Indians and settlers to have the same rights of land ownership, citizenship and protection as each other. Penn passed further laws to prevent unscrupulous settlers taking advantage of the Indians' ignorance of the incoming people's business methods. In spite of this, to the Indians the concept of land ownership did not exist: it was simply a question of occupation. Accordingly, European immigrants found it easy to cheat the Indians out of their land by purchasing large, valuable areas in exchange for trivial sums or objects of little worth. The Indians were displaced from their homelands and suffered greatly in consequence, not least at the hands of those who followed Penn to power – including, sad to say, one of his sons.

The Quakers, on the other hand, always sought to give fair values to the Indians. In comparative terms, the Quakers' deals were indeed fair, but the result was still the creation of huge personal wealth for them and for all who came into possession of the fertile, productive lands along the coast, inevitably putting pressure on the Indians to retreat further and further back into inhospitable new territory.

In Pennsylvania, even after Quakers became a minority of the population, the electorate continued to return a majority of Quakers as their assemblymen, until invasion by the French led to the seven years war (1756-1763) in the defence of Pennsylvania. Then, non-Quakers, understandably, could not abide their Assembly's pacifist stance in refusing military measures even for defence.

Against this background, the great Indian Chief, Pontiac, effectively combined all the Indian tribes against the white settlers. Some of these tribes were traditionally peaceful and welcoming to strangers. Others were warlike and, previously, had invaded neighbouring tribes. But the general image of the Indians being, by nature, savage warriors is unjust. There is no doubt that they did practice scalping, including in the conflict referred to below, but historical research has rightly pointed out that "stereotypes are absorbed from popular literature, folklore, and misinformation. ... Europeans were the ones who encouraged and carried out much of the scalping that went on in the history of white/native relations in America." [32]

In 1763, there was a great insurgence as the united Indians spread terror through the provinces. They attacked and took a large number of British frontier forts. Defence led inevitably to counter attack and the committing of atrocities against the Indians. Scottish-Irish frontiersmen from Paxton township – the Paxton Boys – were determined to rid Philadelphia of those who supported the Indians and accordingly made Quakers their prime target. They organised themselves to rid Philadelphia of Quakers, and to have Israel Pemberton, the most senior Quaker figure, turned over to them. In the course of their objective, they coveted an area of rich Indian land, the place of the Indians' "Council fire", and took it by surprise, murdering fourteen. The remainder of the Indians fled to Lancaster, claiming rightful protection and being given refuge in the town's prison, but the Paxton Boys broke in and murdered all inside.[33]

Other Indians, namely those from Wahalowsing, trusting John Woolman, fled to Philadelphia where Friends provided emergency supplies and secured temporary accommodation for them. Eventually they returned home. (Their chief, Papunahung, whom John Woolman met in Wahalowsing in 1763, already knew Quaker ways and had attended Quaker meetings and conferences on Indian affairs at Philadelphia.)

In the face of the Paxton riots, some 200 Quakers went against Quaker pacifist principles and took up arms to defend Philadelphia. But the majority of the citizens were ready to welcome the frontiersmen with the result that armed conflict was avoided and, instead, the full heat of revenge for Pontiac's actions was channelled into highly provocative anti-Quaker pamphleteering.

Pontiac was defeated and the imposed peace required the Indians to hand over all their captives. Not only did this apply to those newly captured but also to all who had become part of the Indian communities over many years. Children were removed from their foster mothers, husbands from wives, friends from friends, many being dragged away by force. Some succeeded in escaping back to their Indian families.[34] But, from now on, fear ruled and the Holy Experiment (which had lasted for three generations) was in tatters.

Despite this setback, Indians' respect for Quakers survived and "No Quaker blood was ever shed by a red man in Pennsylvania, and to be a follower of Onas was at all times a passport to their protection and hospitality." [35]

Quakers' refusal to provide military defence against the invading French was thus compounded by their long-established friendship with the Indians. Public opposition to Quakers intensified, pointing to the hypocrisy manifested in what was perceived as a spurious Quaker peace testimony. As is common with public opinions, oversimplification and generalisation meant that all Quakers became tarred with the same brush when, in reality, it was only a minority who could be accused of hypocrisy. However, in this instance there was some justification since this minority included some very wealthy and influential Quakers who, in the judgment of the public, wanted to maintain their lucrative businesses and their sumptuous lifestyles without contributing war taxes or engaging in military service but who, unavoidably, would benefit from the military defence of the province in which they lived.

There was also the hypocrisy of the 200 Quakers mentioned above who had taken up arms ready to resist the 'Paxton Boys' and who were not disowned for breaching such a fundamental Quaker principle as pacifism. Even during its heyday of political power, Quakers had, in effect, authorised war taxes by approving large appropriations of public money "for the King's use", shielding behind their very narrow, literal (and convenient) interpretation of "render unto Caesar the things that are Caesar's and unto God the things that are God's".

In a short space of time from 1755, most Quaker assemblymen, urged on by Philadelphia Yearly Meeting, had concluded that their positions as elected representatives were untenable and they resigned from the assembly, thus changing for ever the face of government in the colony – a change that many non-Quakers also were sorry to see. Moreover, because of the requirement both to recruit men to fight and to raise war taxes in all colonies for defending English possessions, Quaker representation in assemblies in the other Quaker strongholds also fell away.

### *Reformation*

In parallel with these aspects of American Quaker history, from about the turn of the century there had been an increasing trend away from the observance of Quaker principles ("discipline") until, in 1755, Philadelphia Yearly Meeting initiated a process of reform that was to last right up to Independence and beyond. It was tantamount to a process of cleansing. Numbers of Friends dropped quite substantially, but, in the fullness of time, because of its restored quality, Quakerism regained its strong appeal.

The meetings for discipline are illuminating on this aspect of 18th century Quakerism, ranging, as they do, over:

Marriage delinquency (nearly 40% of the total).

Sectarian delinquency:
Drunkenness; military activity; non-attendance at meeting and then a long list of lesser delinquencies, including loose conduct, profanity, quarrelling, entertainments, neglecting family responsibilities, contempt of the Meeting's authority, gambling, disapproved company, business ethics, ignoring 'gospel order', oaths, courting and fraternising, lying, disobeying parents, dispensing liquor, theology, dress and speech, printing, Sabbath-breaking.

Sexual delinquency:
Fornication, including with fiancé(e), incest, adultery.

Delinquency with consequences for third parties:
Debt, assault, slander, slaveholding, fraud, theft.

The disciplinary procedure – placing the offending Friend under "dealing" – required Friends to be appointed by the appropriate meeting to meet with the offender so as to discover and/or to point out the error of his or her ways. Offenders then had the opportunity to formally apologise – to "condemn" their behaviour (and to amend their ways) – and were only disowned if they failed to do so. The apologies were made public within the meeting and, depending on the errant Friend's status, could also be publicised externally. It was practically unknown for Friends ever to take each other to court under the law. Some transgressions, such as "marrying out" were irreversible and these, together with those not producing the required apology, resulted in disownment, the scale of which was considerable when viewed in a modern context. The statistics cover more than 13,000 delinquencies. The overall percentage of disownments totalled 52%, or 6,800.[36]

This reformation provides the main backdrop to Rachel's time in America. The Pemberton brothers (Israel, James and John), each in their own way, were key players along with many other well-known Quakers mentioned by Rachel in her journal. By now, Quakers had almost completely withdrawn from politics, but much hostility towards them remained and, indeed, was still to follow in the period up to American independence, bringing with it more sufferings.

Once its political facet had gone, coupled with the consequences of its reformation, Quakerism developed as a purely religious group, closely akin to the 'conservative' (traditional) form of Quakerism that still exists today, continuing its strong peace testimony and deeply involved in an impressive range of social issues quite disproportionate to the size of its membership. Prominent among these was slavery (covered in chapter 6).

*Independence looms*

Rachel's visit was only five years after the end of the French war and the defeat of Pontiac (both 1763) and six years before the Revolutionary War, reflecting the growing and overriding ambitions of the majority who wanted to use conventional, military means to remove English rule. The official Quaker line – loyalty to England ('rendering unto Caesar'), to be broken only when it conflicted with loyalty to God – marked them out as traitors. They were also accused of being hypocrites when instances of those Quakers who supported independence were levelled against them. This, their refusal to swear allegiance to the new, independent constitution and their refusal to pay taxes for wars resulted in some Quakers having their goods distrained and in further persecution and imprisonments one hundred years after many rights of religious toleration had been hard won. American independence effectively ended the extensive process of Quaker religious visits between England and America.

~~~~~~~~~~~~~~~~~~~

There was much for Rachel and her companions to ponder as they now finally left England for their momentous journey into both the known and the unknown.
~~~~~~~~~~~~~~~~~~~

## Chapter 4

## OUTWARD VOYAGE

Rachel and her three companions set sail early in the morning of 6th day, 26th of 8th month 1768. Although the wind *was boisterous such that I was unable to sit at Dinner*, it later abated and Rachel went on deck to drink tea *after which my mind was comfortably drawn into silence, and returned to the Cabin in an humble frame, waiting for the income of Divine Life, which is indeed the only cause of rejoicing, and by which every enjoyment is sweetened.*

7th day the wind was fair; they had an "exceedingly pleasant sail" along the Coast and got clear of "the lane" (the English Channel) that night.

On 1st day (2nd week of voyage) Rachel and James Buck were sick and remained so until 5th day when she was a little better and drank tea with her three companions and *The kind Captain came and sat with us tho' I could not but view him in Martha's state cumbered with many things, being anxious that every thing that was necessary might be got for us ... and I had inwardly to praise the lord for his mercy ... and humbly to beg the continuation of his Divine protection upon the Watery Element ... after which my mind was covered with great sweetness and I rested well.*

6th and 7th days were *very pleasant and the wind favourable ... the Visions of the night was pleasing in which I had secretly to adore and magnify that great name.*

*On first day the 4th of 9 Month* (3rd week of voyage) *we had a Meeting for the Worship of Almighty God, at which all the hands that could be spared attended. Things were opened to the several States present greatly to my admiration and I hope to the advantage of some persons – tho' some of them seemed very raw yet behaved well and all very kind and Civil to me; the meeting ended in prayer and praise, our minds being filled with humble thankfulness before the God and Father of all our Mercies who graciously favoured with the Income of his Love and Life giving presence to our mutual comfort and Edification.*

For the rest of that week, the winds were strong and the seas high. Rachel was sick and only a little better on 7th day. Being still unable to sit up on 1st day (4th week of voyage), there was no public meeting but it was a little calmer in the evening and William Coleman proposed sitting a while in silence *in which circumspection and care in all our words and actions was strongly recommended, and not to be ashamed to confess Christ before men, but to be bold for his truth, as it was such only that he would confess before his Father and the Holy Angels ... concluded with humble thanksgiving and praise for the many mercies and unspeakable favours extended to us upon the unstable Ocean ...*

2nd day was fine with the wind favourable and on 3rd they passed Corvo (the northernmost of the Azores). In the evening *my mind was much favoured with the gracious overshadowing of Divine Love to the breaking of my heart and tendering my Spirit in a sense of my own unworthiness.* The 4th, 5th, 6th and 7th days continued fine when *nothing remarkable happened; only catching two Dolphins; as I had never seen any before it was very agreeable to me, and I [did] eat of it with a pretty good gust and found no bad effect from it.*

*On first day the 18th of the month* (5th week of voyage) *we had a Meeting to which a few of the hands on board came; in which I had to point out the danger there was in laying Stumbling blocks in the way of the weak mentioning the expression of our Lords that offences would come but to love them by whom they came that it was better that a Millstone had been hung about their neck than offend one of these little ones.*

The weather continued pleasant but there was almost a calm until the 7th day when the wind picked up a little in their favour. On 1st day

(6th week of voyage) they had a meeting attended by a few of the ship's company when the theme of Rachel's ministry was on *he who sat in the Ship and taught his people.* On 2nd, 3rd and 4th days the wind was contrary and squally, the seas were high and they made little progress as they were *tossed back and forward upon the unstable Ocean.* It made Rachel poorly again, yet the little Quaker family sat together on the evening of 4th day *and tho' tempestuous without yet a quiet serenity within was graciously proclaimed by Him who speaks and it comes to pass and commands and it is done.* 5th day the wind was still against them but on 6th it was a little more favourable followed by a southwest wind on 7th when they went forward.

*On first day* (7th week of voyage) *an uneasy motion attended the Vessel yet we kept our Meeting as usual to our mutual satisfaction tho' I was very low viewing my own weakness in that lonely situation, deprived of all outward help to bear a part in the work by Public testimony, yet I hope not alone in a spiritual labour and inward travel of Soul for the arising of Life which proved to me a great help and strength in my lonely stepping along.*

They spoke to a vessel from New England, which had left only six days previously, and confirmed their bearings. Little did they realise that it would, in fact, be fifteen more days before they could set foot on shore. On 2nd day they caught a shark and there was a little drinking rain. They spent six days with the wind in the wrong quarter *– all lying days the wind continuing ahead and we a trembling on the midst of the great Ocean.*

*It brought me after to a close inquiry into my own Actions and a fresh concern Seized my Spirit that I should not leave the Vessel clear without having another opportunity with the hands on board who had not been so frequent in the attending our Meeting as might have been desired, and on 1st day the 9th of 10th month* (8th week of voyage) *all that could be spared came and sat with us in which I had a full opportunity to open the way of Life and Salvation to them with earnest desires they might be prevailed with to lay hold of Divine Mercy which was afresh extended for their help; and the great disadvantage of evil company was laid before them. The Meeting concluded with grateful acknowledgements to the Divine Author of every good & perfect Gift, whose mercies are more in number than the hairs of our heads, and that we may walk worthy of so great Salvation is the earnest breathing of my Spirit whilst I am penning this.*

2nd, 3rd and 4th days there was still little progress – a calm, interrupted by a short storm of thunder and rain, and they were "in danger of thinking time a little tedious". During the night of 5th day, the wind came round to the northeast and gave them fresh spirit and hopes. About 12 o'clock on 6th day they took a pilot on board and got to within the Capes of Delaware about 8 o'clock and cast anchor in the bay. On 7th day, they heaved anchor but the wind was contrary again and lost them the little that they had gained on the tide.

Rachel wrote a letter home, ready for the earliest possible despatch from Delaware:

> ***I want not inclination to transmit ye Earlyst account I am capble to one I know will be anxious to hear – proble*** [probably] ***may think ye time Long before its Receivd of our Safe arrival in ye Bay of Delaware after a passige of 7 weeks wanting one day from Leving ye Land till we got within ye Capps*** [Capes] ***which was Last night wear*** [where] ***we ancord & this Morning Wighed ancor & are now sailing up ye Bay with Little wind & ye Day pleasant – yt I coud not Imploy myself more agreable than in pening this account to My Dear husband and Childer who I dou[b]t not with their father haith often bin Solicitous to know how it haith fared with their Mother Upon ye Unstable Element upon which she haith Dwelt so Long ... my first Entrance upon this anxious task ye aspect was indeed gloomy having no femal[e] aboard but My Self – but have Now Reason to believe it was all in Wisdom – Every thing haith bin Maid much Esier than I could Expect – as their*** [there] ***was an inclination to oblige Each other ... I was much tryed with Sickness at times for upwards of 5 weeks – yt had Little Relish for food of any sort – Animal food became***

> ***Lothsome and Tea had not its Usual Relish – yt watter Podige*** [porridge] ***became an acceptable Dish – I Breakfastd & sup[p]ed of Em for near 2 weeks with great Contentment & thankfulness upon My mind – being quite satisfied having No Desire for any thing Else tho we abounded with plenty of Every thing Rather Elegant than otherwise. We had Both Rosted and Boild almost Every Day – we never mised ye one but seldom Both as well as Variety of Licor of Both wines & Malt as good as at Land - & all things in good Order with proper attendents ye Steward a good Natured obliging young Man.***

Finally, at around 3.00 pm on 1st day the 16th of 10th month they reached Newcastle and were able to go on shore using the pilot boat. Here *we got a little refreshment whilst the horses were got ready for us to go to Wilmington which we reached agreeably about 6 o'clock where we met with many kind Friends that were glad to see us – the Joy seemed mutual and especially once more to see my Old acquaintances Elizabeth Shipley and Esther White who were truly near to me in Gospel Labour. We lodged with Widow Harvey who with her children was exceeding kind – here we also met with two Valuable Women friends one from Carolina the other from Virginia. On second day morning we visited Elizabeth Shipley who had been poorly and tho' getting a little better is yet in a weakly way. Our Meeting was like that of Mary and Elizabeth when the "Babe lept in her Womb for Joy". The Season was most comfortable in which with awful thankfulness we had to offer the sacrifice of pure praise to the Father and Founder of all our mercies who had been with us upon the great Ocean and preserved through every danger and supported thro' many trials far above our desert the remembrance whereof deeply humbled our mind.*

It does indeed seem miraculous that all the detailed preparations made with Friends both in England and in America, followed by the long, unpredictable voyage of some 3,000 miles by sailing ship, did at last bring them here to their horses and to the succession of American Quakers, including several Wilson relations, awaiting them on their even more unpredictable journeys through the provinces on the eastern side of this vast continent. Including the waiting days at The Downs and Dungeness they were actually at sea 61 days, during which time Rachel was either "poorly" or "very poorly" for at least 18. And one wonders how the crew of the ship felt about their 'first day' meetings on board with this remarkable Quaker woman preacher and how they took to the silent parts of the meetings as well as to her vocal ministry.

As a Quaker minister it was only to be expected that Rachel would feel drawn – indeed to see it as her duty to God – to minister wherever she went. Her ministry, in the way that she describes it in her journal, is couched in much scriptural language and resonates strongly with the preaching of the first generation of Quakers.

What she does not describe is the unique nature of the Quaker experience – the sense of revelation – brought by the early Quakers. This was that Christ is come to teach his people himself and that God dwells inside each and every one of us. For them, God came to be known directly without the offices of any priest or other intermediary and, moreover, it did not depend on having read the scriptures. To use a modern description, it is the "experience of an indefinable power, a power that we believe fills the whole universe and can enter into the core of our being if we will open the door. 'Behold I stand at the door and knock' said Jesus. When the knock comes (in whatever form that may be) we have to decide whether to go with it, for we have to trust in the power before it will work, not the other way round. ... when a 'knock' is accepted, when the person is 'convinced', there comes a sense of a real indwelling presence, of a 'friend', a 'comrade', a 'guardian', an incarnation of the unknowable God through whom one can pray." [37]

Rachel was a truly wonderful and very human person, accepting every 'knock', and this clearly 'reached' those who flocked to her meetings.

## Samuel Rowland Fisher 1745-1834

Samuel Fisher, was the son of Joshua Fisher who, in 1746, established a large mercantile business of that name in Philadelphia and who, shortly afterwards, started the first line of packet ships to sail regularly to and from London. Joshua's grandfather had come to America on the same ship, the *Welcome*, that first brought William Penn.

The *Pennsylvania Pacquet* was already in commission by 1760, this being the year when Jane Crosfield sailed on it to make her religious visit to America.

Quakers pursued their witness and their commercial businesses as a single whole in their lives of service to God. Thus we find Samuel, by now the owner with his four brothers of a large business, giving up his time to be Rachel's 'companion' for the first part of her religious visit. And in a business letter in 1769, dealing with a particular consignment of linen from a Quaker in Ireland, he adds:
"Our Friend Rachel Wilson having nearly compleated her Visit to this Continent to great Satisfaction to People of all Societies, & so great an Openess has appeared in many Places that we have reason to believe that [these] her acceptable Visits will not be easily erased from the Minds of many but prove everlasting Benefit."

In the fullness of time, Samuel Fisher and two of his brothers were exiled for holding fast to their pacifist principles and refusing to take the oath of allegiance in 1777 during the Revolutionary War.

## Chapter 5

## IN & AROUND PHILADELPHIA
## OUTWARD TO LEESBURGH

Despite the weather being very wet and Wilmington Friends encouraging her to stay, Rachel was eager on that 2nd day, 17th of 10th month to set out on her mission and *my kind Friend and Companion Samuel Fisher procured a Chaise in which we got agreeably along, yet not without some danger but escaped without harm; our kind Landlady and her Son accompanied us, also the two Women Friends.* They dined at Chester and dried themselves; then, with the rain still falling, they proceeded by carriage to Philadelphia.

Rachel travelled in or around Philadelphia for the next 24 days, attending meetings for worship of all sorts and sizes on almost every day, meeting a great many Friends, including several personal friends and relations, and visiting the sick.

As well as in Philadelphia itself, Rachel travelled to Shrewsbury, New Jersey, via Bristol, Allentown and Freehold (74 miles); then back to Allentown (34), via Freehold; Crosswicks (distance not recorded); Burlington (14 miles involving crossing the river into New Jersey) and Philadelphia, (20 miles); next to Abington; Horsham; Byberry; Germantown; Fairhill; the Hill and the Bank. The meetings ranged from large to small and encompassed 'morning', 'afternoon', 'evening', 'weekday', 'preparative', 'monthly', 'quarterly', 'yearly', 'select' (elders and ministers), 'youths', 'Negro's Meeting' and a marriage.

She had just one day off when she wrote home and also to R. Chester: ['ye'='the'; 'yt'= 'that']

> ***I wrot thee after I got into ye Bay of Delaware in hope to have sent it by Captain friend of which was Disapointed by ye wind being too high to get it on Board but now in Expectation to get Em away by the way of Bristol – as I wd not wilingly Miss any***

***opportunity of Conveying thee intelegence I know will be so acceptable of our Safe arival hear ... I never was Better in my health than since I Landed. Ive Lost a litle flesh at Sea yt what I can very well spair – if it should be a little more I should not bemone ye Loss whilst ye Blessing of Health is injoyd ... Poor Brother Anthony*** [Isaac's brother] ***Came to me yesterday – his aperance was Rather affecting – yet thayr is a family Resemblance in him Something of ye onest & Valuable Father in his face. Ive seen none of his Childer – he told me he had [a] son Moved hear but I find [him] not among frds*** [Friends] ***– he also tould Me Cous David Wilson was Dead this summer – I gave him a Little Matter as he had come 12 miles to see Me – and if thou Chous*** [choose] ***I should hand Em a litle more by way of present I dou[b]t not itl be acceptable – tho he seems prety healthy & able to work – tho Looks old & Shab[b]y. Ive not yet seen Cous John Wilson.***

Next she deals with her finances and then

***My Dear Love to John and Doly, George and Deby & I hope my Little Name Sake thrives ... as for Isaac*** [daughter Dorothy's son born 1765] ***if he can Reme[m]ber his Grandmother ... My Dear Love is to him and she wd have him to be a good Boy ... Benj Birkett is still hear & I hope behaves well – its an orderly family ye young pepol yt are arived at Meeting all Religously inclined – good examples – yt I think it may j[o]ustly be Esteemed a favour he fell into such hands – at Every Branch of ye family Exceding kind and Desirous of my Staying with Em.***

Philadelphia was America's largest city at this time and also the principal powerhouse of Friends as brought to life by this selection of journal entries for the days spent in and around Philadelphia:

*First day was at 3 Meetings.*
*I met with many of my old Friends here with whom my mind was easily united in Gospel Labour.*

*I was at the Marriage of ... at the great Meeting house ... I had to tell them it was a truth worthy of our remembrance that the Lord looks not as Man looks in which I was opened above my expectation.*

*We lodged at ... and we had a sweet taste of Divine Love together. ... their Select Meeting was not large, yet favor'd with the overshadowing of Divine good, in which my mind was enlarged to set forth the beautiful Order of the Lord's House as all his servants move under his Divine direction and earnestly desired there might be neither rent nor schism found amongst them.*
*... dined with Widow Williams and her Children – her Husband being dead only the week before in the small Pox and neither she nor her 10 children had any of them had them – it was a season of renewed favour.*

*On 3rd day attended the Select Meeting at 9 in which our minds were deeply baptized together; at 11 the parting Meeting came in which was large and open in which the great Love of God was set forth in sending his only begotten Son for our Redemption, and the Meeting ended in prayer and praises for the unmerited favors thus plentifully outpoured.*

*Many Friends accompanied me on fourth day to Allens Town 20 miles, had a Meeting in the Inn where the people behaved well and things were pertinently spoke to tho' I did not think had so great a reach as at Fresholt* [Freehold].
*... at Croswick* [Crosswicks] *there were a large Body of Friends and many of their neighbours came in. James Thornton first appeared* [i.e. ministered] *in an acceptable manner. I had also an open time amongst them my mind being set at liberty both to Friends and others in the renewing of Gospel Love which was fresh cause of admiration and thanksgiving – I had chiefly to treat upon "that if thou doest well shalt thou not be accepted and if thou dost not well sin lieth at the door".*

At Philadelphia Monthly Meeting: *I had to set forth the beauty of the Lords House and the Orders of his servants and the necessity there is for all to mind their own business and be content with their own allotment for the presentation of good Order and to war against a Spirit that would find fault with each other without the great Masters Order.*

*... after Meeting in the evening ... I had to desire the youth present to mind the present Visitation and watch with circumspection and fear that they might not pull down what their parents had built up.*

*On 2nd day we went to Abbington ... 12th was their Monthly Meeting and large things did not rise high yet I was able to get through what was upon my Mind to some degree of Satisfaction. The Meeting of Business was the most unsettled I ever saw which I could not forbear remarking and the great hurt it did which I wish may be regarded.*

In a reference, one assumes, to 'marrying out':

*The great disadvantage of being unequally yoked was pointed out and how necessary to ask Wisdom of Him that giveth liberally and upbraideth not even in the weighty affair of Marriage.*

*... visited Cousin Wilson's ... Also one Thomas Wood who was near 100 years old and who had been a useful Friend.*

*At German Town ... where many Friends from Philadelphia accompanied me, the Meeting House being too small to contain the number I had close work with the Babylonish garment and the Wedge of Gold, and with the indulgence of things forbidden.*

*I was at their Select Meeting ... where several living testimonies were borne. My Mind was deeply humbled under a sense of my own weakness and unworthiness of the favors received which I had to express in a broken manner yet very affecting. The Meeting concluded with humble prayer – Dined with Isaac Greenliff after which many friends coming in, tho' I was very low, we were greatly favoured together – and also at Hugh Forbes after which I went to John Pemberton's where viewing a Plan of the Meetings my Spirit was greatly overcome that I could not refrain from weeping Tears*

*under a sense of my own unfitness and Lonely situation which was a preparation for what fell to my Lot.*
*... drank Tea with Widow Warner and visited her Mother an innocent Woman in her 90th year – after was at the evening Meeting which was exceedingly crowded both within and without doors; in this Meeting I had to mention the expression of Paul to Agrippa when he said "thou almost persuaded me to be a Christian" – accompanied with strong desires for those present that they might be not almost but altogether what the Lord would have them to be.*

*Third day was the Youths Meeting which was large and in which Divine Goodness was graciously pleased to overshadow with his Love and life giving presence.* (The Youths Meetings were attended by members of all ages, their specific purpose being to urge the youth of the meeting to be faithful.)
*Mary Pemberton took me in her Chariot to Anthony Diehase's whose Wife had been long confined; her Sister being also present I was opened to speak to their States in a particular manner with which they expressed their thankfulness – After we went to the Hospital where there were many sick and disorder'd people who seem well taken care of ... After we went to Wm Coleman's whose Wife had been poorly some time and looked to me as if it would be her last Illness, with whom we were comforted together.*

Earlier in her travels, she met another Friend also terminally ill: ... *sitting awhile with Samuel Smith who had been confined for above 2 months and the use of his Limbs had been taken from him and to me it seemed as if it might be his last Illness. I was engaged in supplication on his account and I believe it was a comfortable season to the afflicted Friend as well as to his Wife and Children.*
*The Negro's Meeting began at 3 when many of them appeared and kind Providence favour'd with his ancient Love that pertinent advice and counsel was achieved with which several were much affected.*

Friends made great efforts to attract and include African slaves in their meetings, although they were surprisingly slow to establish full equality – African Americans still sat on a separate bench at the back, as was the practice in other denominations. [38] In Philadelphia Yearly Meeting, they could apply for membership from 1796 but the uptake was low, one reason possibly being that the quiet of a Quaker meeting did not appeal as much as other forms of worship.

One vital arrangement was made on 3rd day of 11th month reflecting the standard practice in those times for women Friends travelling in the ministry to have a designated woman companion: *That afternoon consulted about going forward to the Southwest. Esther Fisher was thought proper to accompany me as I was quite free in my own Mind with her Company.*

Her time in Philadelphia now fulfilled, Rachel completed her journey across the south eastern side of Pennsylvania: 28 miles to a Friend for the first night followed by 22 miles to Meeting at Sadsbury *which was but Low yet revived a little towards the conclusion*; next, 12 miles to Moses Brimstone's *where we were kindly entertained*; then 2 miles to Meeting at Lancaster (on 7th day, 12th of 11th month) and 8 miles to her host where she met with Sarah Morris *who had given up to accompany me through this Journey, which I cannot but esteem an additional favour.*

*This evening we had a taste of the pure Celestial Streams of Divine Love opened to us for our encouragement. On first day morning the Meeting was not large nor very open; I had to speak to the great advantage of Silence.* She met Thomas Lightfoot and his wife, having not met the latter for 14 years *and it was truly pleasant to meet in that Love which first united us in Gospel Labour.* Their journey continued for 10 miles to the ferry over the Susquehanna and the further 12 miles to York.

*On third day morning had a Meeting at 11. Sarah Morris first appeared with that of the seed falling upon different sorts of Ground – which also fell to my Lot to enlarge upon. After this Meeting an engagement fell upon me to have one in the Evening which began at 8 to which many of the Towns people attended and seemed well satisfied. They appeared to me several of them to be in a seeking state to whom Divine regard was manifested.*

Next morning, Esther Fisher (her first companion) returned to Philadelphia while Rachel and her other companions journeyed on to Newbury where the small meeting house scarcely contained all the Friends who attended. Another Friend ministered first, referring to the parable of the ten virgins, followed by Rachel desiring that one should be as anxious for inward wealth as for outward wealth. On 5th day they had a large meeting close to Warrington and Rachel ministered on *the great favour extended to us poor unworthy mortals* and *setting forth how much it required our circumspection and ... the disadvantage that attended giving way to our own unruly tempers as well as the danger of letting in hardness one against another.*

On 6th day they attended meeting at Huntington – it *was but small, many of the Men being at their Court at York, it was a little trying in that being in deep Poverty yet for sometime before the Meeting concluded things rose above my expectation.* They travelled to their hosts and had *a sit in the Family; the Son and Daughter seem'd Raw, though pure and loving.* The practice of visiting preachers was to have "settings" in the evening with their hosts' families and to experience the spiritual uplift that these gave. The frequent mentions in Rachel's journal to her having "a sit in the family" are clearly references to these "settings".

They stayed over there on 7th day. First day meeting was at Menallen where many gathered, both Friends and others, *and the way to the Kingdom was opened to them by the preaching of the Gospel when John saw the Angel that flew through the midst of Heaven.* They continued on their way: 2nd day, to Pipe Creek, 3rd day to a Friends' home, 4th day to Bush Creek and 5th day to Frederick[town] where *we lodged at an Inn [and] had two Meetings in the Court House, to which many of the Town's people attended, and seemed well satisfied. We drank Tea with the Parson's Widow who was very friendly; the Curate came and sat with us, who expressed his satisfaction with the Meetings, and the Doctrines he had heard.* 6th day: they crossed the River Potomac into Virginia and reached Leesburgh, 22 miles.

In addition to the Meetings mentioned at Sadsbury, Lancaster, York and Frederick, there were meetings all along the way with their Quaker hosts and hostesses. One can sense how encouraged they felt by, for example, the people who came to Frederick seeming to be "in a seeking state"

So far, therefore, Rachel had briefly set foot in Delaware, New Jersey and Maryland and had visited Friends and Meetings extensively in Pennsylvania. During her 24 days in Philadelphia, she attended 28 meetings for worship (including those for business and marriage). She 'appeared' at more than half of them and recorded only one of them as having been not very large. She and her companions were now in Virginia and one can picture them reliving the greatly differing receptions that had been given in the American colonies to the early Quakers who revealed their radical (and to some people alarming) experience of the inner light.

During their travels, they continued to enjoy the same warm welcome from their American hosts as did those who had gone before them:
"... their hospitality to travelling Friends who visited them was genuine and hearty. The visitors were given the best of everything, often including all the beds in the house, while the family slept on the floor. If there were only one room, that would be placed at the disposal of the guests, and the family would betake themselves to the shelter of a covered wagon or a barn" [39]

## Chapter 6

## VIRGINIA

6$^{th}$ day, the 25$^{th}$ of 11$^{th}$ month 1768. Having arrived at Leesburgh, Rachel had an evening meeting in the Court House to which many of the local inhabitants came. She ministered to them followed by a local Friend *pressing her desire that all might be sensible of the great Love of God in sending his Servants and Messengers amongst them. By this time I was filled with a sense there were many seeking souls, to whose states I was opened.*

She stayed overnight with local Friends and on seventh day went to their meeting at Fairfax which was "large and solemn". Here she met Sarah Janney who had *been under an engagement for some time to have a religious visit to the Southern parts that when she heard of my coming revived the concern and as my Dear Friend S Morris did not have strength to go forward, it appeared to me providential to have a companion under the same engagement with whom friends were well satisfied, that she had a certificate readily granted.* Rachel stayed for meeting on first day, which again was large and, afterwards, went back to Maidstone Ferry. On second day she proceeded to Goose Creek where the little meeting house did not hold half of the people who came and, later, she said good-bye to her companions Sarah Morris and Thomas Fisher.

While at Fairfax and Goose Creek, she took the opportunity to write a letter home so that these two Friends could despatch it for her when they got back to Philadelphia:

> ***Samuel Morton, Thos Fisher & Sarah Morris haith accompd Me So far ... am Lick*** [like] ***to get afresh Companion hear ...am well taken Care of having Every outward help Necessary – or yt Can well be procured & Every thing is Made Ese*** [easy] ***yt I find no Difficulty but what I Can Esely Despence with – being favoured with health & good aptite I want no fine Sauce to Relish My Food – as to Drink Cyder it agrees with me very well & yt is pretty Comen in Most places – tho Ive bin at Some places to hear***

> ***they had not yt or to Malt Licor. Ive seen none since I Left Philadelphia Nayther have I any desire after it yt one thing suted*** [suited] ***to another – Ive got an Excelent hors yt Carr[i]es Me Exceeding Ese – ye American horsis do Exceed ours for Ease – yt am well suted ... My Companion this Long jorney is Sarah Janney, Proble*** [probably] ***Thos Gawthrope or Jane Crosfield may know her – I mett with many Remembered them – My Dear Love to them.***

The reference to the quality of the American horses is interesting. A very substantial Quaker business in Rhode Island included a horse-raising plantation where there was a unique breed of horses of Andalusian origin known particularly for their speed and easy pacing. They could pace a mile in just over two minutes and cover 100 miles in a day without harm to themselves or their rider.[40]

> ***If I should not have an oportunity to write againe til I get to Charlestown I wod not have thee Unese upon my account. I hope I shal not sufer – ye Great Master in whos servis I am ingaged is altogether able to qualifie for Every ingagement he Calls to yt I am quite Resigned tho my path seems Different to some – having not only to Visit frds but others in order to gett a Litl peace as I go along yt have had several Meetg in fresh places Much to My satisfaction and I have reason to believe to ye Benefit of those We have Visited yt have Left all behind Me Ese which I am Desires*** [desirous] ***of as I go along yt I may not Look Back with pain – not to Make More haist than good speed if I should be Detaind a few Months Longer than Some May have performed ye Visit in. I find I am to Look to My own Benefitt Singly Eying ye Pointings out of Divine wisdom.***
>
> ***My frds wd have Left us this Morning – but concluding to go with us to Goose Creek when we had a Meeting to Day – ye meetinghous so small did not contain half of ye pepol & sharp frost yt I could not but be in pain for them yt stood out – but***

***when Meeting was over I found they had got 2 fires to stand or sit by – yt they wear better off than I Expected.***

Her letter explains that the Gap and Winchester were next on their planned itinerary, then Hopewell Monthly Meeting

***after which we shall have Longer Stages till we Reach North Carolina tho I hope we shall not be Exposed to Lodge in ye woods – hears*** [here's] ***great improvements in these Backparts – their*** [they're] ***now Prety thick inhabited – how Long this journey will take is Uncertain. I can form Little or no Guess it may be 2 or 3 Months before I Reach Charlestown. Its a great tract of Land to go over. I must bid farewell tho when I settle down to write thee I hardly know when to Leve if I can get a Little time – which is at present presious – I now absent My Self from Many fds – to finish this – My Dear Love to all our Childer and Relations as if Named also Ruth – with as much as I can give to My Dear husband from thy truly affectionate wife. Rachel Wilson***

Virginia was a different world, as John Woolman discovered on his religious visits in 1746 and 1757. He entered a land of individual homesteads and plantations with never a group of houses large enough to count as a village or settlement in the whole of his first journey. Even in 1760, Thomas Jefferson (governor of Virginia 1779-81 and subsequently 3rd president of the USA), when he left home at seventeen to go to college in Williamsburg, had never seen a settlement of more than a dozen houses. He was impressed by Williamsburg, the seat of government, consisting of 200 houses. They were poorly-built, wooden structures and the streets were still earth. Yet the population of Virginia then equalled the combined total of Pennsylvania, New Jersey and half of New York.[41]

~~~~~~~~~~~~~~~~~~~

Twenty years before Woolman, the ratio of settlers to African slaves was 10:1 whereas in 1746 it was 1:1. A description of 100 years before that is still more striking:
~~~~~~~~~~~~~~~~~~~

"A lot of water had flowed down the James River since that hot, moist day in August 1620 when the Dutch man o' war, curiously, nosing up to the new settlement, had made a handsome profit, offering to exhausted English gentry a batch of twenty Negro slaves for sale." [42]

Woolman, in his journal, described Virginia where the plantations were of "the bewitching Vegetable Tobacco". African slaves – men, women and children – toiled unenthusiastically all day between the rows, supervised by overseers whose job it was to extract, by fair means or foul, enough output to satisfy their masters. An account of what Woolman witnessed reads: "The bare legs and feet that presently scuffled along in the dusty road [at the end of the day's work] were thin and stricken with sores. There were no fat ones among them." [43] Much remained the same as Rachel now travelled along in this the colony where slavery was most widespread.

Quaker concern for their fellow human beings was manifested both in their dealings with the native Indians and in their position over the possession of African slaves. For over twenty years, John Woolman had been active in America as the Quaker leader against slavery, but Rachel was ahead of the year when the efforts of Woolman and other abolitionists came to fruition in the Philadelphia Yearly Meeting minute of 1776 to "deny the right of membership to such as persisted in holding their fellow-men as property". In 1769, many Friends were still slave owners who were content to follow Fox's 100-year old direction to Friends "as to severall things as to ye [the] well ordering and manageing theire affaires" namely: "trayneing up theire Neigors in ye feare of god bought with their money & such as were borne in theire families so yt [that] all may Come to ye knowledge of ye Lord, yt so ... we will serve ye Lord & yt theire overseers might deale mildely & gentley with ym [them] & not use cruelty as ye manner of some is & hath beene & to make ym free after 30 years servitude ..." [44]

In 1746, "John Woolman visited Maryland, Virginia and North Carolina, and recorded that slavery appeared to him 'as a dark gloominess overhanging the land.' Three years later he again visited these southern Meetings of Friends. Travelling as a minister of the Gospel, he often sat down at tables of slave-holding planters, who were accustomed to entertain their friends free of cost, and could not understand his scruples against receiving freely for food and lodging which he looked upon as having been gained by the oppression of the slaves. Wherever he went, he found his fellow-members entangled in the wrong of slavery. Elders and ministers, as well as the younger and less esteemed, all had their slaves." [45]

All this time, Woolman had been using the utmost tact in persuading his fellow Quakers to listen to him. Many were successful, wealthy businessmen who were benefiting from slave ownership and many held high office in American colonial administration. It was also common to find single slaves in modest households and small Quaker businesses.

Woolman's particular strength was in his logical, clear-sightedness. Friends, by and large, had been endeavouring to preserve some sort of status quo, taking positions in arguments that often were heated. There was general agreement that Friends should not trade in slaves (i.e. buy and sell them as a business) but many had been resisting the argument that they should not even buy slaves (or indeed sell them when no longer required). They were also resisting granting immediate freedom to existing slaves, although there were plenty of examples of freedom being given at the end of a very extended term of service (e.g. 30 years). Then there was their argument that Quakers were good masters, treating their slaves fairly and providing them with a better life than they could have expected back in their African homelands or from other slave-owners. Woolman saw straight through all these arguments to the root of human dignity – the free rights of every individual of whatever origin or means – as given to all from God. There should be no such thing as slavery.

He confined his attentions to Quakers – a massive and daunting task in itself. He was present at Newport Yearly Meeting in 1759 when message was brought in to a Quaker that his ship had just arrived and required his immediate presence to supervise the unloading and sale of its cargo of slaves. The meeting was full of hundreds of prosperous Friends, as well as some visitors from England holding travelling "certificates", who all witnessed the incident. Woolman felt sickened. By contrast, about this time, another shipowner (possibly not a Quaker, but connected to them), when he personally watched his ship being discharged of its human cargo, was so moved to tears that he set free all of his share of the slaves – the "miserable wretches" – provided for them and subsequently traced as many of the others as he could in order to buy them and likewise provide for them.[46]

At an individual level, there had been an instance of a Quaker who cared for his slaves in a way that enabled them to marry and have a family but later sold the wife/mother when her services were no longer needed.

Another example was provided by the Quaker family with the horse-raising plantation mentioned earlier where that part of the business alone had as many slaves as horses. Quite apart from home sales, the business had exported as many as 100 horses in a year. The total business at its peak extended to 12,000 acres (a typical farm being no more than 300 acres) and the family was then the largest slave-owner in Rhode Island. They produced no fewer than four Lieutenant-Governors of the colony.[47]

It is shocking to realise that with the huge natural resources then being opened up in Africa and the Americas, the intercontinental trade that developed was greater in slaves than in anything else. As many as 100,000 slaves were traded by the English alone in a single year. Since 1680, there had been something approaching 2,000,000 slaves transported to America. The company that originally had the monopoly in this trade was once so important to the English economy that, in 1730, to ensure its continuation, Parliament approved a subsidy of £10,000 per annum. In 1750, "fearing the injurious results of a declining Negro trade", it liquidated the company and introduced a Regulated Company. This, in recognition of the commercial risks that they were taking, granted to the proprietors a monopoly in their particular trade and gave a large and instant boost to their business, especially in supplying slaves to the southern colonies. It made easy money for the traders, Newport merchants being the principal beneficiaries.[48]

In Virginia, the Governor received a directive from the King (James II) commanding him, "upon pain of the highest displeasure" to withhold assent to any law that would in any way obstruct the slave trade.

How much influence did Woolman have on Friends during the twenty years since starting his quiet, sensitive, tactful campaign to open his fellow Quakers' hearts and minds to the truth behind their slave ownership? Had those Friends that Rachel was now visiting met him and how had they responded? Rachel's journal, so far, has not mentioned Friends' slaves.

But Quaker realisation of the evil was already spreading. Yearly Meeting in Virginia had condemned the trade back in 1757, the year of Woolman's second visit; then, in 1764, it had laid upon Quakers a duty of kindness towards these their 'servants', of educating, feeding and clothing them. Only the previous year, Yearly Meeting had taken the next big step by banning Quakers not only from trading but also from purchasing slaves. The whole issue was thus highly topical and controversial at this point in Quaker history.

~~~~~~~~~~~~~~~~~~

On third day, 29th of 11th month, Rachel and her companions were at the Gap, *begun at 10 which proved satisfactory amongst a mixed multitude.* They came over Shouden, to Samuel Pleasants' *where many neighbours came in, and we were much favoured ... In the Morning before we took leave, our minds being covered with sweetness, a little tender advice sprung up very seasonably to the tendering our Spirits together.* They reached Winchester on 4th day in time for a meeting at 5, held in a large room at an inn, to which *the*
~~~~~~~~~~~~~~~~~~

*people came pretty fully, that it was much crowded, and they behaved well, mostly very solid, being covered with Divine Nature and things were opened to their different states in a manner above my expectation, and the wonderful Love of God acknowledged, that after the meeting was over, a solid Woman came to me and told me she had something to impart to me – 'She had some time before had a dream, That a Babe was sent to them that told its Errand, and then was taken from them again, which was fulfilled in me that night'.*

Increasingly, their journey became characterised by stopping with local Friends in their homes in isolated places and isolated communities, holding their meetings with them in the company of many neighbours who also came along, and enjoyed Friends' company as they rode with them to the next port of call. Occasionally, they had to lodge overnight at inns.

Rachel continues: *On 5 day of the week 1 of the 12 month had a Meeting at Richard Jostles ... Friends accompanying us 10 miles the day proved very Cold – we rode 10 miles after to Joseph Steers, I never was more pleased to get Lodgings, the Wind was so sharp, and though their House was open and unfinished, we got no colds for which favour with the many confines upon me, may I be humbly thankful. On 6 day was at Back Creek 8 miles, had an open Meeting – dined at John Pugh's, with many Friends, where we had a solemn Season – Wm Jolliff & Wife meeting us we returned with them.*

*On seventh day was at Middle Creek, 10 miles; had a Meeting in a Friend's House, in which I had to desire we might wait, as with one accord, for the inducement of the Holy Ghost, as the necessary qualification for acceptable Worship, as well as Ministry; in which we experienced comfort and consolation – the Meeting ended well. We dined with the Friends and a few words were drafted in the Family before we left them to satisfaction. We returned to William Jolliff that Night, Sarah Janney my Companion, her Husband and several other friends, that we were 12 strangers in the House, and all kindly entertained.*

*First day was cold and Snowy, yet the Meeting was larger than might reasonably be expected, yet it was a Suffering time. In the afternoon had a comfortable season in the Friends family to our mutual refreshment. 2nd day was their Monthly Meeting – the Morning Sacrifice was season'd with the Salt of everlasting Covenant – the Meeting was Pretty large, and rather more open than the day before, yet there seem'd something that hinder'd the running of Shiloh's streams.*

*The Womens meeting more favoured, as also at Table – That evening we had some conversation with one of the Burgesses, who expressed his satisfaction pretty fully with our Visit, and wished it might be successful.*

*On third day rode 12 miles to David Brown's where we had a Meeting, to which many of the neighbours came, amongst whom we had a full opportunity, and many so reached to, that they were brought to acknowledge to the Truth – We came afterwards to Crooked Creek 8 miles to Robert Hain's where we had a favoured opportunity in the Family.*

They continued to Crook or Crooked Run (4th day), a wet day and the meeting large and "middling well", then to Stowerstown where they lodged at an inn and had a meeting attended mostly by Dutch people who "behaved well" and several were "reached to", also at Milentown, and a further meeting that evening at their host's. Next they were at Jackson Allen's for a meeting at Smiths Creek to which many people came. It was now 6th day.

*We thought of going forwards after but finding a stop in my mind concluded to stay over first day and came here with Thomas More, 9 miles, had a very comfortable opportunity with their family and was strongly advised to be careful of their Company – there were many young folks, and I fear in danger, though they behaved loving – We had a Meeting there on first day morning to which many of the*

*Neighbours came, it was long in gathering, which was a sensible loss* [i.e. a sense of loss] *and I could not help remarking it, yet it turned out well, that we had great cause of humble thankfulness, and left them easy.*

*On second day came to Stantontown,* [Staunton Town] *40 miles, dined by the way at John Graton's, one that kept a store upon the road, he was very kind. Jackson Allen and Reubin More went along with us, we lodged at an Inn, there was no friend near – As my mind was much engaged to have a meeting with them, they being all strangers to us, and our principles, we applied to the Sheriff, who readily granted us the Court House to hold a Meeting in, and came with two others and sit with us a little in the Evening, and attended the Meeting next Morning* [3rd day] *with most of the little Town, and some of the Country, which is pretty thick inhabited thereabouts; the Meeting was overshadowed with Divine good, my mind deeply humbled under a sense thereof, that I had earnestly to beg the Lord would be with us and open the hearts of the people, as he did his Servant Lydia formerly, to receive his Word – which prayer was graciously answered to my admiration and thankfulness; many of them came and dined with us, and staid till they saw us upon Horseback, the Sheriff was so kind as set us on our road a few Miles, and invited us kindly to his House. We came that night to Richard Williams near Rockfish Gap, 12 miles, an Inn, where a few of the neighbours came, to whom the way of Truth was declared.*

Notwithstanding Rachel's reference to "pretty thick inhabited", human habitation in these parts was sparse and scattered; it was mid-winter and they were in unfamiliar terrain. Rachel's spirit, as always, was indomitable.

*In the night the Snow fell which was rather discouraging to set out in, but not being easy to lay by, we set forward* [4th day] *and with Difficulty got to Thomas Stogton's, 16 miles; he was not at home but his Wife and Children received us kindly, being glad to see us , as they had but few Visits from Friends living at such a distance from any that bear our name, and being about 8 miles from any Meeting – that evening we had a sit in the family and some few neighbours – The Snow lay thick upon the Trees, so that it was scarcely possible to go forward. The Friend did not get home till noon next day* [5th day], *that we concluded to stay another night and had another Meeting, which was large and to satisfaction; that we had renewed cause to praise the name of the Lord, and magnify his power that was graciously made manifest for our help and encouragement to persevere in an humble dependence upon Him, who never fails those that trust in his Divine Aim.*

The battle with the elements continued:

*On sixth day Morning we set forward on our Journey though the prospect was very discouraging the Snow was so thick, and the Trees so laden, and many broken down, that the Road was almost stopt up in places; my Horse being full of Spirit brush'd through, that I was often in danger of being brought off and before I had rode one mile, a large Tree, under which there was not enough room for him and me, took me quite off, and I fell into a hollow way with my head downward where I must have perished, if help had not been at hand – but my kind Companion was soon off his Horse – ready to assist, being strong and willing to exert himself for my relief, he soon got me out of the Snow, and I found myself able to walk, though my Leg was much crush'd. I got up on my Horse and made a Shift to ride 15 miles to one Samuel Woods who kept an Inn, where they behaved kind and got my Leg bathed and gave it what relief I well could. Having a mind to sit with neighbours that inclined to come, notice was given, and a large Meeting we had in the Evening ... though one or two behaved light, and did what they could to make others so, which I could not but openly reprove ... the Meeting ended with prayer ...* [7th day] *Having a desire to be at Southriver, we got up, tho' my Leg was so bad I was rather fearful I could not bear to ride, yet not easy without pushing forward, and I bore it above expectation, and got 17 miles to a place called the Court House, in Hamerst* [Amherst] *County, where we dined, after which rode 20 miles to an Inn –Batty Harrison's where we had a meeting with the family.*

And next for something completely different. They crossed James River and got to first day meeting in good time. Here they discovered to their surprise that local Friends had allowed two Baptists to preach. Since the central Quaker tenet was (and is) the individual's direct access to and experience of God, without reliance on a minister or priest as intermediary, and with spoken 'ministry' being the individual's response to God's inner power, appointed preachers or ministers were anathema to many a Quaker.

*... at first* [this] *affected my mind pretty much, yet it was evident there was a Divine hand in bringing us there that day, and the testimony of Truth was exalted over the heads of gainsayers. One of those called Baptists came to me, said he was glad I was sent to visit the people, and it was in his mind that day, whilst I was on my feet, to give me a little money as Providence had blessed him with plenty. I told him He* [i.e. Providence] *had done to me too, and I had rather wherewith to be helpful than needful, and I never grudging to spend it in the cause of Truth, and I hoped I should ever keep my hands clear of taking bribes. He used some Argument to engage me to take it, but all to no purpose.*

*After this they drew the people into the Meeting house, it being very cold, the Snow upon the Ground, and many of them had come many miles to hear them. I got up on my Horse, but could not with ease go forward, so alighted and went to the Meeting house, where the same man that offered me the Money was upon his knees, with a good deal of Zeal or fire that seemed to me to be of his own raising, his name James Child, the other Christopher Clark, immediately stood up with his Testament in his hand, taking his text – You search the Scriptures, in them you think to have Eternal Life, but you will not come unto me that you may have life, which he drew into three heads or parts, and went on a pretty while, all which time I stood, tho' my leg was so bad, I was fitter for my Bed to all human appearance, yet inwardly supported that I felt but little pain; the other spoke directly, pretty much in praise of what they had heard that day, and that he thought he should not have opened his mouth that day, but now he believed it his place, and was just going to open his Testament. As my mind was full I craved a little time which was granted, in which I had to point out the necessity of silence before we could learn Christ Jesus aright and how inconsistent to take the expression of David in their mouths, when they have no knowledge of his expression, it appeared to me making use of a lie. I then found myself easy and came away exceeding thankful.*

They continued their journey in severe weather, stopping along the way with Friends, having meetings with all of them and their neighbours, enjoying their support as they accompanied them along the different sections, all very mindful of Rachel's badly injured leg. 2nd day was spent resting it; 3rd day brought them to New London when it was very wet and then to two stretches of much raised water that *was difficult and wet me much, but got safe through.* Given the weather, several people could not make it to meeting but, even so, more local people than Rachel expected turned up. They lodged with a Captain Ward and then, on 4th day, the *weather was cold hail and snow all the way ... the snow so thick and my leg rather inflamed with riding we were most easy to rest a day* [5th] – *S Gilbert and his Wife and Children all kind, and desirous of our Stay tho' he never pretended to come amongst Friends.*

6th day, the snow was still very thick and they had great difficulty crossing the Staunton River which was frozen at the sides making it hard to get to the boat, especially with *only a Negro girl to help us* apart from the accompanying Friends. They got over at the third attempt but *staying so long in the Snow was not a little dangerous to my leg but I bore it better than I could have expected.* Their host for the night *had formerly joined friends but, I fear through unwatchfulness, is fallen away, yet he and his Wife received us kindly and we had a Meeting in the family to satisfaction.*

7th day they crossed the River Banister, "not without danger", and on 1st day attended their host's Meeting *in which Divine Goodness was Graciously pleased to favour with his heart melting Love to the*

*Solacing our Souls in humble thankfulness. That evening we reached Richard Kirbys 15 miles, had a meeting with them on 2nd day morning to which many of the neighbours came to their comfort & edification, being like the thirsty ground that drank in of rain with eagerness. That evening had a meeting at Wm. Paine's 5 miles thro' heavy Rain: not many attended. Though I thought not so open as in the morning, yet the people seemed well satisfied as some necessary truths were opened to them.* They had another meeting that evening with a good attendance despite the atrociously wet weather.

They were now about to cross into North Carolina, having stopped nowhere sizeable since Winchester, at the end of 11$^{th}$ month, four weeks earlier.

## Chapter 7

## NORTH AND SOUTH CAROLINA

There is a wealth of old maps held at the National Archives at Kew in London where I have spent fascinating and frustrating hours trying to relate Rachel's journey to modern road maps on which many places, especially the creeks and early settlements are not shown or have long since acquired modern names. It was a long time before I found Hogans Creek on an old map in the right position to tally with "hogins creek" in Rachel's journal. Also, it is clear that Rachel wrote down names, of both places and people, according to what she heard her hosts say. For example, at the northernmost part of her religious visit she reached "Morienique" – Merryconeeg, ME – on the far side of Casco Bay, or "Shapquer" – Chappaqua, NY.

Some of the maps are restricted to colonial boundary disputes; others to strategic military lines. Several show the names of individual settlers and their pieces of land and, pushed further back, the areas occupied by the American Indians. Another gives a plan of the infant City of New York with New Broadway Street ending at an area of "marshy ground" and "Fresh Water Pond", the Quaker Meeting House being just off this street in Crown Street. There are numerous annotations such as "very good land" The most comprehensive one I saw was "An Accurate Map of North and South Carolina With Their Indian Frontiers, Shewing in a distinct manner all the Mountains, Rivers, Swamps, Marshes, Bays, Creeks, Harbours, Sandbanks and Soundings on the Coasts, with The Roads and Indian Paths as well as The Several Townships and other divisions of the Land in Both the Provinces, the whole from Actual Surveys by Henry Mouzon and Others" published 12$^{th}$ May 1794. The scale is 8½ miles to 1 inch, providing an incredibly detailed picture of the vast, undeveloped areas that Rachel and her companions were about to enter. Creeks and rivers abound; tracks are scant; places, apart from the few like Charleston, comprise only a few isolated dwellings plus a Court House (often with no place name), a collection of Chapels and, here and there, a Quaker Meeting House, the most noteworthy being at New Garden Settlement (with another Quakers Meeting House close by), now Guilford, Greensboro but not even boasting a Court House.

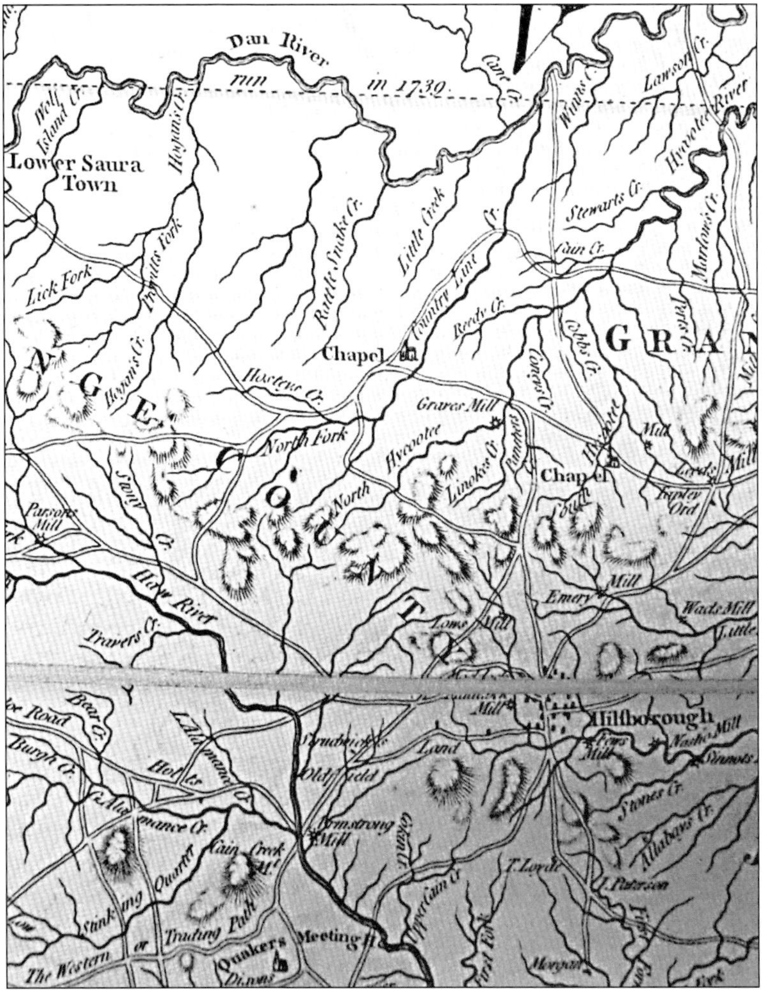


Part of 1794 map showing Hogans Creek (top left quarter) and Hilsborough (bottom right quarter) *National Archives UK, map ref. M.83 WO78/5757*

And so, without the benefit of any such map but with the local knowledge of their Quaker hosts, Rachel and her two companions entered the next stage of her religious visit. Despite being accustomed to the harshness of winters back home, when the lakes of Westmoreland regularly froze over, the winters on this continent were something different. A river the size of the Delaware could freeze in a single night and the Atlantic could freeze as far as the eye could see. In the shallows, the salt water ice could be three feet thick. Normal life and business largely hibernated in the more northerly colonies and wars were held in abeyance to be resumed only when spring arrived. One recalls that another Westmoreland Quaker – Jane Crosfield (Rachel's travelling companion in England in 1744-45) – paid a religious visit to those parts in the winter of 1761 and found out the hard way. She had met John Woolman when she came to America and he had been dismayed at her and her companion setting out for New England at that time of year: no woman should attempt it, he had urged.[49]

It was now 3rd day, the 27th of 12th month and the first obstacle was Hogins (Hogans) Creek as mentioned in Chapter 1. The full journal entry reads:

*William Payne set us to the River Dan, 12 miles, which we ferried over without much danger, though the water was high and the current Rapid. We could not cross Hogin's Creek at the usual place, the water was so high that we went a By path that night, 15 miles, in the woods with some difficulty and lodged with a friendly man, a Presbyterian, his name Robert Shuttlefield. His son was remarkably kind and wished it had been in his power to have done better for us; he gave up his own bed for my companion and me and spread Skins upon the ground for Samuel and Micajah and himself so that we put on tolerably well. In the morning* [4th day] *he helped us over Hogin's Creek, swam our horses and we went over on a Log though not without fear, our saddles & bags being first borne over. After we got well to the main Road but the heavy rains had made them deep & troublesome. After we had rode about 4 miles we called to inquire the way and, whether through mistake or designedly I know not, we were turned out of the way and we rode to where we apprehended we should have crossed Haw River – but upon inquiry found we had come 4 miles out of our Road in heavy Rain, at the same time, fearing the River would be impassable, made it painful work, yet there was no time to hesitate, that we made the best of our way through the rain and got safe over the River, though much wet, the water so high it came up one Leg above the ankle. We called at a little house on the other side and tho' we could get no Refreshment yet we dried ourselves a little and went to an Inn where we fared pretty well and 4 miles further to Lodge, which looked discouraging at our first entrance, but they improved and grew very kind and did their best for us. The landlord seemed desirous of a little conversation with us about points wherein we differed from them, and as he seemed rather to search for information than to quibble, I found freedom to answer both to that of Baptism & the Supper, with which he seemed satisfied & I was quite easy in my mind. In the morning* [5th day] *he would take nothing for my eating and went with us to set us over Ready Fork. As we could not ride it, we went over in a canoe and our horses swam. Whilst we were getting over there was what is called a Whirl Blast that brought down several trees at a little distance and made a noise like thunder yet we escaped without harm though our horses were a little frighted; this was fresh cause of thankfulness to the preserver of men that had so eminently preserved us both by land and water. We reached New Garden Settlement about 2, 15 miles, we called at Henry Balingers and got a little refreshment where we had a melting season in supplication; then to Eleazar [Eleanor] Hunts about a mile where we were kindly received and entertained with great hospitality. The season has been so wet, they scarcely expected we could have got along; we were truly glad once more to get among Friends.*

Samuel was Samuel Moreton – the male companion to the two women for this stage of the journey – while Micajah was a local Friend, Micajah Ferritt, who joined them for about two weeks. On 6th day, the 30th of 12th month, they called on several local Friends.

*On seventh day was their Monthly Meeting, which was large, attended by a number of well concerned Friends for the preservation of good order. They had under consideration the dealing with offenders in regard to marrying out of our Society, and as there was some difference of sentiments, they desired our assistance, in which I was enabled [to lay] before them our practice, as well as the great disadvantage of mixed Marriages, which seemed to have a great effect, and brought a general assent to the Truth.*

As the colonies developed, several of the Quaker population that dominated the island of Nantucket and its whaling industry sought greener pastures, with quite a number (at least 72) moving in stages to North Carolina to form a Nantucket community based around New Garden Meeting. William Hunt, nicknamed the "Pied Piper", founded the meeting, while in the near future John Macy would be leading another migration. Rachel met Hunt here and Macy when she reached Nantucket.[50]

The next day was 1st day, the 1st of 1st month 1769 and Rachel attended their Meeting. On 2nd day there was a meeting at Deep River where so many came that the Meeting house was not able to contain them all and many were left out of doors. On 3rd day they set off for Mordicai Mendenhall's where they had a meeting in his house which was only large enough for half of those who attended.

*We came afterwards to Wm Reynolds, 21 miles, my leg continuing bad, the wound not healing. Riding and Standing rather inflamed it, that I was like to be discouraged, but my good Master enabled me above my own expectation.*

4th day they went to Centre – *a pretty large house and quite filled, mostly Friends.* 5th day they were at Providence where, once again, the house did not hold everyone and the Meeting was held "without". After this they visited two more Friends and lodged for the night.

*On sixth day were at the Meeting House at Rock* [Rocky] *River, which is seldom made use of, belonging to one that had missed his way, friends found it their duty to testify against him, and the wrong spirit getting up had almost laid waste that Meeting, yet favour seemed to be extended though things were closely spoke to they were all loving and seemed pleased with the opportunity.*

7th day was Monthly Meeting at Cane Creek and they stayed over to first day for meeting for worship which was large and Rachel's mind was *much enlarged in Doctrine, which flowed freely that day, with Consolation to the honest-hearted and reproof to the careless and Lukewarm.* In the evening they had an "opportunity" with several young people. They made it to the small meeting at Hawfield on 2nd day, *the few there was were dilatory in gathering by which the Meeting suffered loss* and reached Hillsborough by the end of the day.

This is the first town shown in a general atlas since Winchester, 42 days before. The proliferation of Quaker meetings as they crossed the full depth of Virginia and now Carolina was a remarkable legacy from the missions, one hundred years previously, of the first generation Quakers, including George Fox himself. The names of many of these early meetings' are those of local creeks.

In his Journal, Fox recorded: "I determined to pass through the woods on the other side of Delaware Bay, that we might head the creeks and rivers as much as possible."

Another extract reads:
"A tedious journey through the woods and wilderness, over bogs and great rivers. We took horse at the head of Tredhaven Creek and travelled through the woods, till we came a little above the head of Miles River, by which we passed ... and so to the head of Chester river, where, making a fire, we took up our lodging in the woods. Next morning we travelled through the woods till we came to Sassafras river, which we went over in canoes, causing our horses to swim by. Then we rode to Bohemia river, where, in like manner,

swimming our horses, we ourselves went over in canoes. ... Then we had that wilderness country, since called West Jersey, to pass through, not then inhabited by English; so that we sometimes travelled a whole day together without seeing man or woman, house or dwelling place. Sometimes we lay in the woods by a fire, and sometimes in the Indians' wigwams or houses." [51]

These, of course, were describing Fox's travels in another colony rather than where Rachel was now, but Rachel's descriptions of her journeys so closely mirror Fox's that one senses the presence with her of Fox and the original Quaker pioneers.

Following Hillsborough Meeting on 3rd day, the 10th of 1st month 1769, they came to Spring Meeting on 4th day. The meeting house was so small that they met in the larger space offered in a Friend's house in order to accommodate everybody, some of them having come from Cane Creek. On 5th day they continued to another Friend's house, calling in on a friend on the road and crossing Deep River en route. Next morning they crossed this river again, both going and coming back, by canoe in order to attend the local meeting *in which I had earnestly to desire that they might wait, as with one accord, for the fulfilling of the promise, or to be indued with the Holy Ghost, as the proper qualification for worship, as also for the Ministry, to which I had to speak pretty closely – And afterwards, I understand there was a Baptist Preacher who seemed affected. Many Friends returned with us to Cornelius Tyson's, with whom we had a comfortable season, as also we had the evening before with the family and friends that came with us from Spring Meeting and Cane Creek.* [3 others] *also came with us to Holy* [Holly] *Spring.*

*On seventh day, 25 miles to Thomas Cox's had a sit in the family tho' I soon found all was not right, they had too much joined in with wrong Spirit that was at work to lay waste Discipline and all Order, raising heats and Broils and sitting at a distance one against another. I had to lay open the tendency of such a disturbed Spirit, and Truth came over them.*

*On first day was at their Meeting in which my mind was enlarged to speak to the state of that Meeting in a particular manner. Came back to John Cox's, where we lodged that night, several Friends came to sit with us in the evening with whom I had a full opportunity to clear myself and I hope it will be a season to be remembered. That day I suffered much in my Leg, that many Friends thought it scarcely prudent to proceed on so long a Journey, till I was a little better, the weather being very unsettled and the Waters high, yet I found no freedom to stay.*

So they travelled again on the second day, even though it was exceedingly wet. Next day they were joined by Cornelius Tyson and other Friends; the weather was much better but they got very wet crossing the much swollen Hedge Crook Creek, reaching another Friend for the night at the Peedee River, where they dried themselves. Many neighbours came to the Meeting there on 4th day.

*On fifth day ... we had opportunities at friendly people's houses on the Road, with which they seemed well satisfied and thankful for the opportunity. The weather turning from Cold to Hot, it affected me with a feverish complaint and settled in my lame Leg and thigh that I travelled in great pain.*

*On seventh day the 21st of the 1st month 1769 was truly glad to get to the Widow Wiley's, about 13 miles to Wateree. That night I sweat freely, by which I was a good deal relieved in my Body, yet very lame, that I could scarcely point the Ground, but here I was suitably provided for. One Joseph Kershaw, a Store keeper, tho' not under our name, sent his Chair to take me to Meeting, and after to his own House to Dine, where we had a solid opportunity at Table; also in the evening before we came away, he frankly offered his Carriage to go to Charlestown, which I could not but think a little extraordinary, and as a particular favour in any Situation, so seemingly unfit for Travelling on Horse back, that a way should be prepared for me to get along in so unlooked for a manner, as our Horses were all unfit to go further, their Backs were so crushed, that we wanted rest both ourselves and our Horses.*

*We had another Meeting on 3rd day and my Leg mended so fast, that I was able to walk, and so set out for Bush River. On 4 day morning being able to ride on Horseback, we accepted two of Joseph Kershaw's Horses, one of Samuel Milhouse, and left our own at the Widow Wiley's till our return. Zebulon Gant and Isaac Pidgeon and Wife, and Mary Kelly, all accompanied us.*

Early on they missed their road, not knowing in which direction they were heading or what dangers might be lying in wait for them. They had to spend two nights lost in dense woods, finding a cabin each night. It was still 1st month (January). The men slept outside the first night and the women inside while *the second we all lay in a Cabin, and had a sit at both places to satisfaction.*

On 6th day they reached Samuel Kelly's where, having been spared any misfortune in the woods, their evening "opportunity" was rudely interrupted, while Rachel was speaking, by the intrusion of *many of those who are called Regulators ... tho' they themselves wanted regulating, with whom I had a pretty full opportunity to lay before them the inconsistency of their practice with the Doctrines of Christ.* Regulators were organised groups of frontier settlers in the Carolinas, who, in 1768, had begun to protest against their lack of representation in the colonial assemblies. (Three years later, the Regulator movement was crushed by the British Governor of North Carolina, William Tryon who, later that year, became Governor of New York.)

7th day was their monthly meeting and they stayed over for Meeting on 1st day. They then took four days to ride to Charleston: 2nd day, 35 miles; 3rd day, 35 miles (where their Lodgings were "but middling"); 4th day, 50 miles; 5th day, 45 miles (lodging at a tavern), making, by Samuel Kelly's account, an overall total so far on their journey of 1,318 miles. Henry Laurens, a Huguenot merchant and planter who relied on Quaker business associates, rode out of Charleston to meet them, immediately recognising them as being "conspicuous by their plain style of dress".[52] In later years he became a moderate leader of the Revolutionary movement in the South, was elected to the first Provincial Congress in 1774, and served on many important committees in the Continental Congress (1778-81). He was captured by the British in 1780 but then exchanged for Lord Cornwallis in 1782 and played a valuable part in subsequent peace negotiations and, from 1783 to 1784, in representing American interests in England.

There was a crowded meeting at the Friends Meeting House on 6th day. Rachel spent 7th day in writing home and, in the evening, *a West India Merchant desired to Dine with us which proved a favourable season.*

Here she at last received news from her "Dear Husband" and wrote:

> ***Charlestown 2 mo 4th 1769***
>
> ***At my arrival here I mett with thine of ye 30 of ye 9 month which gave me ye account of ye Departure of our Dear Child which tho Long Expected & in good Degree prepared yet it was affecting at this Distance – tho I am far from Mourning or ye Least Repining at ye act of providence but rather thankful with thee he went so quiet at Last and you so supported under ye trial. Theres something in me yt would have Li[c]ked to have bin present & Bore a part upon ye occation if it had bin ye Divine will – but in yt I have no Caus to Dought*** [doubt] ***of being in my place.***

(This refers to their 18 year old son, Anthony, who, as mentioned earlier, had "scarce a days health in ten years" and who died on the 20th of 9th month 1768.)

Rachel wrote that she was becoming

> ***... Experienced in my Stepings along through this Wilderness Country as it haith bin My Lot to Visit ye Back inhabited in Many plaices wear no Inglish had Ever bin before ... have bin Supported far above My Expectation Both in Body & Mind. We***

> ***were always kindly Recd & Entertained in ye Best Manner they were Capable of & with which I was thankful: for having never bin Exposed to Lye in ye woods yet our Men Companions was [out] one Night but I got Under Cover & a tolerable Bed & I Expect from accounts ye worst part of ye Jorney is over in yt Respect but what Ive yet to Meett with is wisely hid from Me; its Enouf to Step on from day to day Depending upon ye Arm of power yt is altogether sufficient in Every Imergency & qualified for Every Servis he Calls too.***

She continued her letter with heartfelt thanks to her companions, Samuel Moreton and Sarah Janney and to the many Friends along the way who had ridden with them for stages of the journey for 70, 80 or 100 miles through the woods. Her experiences, she said,

> ***wd be too Bulkee for a Letter. It May Suffice to say we have Never bin Detained by water nor Stormy weather, but what we have had Meetings or Riding Every Day & Mostly Both before we reached North Carolina.***

Her letter then related the atrocious, wet weather that made the various swollen creeks and rivers almost impossible to cross and the appallingly bad road to New Garden, many Friends having expected that it would have defeated her.

> ***I said Litl but thought Imposability was not Required at our hands but as I was Solidly Riding along Unexpectedly it Arose in my Mind 'the way will be prepared for thee' & I said in My self 'good is ye word of ye Lord – I Believe in it'. I was prety Closly tryed often yet I Never Dou[b]ted ye truth of ye promis which indeed haith bin amply Verified.***

She recounted having left their exhausted horses at Wateree, this being the point when she had declined the offer of a lift in a carriage for the last stage into Charleston, but instead had accepted the loan of replacement horses

> ***... having Brought us so many hundred Miles ye Weather was then prety Warm & our horsis feed high with Indian Corn their***

***Backs was so ful of Warbls not fitt to put a Sadle upon Em. Ive not seen any thing since I came to America I should Lick*** [like] ***so well to bring home with me as me*** [my] ***hors if it should prove fit to Carry me through. I Never traveled on one so Ese*** [easy] ***& went with so Much Spirit before his Back was hurt. 6 or 7 Miles an Hour he went with Ease .***

***I thought this a Long time to have bin without Recving a Line from thee – it was 12 weeks from My Leving Philadelphia til our Reaching this place & there was no oportunity of Meeting me with thine before, nayther have I had any oportunity of Conveying one to thee before this since yt wrote from Fairfax, which I dout not will have ye same aperance to thee: but I ...tly hope thoul be suported under Every trying Dispensation of Devine providence yt may be Permited to attend during ye time of our Separation.***

and she added her dear love to her family and friends, listing them by name.

On 1st day they had two Meetings in the Baptist Meeting House.

In the morning it *was large, the subject treated upon was 'that Light is come unto the World, and Men loved darkness rather than light, because their deeds were evil'. The Meeting ended with prayer and praises for the many Mercies and Blessings bestowed upon us poor unworthy Mortals. The afternoon was crowded, yet the people behaved generally well. I had to set forth the difference betwixt us and other Denominations, in regard to the manner of our waiting upon and worshiping Almighty God, as also, to point out the great Love of God to Mankind.*

It must have felt strange to be back in a major town. All at once they were exposed to the pace and trends of modern 18th century life – fashions, diversions, temptations – and a sense of having to compete for people's attention.

Fifteen years before, Mary Peisley of Ireland and Catherine Peyton of England had made a religious visit to these parts (and to the American colonies at large). At Charleston "they found a tiny, not very flourishing community of Quakers [that] had dwindled in membership; for several years they did not even hold meetings. These Quakers lived in a pleasure-loving culture whose leading citizens belonged to the established Church of England. ... It seemed to the British visitors that Charleston was functioning 'like a city of refuge for the disjointed members of our Society, where they may walk in the sight of their own eyes, and the imagination of their own hearts, without being accountable for their conduct, and yet called by the name of Quaker'".[53] The process of reformation since then had much improved the observance of Quaker discipline, but there was still more than a hint of worldliness when Rachel came to meet Widow Ragg's girls and on the day of the races.

*On second day Colonel Henry Lawrence* [Laurens – see above] *and Philip Myer's Wife and daughter, and two or three more Young Women, came to see us, with whom I had an opportunity to declare the way of Life and Salvation. We dined with Captain Pickles on board his Vessel, where I was concerned at Table in Supplication. After which went to the Widow Ragg's, several of her daughters being present, was covered with Divine Love, and drawn into Silence, in which they all settled down, tho' grand and great in their appearance. It had an effect to hinder me from doing what I believed to be my Duty in Love to their Souls; the truth came over their Minds, and they expressed their satisfaction with the Visit.*

Henry Laurens was deeply moved by Rachel's spiritual witness – attending her meetings, hearing her pray at table and engaging in conversation with her. Another influential Huguenot merchant, who had not been to a Quaker meeting for 50 years, also made a point of going to hear Rachel. Both of them wanted the opportunity to entertain Rachel and her companions and, along with others in Charleston, were truly sorry that the shortness of her stay precluded this. He wrote "I have not known Strangers, at any time come among us, meet a more Cordial reception, nor do I remember to have parted from any with more regret." His life became more focused on spiritual aspects following Rachel's visit and he was the first influential person in South Carolina to publicly come out against slavery. He noted that Rachel, at her meetings, was "attended by many of the best Inhabitants" [54]

*On third day had a Meeting at 10 which was larger than expected, being their Races, which is too apt to draw away the minds of many into folly and Vanity. I had first to appear in Supplication, after which my Companion stood up, setting forth the advantage that would attend, if they were properly concerned to make use of the present opportunity of divine favour that they might experience a happy preparation for their final change, upon which I had to enlarge, with reviving in their Ears the Solemn Message that was sent to the good King Hezekiah, 'set thine House in order for thou shalt die and not live'. Also setting forth the great Love of God to Mankind, in favouring them with a manifestation of the Spirit of his Dear Son Christ Jesus in their own hearts, also sending his servants and handmaids, rising early and lying down late, exposed to many hardships, under a sense of Duty to Almighty God, and for the good of Souls, thus to call unto them in the Love of the Gospel, that they might be turned from darkness to light, and from Sin and Satan to the power of the living God.*

Her journal continues in like vein for as long again and concludes *my mind was deeply humbled and in the renewing of Divine Love, in so remarkable a manner to the people, not only in Public, but even from House to House, that had thankfully to acknowledge his Mercies which far exceeded our desert.*

Rachel and her companions left Charleston on 4$^{th}$ day feeling uplifted and fulfilled and were taken by chair 30 miles to Moncks Corner, accompanied by their kind Landlord and Captain Pickles, and had a meeting at their inn that evening *to which the neighbours came, but appeared to be a Raw ignorant people, yet they behaved still and quiet.*

There was another vessel ready to sail from here so, before again heading off into remote country, Rachel seized the opportunity to finish a letter home that she had started in Charleston.

> ***I was not willing to Neglect so favourable an oportunity its what Ive bin Long Deprived of and its Lick shal be again when I Leve this place ... tho surrounded with Company its More agreable to Convers with thee tho at this great Distance as my Mind was Never nearer United to My Dear husband than now ... can tel thee I am favoured with a good State of health and inabled to bear traveling Bravly. I expect itl be betwixt 3 or 4 months before we can reach Philadelphia if favourd to get well along ... I wd not have thee Unese about me. I hope I shal not suffer ye great Master in whos servis I am ingaged is abundantly able to suport through Every trial Ye waters are ye Most Unpleasant ... ye Roads are Generaly Prety good & as to Eating & Drinking things it haith bin maid Eser*** [easier] ***to Me than Ever I Expected. Ive tasted but Litle Malt Lickore since I Entered America ... Many weeks Litle Els than Milk & water, yet quite Content. I thought this hint wd not be Desagreable ... time will not admit to inlarge at present...***

... ending, as usual, with her dear love to her husband and "childer".

On 5$^{th}$ day, they visited a sick Friend on their way to Nelsons Ferry and Santee Swamp – *a dangerous place, about 3 miles over; in a flood it is covered with water, that they can go with a Boat. We got well over only in one place so deep as wet our feet. We had but poor lodgings that night but next night [6$^{th}$ day] got to our kind friend Widow Willy's where we left our horses – from Charlestown 120 miles.*

They stayed over for first day meeting and then rode to Links Creek. 2nd day, 50 miles, and 3rd day another 50 miles brought them to *one Malay where we had an opportunity with the family with which they seemed well satisfied though not of our profession.* On 4th day they reached Cross Creek in time for the afternoon meeting. *It is a poor place in regard to Religion, there are a few that bear our name, who seldom attend any Meeting.* On 5th day they got to Duns Creek *to which several of the Baptists came and were reached by the power of Truth to the tendering of their hearts, that in the shedding abroad of Divine Love we were comforted together.*

They returned next day to Cross Creek, where their host lent them two horses in order to get to Henry Horn's on the Tar River, 108 miles away. They crossed Cape River at Simmiter Ferry and reached Colonel Smith's that night. On 7th day they went to Dunken Lemons where, on first day morning, *I was not easy to go away till we had sit a while with him and his Wife, to whom I had to open the way of Life and Salvation.* They arrived at Henry Horn's in good time and found that it was Friends' two weekly meeting that day and the few Friends present were encouraged in their faithfulness. A further meeting was arranged for 5 o'clock, attended by many of the neighbours who were generally Baptists, also their Teacher, who was a man of good character. *I had an open time amongst them, pointing out the great advantage of Silence to the knowledge of our Duty to God and one to another and the prevention of confusion in the Church.*

On 2nd day, they overtook a woman who was on her way to visit a sick neighbour. They arrived at their destination, Rich Square, but Rachel was troubled about having passed by this stranger, so they retraced their steps and found her and the sick man who had been confined to bed for some months. Several neighbours were there, too, and they had a "remarkable opportunity" and the man was *very thankful for so unexpected a visit of Divine Love which was so ardently manifested upon that occasion - May I ever have my Ear open to hear the unspeaking word of Divine Wisdom.*

Next day they had a "solemn season" at breakfast before coming back to Dunken Lemons, followed by a "pretty Meeting of Friends" and then going home with John Duke's wife who was "not one of our Society yet very loving to Friends". They travelled 31 miles on 4$^{th}$ day, crossing the Chowan, and on 5$^{th}$ day reached Friends at Little River, 36 miles.

On 6$^{th}$ day, it was their Meeting of Ministers in the morning followed by Meeting at noon which was "but small, yet comfortable".

*I had earnestly to desire we might walk worthy of the Vocation whereinto we were called in all humility and fear. Also to keep their hands clear of purchasing negroes, as believing it was never intended for us to traffick with any part of the human species and that if there were no buying there would be no sellers and that where there were numbers of them Religion was at a low Ebb.*

This is the first and principal reference in Rachel's journal to Quaker slaveholdings.

They attended Quarterly Meeting on 7$^{th}$ day. Meeting on 1$^{st}$ day was large *and I hope ended well, tho' it appeared rather hard Laborious work, that I was much spent.* Next day, they were at another large meeting, 8 miles away at Simmonds Creek, attended by a good turnout of the local inhabitants. On 3$^{rd}$ day, they were at Meeting at Newbegun Creek, the small meeting house overflowing and leaving many people outside. The same situation was avoided on 4$^{th}$ day by meeting in a Friend's house that was larger than the meeting house.

*On fifth day went to Oldneck, 8 miles, which Meeting was very large and satisfactory. I had to speak to different states, particularly to set forth the great disadvantage of mixed Marriages.*

They crossed Perquimens River and were taken in a Friend's chaise to Edenton where they lodged at an inn and next day had a meeting in the Court House

*They seemed a Raw people, not used to waiting in Silence. They stood about the Door for a while, till desired to come in. I was soon engaged in Supplication, by which they were a little settled, yet not much reached so, that before the Meeting was ended, truth gained Ground, and they seemed solid, and many expressed their Satisfaction. There were two Priests, one of them dined with us at the Ordinary, where I was concerned at Table, he behaved civily as did the whole Company, and seemed desirous of our longer stay, but as soon as I found myself clear, I had no desire to linger.*

"The Ordinary" refers to a type of lodging, particularly inns in the southern colonies. It usually meant a set time and price for a meal and it was not uncommon to have to share a bed (sometimes no more than a pallet) with a fellow traveller, especially in cold weather. A Quaker minister travelling in 1750 stayed at one which she described as "a nasty dirty house call'd an Ordinary, where [I] was obliged to lodge but got little Sleep for Fleas and Bugs and scarce anything we could eat." [55]

They stayed overnight with Frances Nixon. Next morning (7th day), they *visited her mother Elizabeth Nixon an ancient Woman, a Publick Friend that has been useful, but had labored under weakness for 8 mos and had not been at Meeting. She seem'd much refreshed with the visit. We also called in upon her Brother and children, who had been a Widower many years; his Wife died when upon a Journey with C Payton. We went afterwards to the Meeting at Wells, 7 miles, which was very large and highly favor'd*, lodging there that night. First day meeting at Pine Wood was also very large. It looked to be their last in North Carolina and provided the opportunity to take a "Solemn Farewell".

Rachel found time to start a letter to Isaac, recounting her journey through "Watery … Peede … Cross Creek … Inns Creek … Henry Horns … Rich Square … Little River … Edentown … etc" plus the various meetings with

> ***pepol of al Denominations willing to come when they hear of a stranger – in this part thayr not many places of worship but frds Meeting houses – hears a fine Body of Frds who Look Lick them Selves which is pleasant to behold. [I look] to be Ready for ye first Vesel and My time is prety fuly ingaged with Meetings and Riding yt I have not had a Spair hour[e] before this for sometime.***

Her letter mentions how often she had perused his "affectionate epistles" with their news of family and friends back home, all "very agreable at this Distance". She had to leave the rest of her letter to be completed later.

Chapter 8

# RETURN TO PHILADELPHIA VIA VIRGINIA AND MARYLAND

On 2nd day, the 6th of 3rd month, they came back into Virginia: 35 miles to Somerton and, on 3rd day, after meeting, 18 miles to Nansemond. Her horse being lame, she had a lift in a Friend's chaise for part of the way. Here, Rachel finished her letter so that it could go on a ship bound for Whitehaven that was waiting for a fair wind.

> ***We are now at one Joseph Scotts upon Nansemond River – Robert Abrams lives with ye frds & Bears a fair caracter. He looks well & is well [situated] as to ye world – he and his master are Both Bachelors – I thought this hint wod*** [would] ***not be Disagreable to Son George in regard to his Couz.***

and she sent messages from others that they both knew here for their friends and families in England.

She felt refreshed but *alas, this did not last long, till a fresh concern fell upon me.* She had intended going to Suffolk on 4th day, but something inside her told her to stay put. She heard of a burial that was to be at Western Branch that day and felt drawn to visit the widow who was a Quaker but whose children had all transferred with their father to another church. The eldest son had sent for a parson who, they discovered, was a good deal concerned at the prospect of Rachel attending and was opposed to her having any "opportunity" with the people. *His Mother and Sisters sat a while with us, with whom I had an opportunity to clear myself, and came away easy.*

On 5th day they made their way to Suffolk followed by meeting at Bucks Creek where they again lodged with Friends. On 6th day they had to detour 20 miles round by Suffolk because the wind was so high, attended meeting there, followed by Chuckatuck and finally to a large meeting at Western Branch . Rachel had an "opportunity in the family" where they were to lodge to speak "plainly" and noted: *there wants a regulation in that Family.*

They left on 2nd day and travelled on to Black Creek where they went to meeting and *a Close exercising time it was, things seemed very poor and low amongst them, that deep suffering was the Portion of the honest hearted.* Meeting the next day was at a Friend's house to which several neighbours came and Rachel found an open door to preach the Gospel. On 4th day, meeting at Blackwater was large. After dinner, Rachel recounted

*My mind was exceedingly oppressed. I had scarcely felt the like; my Companion had the same feeling. In this state we sat down with the family as Friends breathing for liberty, which was happily granted to our mutual relief.*

On 5th day they reached Burleigh and were at monthly meeting on 6th day, attended also by several neighbours; they dined with a Friend whose husband had died only a few days before and had a "precious opportunity in which the great name was praised". It was their overnight host's monthly meeting on 7th day *in which many weighty Truths were delivered to their Establishment in Righteousness – There we met with a hopeful number of well concerned youth, for the preservation of good Order, which was cause of Thankfulness in our passing along.*

They reached Petersburgh that night and attended three meetings on first day, once again enjoying the presence of many neighbours. On 2nd day they were at Gravelly Run and 3rd day at Curles – several of the neighbours *came in and behaved well though not much reached.* On 4th day evening, Rachel wrote home.

> ***I expect thayrs*** [there's] ***several [letters] lying for Me at Philadelphia which I hope to Recv soon now as shall be in a Countrey wear they have a post – which haith not bin ye Case since I left Philadelphia – when I look at it, it apears Long to have heard Nothing from home for upwards of 5 Months – that I am Lick*** [like] ***to admire at My Leg I am so quick, no painful nor Distressing thought taking place upon ye account – but have to acknowlidg Humbly with God thairs not any thing Impossible –***

> ***his works are works of wonder & Marvellous in Mine Eye ...*** followed by as much praise again ***... through ye Many proving & trials yt may be presented to attend During ye time of Separation for ye Lords sake.***

She mentions having met a local townsman from back home:

> ***... I was pleased to see him look so well – I believe he Behaves well & has Lickly to do well if he keeps his place [he] has with one Colonel Job: a man of Considerable account: I promised him to Mention this to thee yt thou Might Lett his wife know – tho he told me had wrot her Laitly & sent her a smal Matter & has in hopes to do More after a while: he seemed a good deal afected about his wife and Childer & to be so far[e] Separated from them yet not without hopes he May be in [a capacity] to send for Em in time.***

She praised her horse again "ye Easist I ever Road" and expected to be in Philadelphia in about a month. She knew that "the great ocean of Divine Love" would see her through the heavy work of traversing Virginia, expecting to reach Williamsburg "ye Metropolis of this province" on 6th day.

On 5th day, a "pretty large" meeting at Winecock was attended by a good many that were "not of our Society" before proceeding to Cobbles Ferry where they lodged at an inn and then came to Skimino and afterwards to Williamsburg on 6th day where they again lodged at an inn.

7th day:
*There are no Friends in this Town. We had two Meetings in a house formerly made use of for a playhouse, the People light and airy that it was close work, yet I hope Truth gained ground, and several expressed their satisfaction with the Meeting; one Woman particularly acknowledged her thankfulness for that opportunity and that the Lord had put it into our Hearts to visit them, a people so much taken up with pleasures of the World. We had a Solemn Season with her in her own House, and two more of note that came and drank tea with us*

*there, that we bid them Farewell in great Love, their good wishes also attending us.*

*I also went with Edward Stabler to Visit the Governor, who received us kindly, and seemed well satisfied , and told me it was his desire to fill up his place properly to do what he ought to do, and not to be biassed by party; this was the substance of what he said, tho' not in the same Words. I answered if this was singly Eyed by him, I doubted not but he would be a blessing to the People. He took his leave very affectionately and wished my Journey might be prosperous.*

Her visit was reported in the 'Virginia Gazette'; the governor was Norborne Berkeley (Baron de Botetourt), a royal appointment (as was normal) and only recently arrived from England.[56]

Later, the travellers arrived back at Black Creek where they lodged. They attended first day meeting there and then rode to The Swamp. After meeting next morning, they reached Picquinocque; next day they continued on to Richmond and had a meeting in the Court House attended pretty fully by the local inhabitants, "reaching" several of them. On 4th day they rode to Genita and on 5th day to Fork Creek, holding meetings in both places although Fork Creek had only a few Friends, being made up mostly of others, and things seemed *at a low Ebb amongst them through unwatchfulness* and finished up at Camp Creek.

*We called by the way to see one of the Assembly men, who was a Man of great Moderation, and had appeared in Friends favour; his name was Patrick Henry; he received us with great civility and we had an open time in the family; he made some sensible remarks.*

~~~~~~~~~~~~~~~~~~

Patrick Henry was the distinguished Virginia statesman, only 32 years old, who was already famous for his Stamp Act speech of 1765. This Stamp Act in Britain levied a duty on all American colonial newspapers, certain other publications and dice to produce revenue for
~~~~~~~~~~~~~~~~~~

garrisoning the colonial frontier. The colonies were vehemently opposed to taxation without representation and the Stamp Act Congress in America in 1765 regarded it as a threat to self-rule, arguing that they could only be taxed by their local assemblies since distance precluded their representation in the British Parliament. The Congress was a significant step towards national unity.[57]

In parallel, Patrick Henry strove to fulfil his vision of achieving religious toleration in Virginia. This province continued to insist on church uniformity and to severely punish Quakers by distraints on their property and by imprisonment (for non-payment of tithes to the established church) long after such practices had been dropped in other previously intolerant colonies, such as the Puritan ones in New England. Henry's vision, as articulated by him, became the draft of the relevant section of the Bill of Rights at the opening of the Revolutionary War:

"Religion, or the duty which we owe to our Creator, and the manner of discharging it, can be directed only by reason and conviction, not by force and violence, and therefore all men are equally entitled to the free exercise of religion, according to the dictates of conscience; and it is the mutual duty of all to practice Christian forebearance, love and charity toward each other." [58]

Before that, Patrick Henry had supported a law, passed in 1776, releasing Quakers from the general requirement of military service.[59]

It would be good to know who all the people of note were that Rachel met in America. She certainly met many of the leading Americans of the period and, like Henry Laurens, they were influenced by her. Benjamin Franklin (the scientist and statesman) remembered her clearly when visiting Westmorland in 1772; likewise Richard Stockton (a provincial councillor, a trustee of the College of New Jersey and, later, a delegate to the Continental Congress) and his wife, Annis Boudinot (a talented poet).[60] There were several auspicious occasions throughout Rachel's religious visit – maybe more than several – but the brevity of her journal entries is typical. There are at least two such occasions that she does not mention at all, including meeting John Woolman. But then Woolman himself was just as brief, even self-effacing, in his journal and made matters worse by omitting to give many of the names of those whom he met and also was often unreliable with his dates.

~~~~~~~~~~~~~~~~~~~

It was now 7th day the 1st of 4th month. They rode to John Bosell's *where a meeting was appointed. The day proving wet, but few came, though more than was expected; they had but little sense of Religion, too much given to pleasure and diversion, they appeared light and airy, yet through Divine Goodness, [I] was afresh abilitated to discharge my duty and set before them in a clear view the end of such indulgences if gone on in, and the Necessity of Repentance, and amendment of Life to turn at the Reproof of Instruction, which is the way to Life, as the day of tender Visitation was yet extended.*

They continued on to Cedar Creek. Next morning, 1st day, the Friend's house for meeting being large enough for only a third of those who came, they had a good meeting out of doors. On 2nd day they went to Caroline, Virginia, for meeting. *Many of them called Baptists attended, and were very loving, strongly inviting me to go to their Meeting which I did not find freedom to join in with.* They had another meeting 12 miles away that night, this time in the Court House and *had some agreeable conversation with the Landlord who is one of the Assembly Men, a solid sensible Man.* On 3rd day they reached Port Royal where there had not previously been any Meeting and had *a satisfactory opportunity amongst the people.*

They left Virginia, crossing the Rapahanack and Potomack rivers into Maryland, then 50 miles to Widow Plummers on 4th day; 12 miles on 5th day to West River for meeting; 6th day, (14th of 4th month) to meeting in the Court House at Annapolis. Here, Rachel's companion since 26th of 11th month, Sarah Janney, left to return home, which
~~~~~~~~~~~~~~~~~~~

Rachel found *a little affecting* having to part with someone *who had been a true help meet in the service.*

It was Quarterly Meeting at Chester River on $7^{th}$ day. On $1^{st}$ day, the public meeting was so large that the house contained only half of the people, *yet it was a precious opportunity for many.* They were invited to a special business meeting that evening to consider the continuation of meetings in that place. It was *unanimously agreed that it was not the time to remove the Meeting, but rather to enlarge the Meeting House as things seemed rather reviving.*

There was another public meeting on $2^{nd}$ day, followed by a further business meeting which was adjourned to the next day. Rachel's second companion, Samuel Moreton, then left for home – *he had been exceeding tender over me and useful upon many occasions; I was often humbly thankful the Great Master had prepared me such a companion.*

After meeting on $3^{rd}$ day, she went to Chestertown for another meeting in the Court House. It was large and solemn in which Christ was preached: *the Way, the Truth and the Life.* On $4^{th}$ day she was at Cicle for their monthly meeting and met up again with Samuel and Esther Fisher. It was an especially joyous moment as they brought *several letters from my Dear Husband and children.* This was nearly the end of her time in the south. On $5^{th}$ day she was at Sassafras in the afternoon, enjoying "great flockings" of the people in these parts. On $6^{th}$ day she was at Wilmington and on $7^{th}$ day reached Philadelphia one more.

It had been late autumn when Rachel ventured into the southern colonies. She had kept going through all the dangerous floods and deep snows of winter, in long successions of isolated settlements and individual Friends between the few sizeable towns on their route, and it was now spring. On her reckoning, she had ridden on horseback something like 2,700 miles.

Rachel's letter home dated 17th of 4th month 1769 in which she finally tells Isaac about her fall from her horse in the snow.

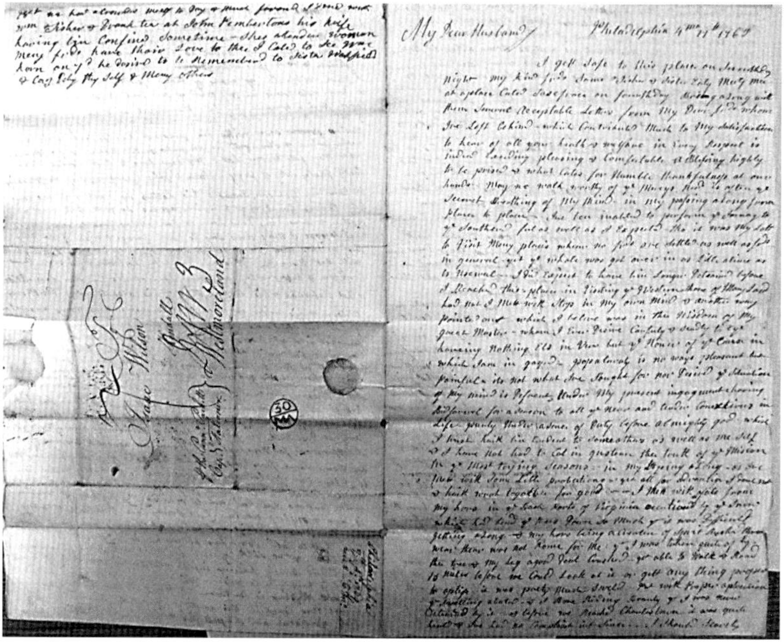

## Chapter 9

## BACK AGAIN IN PHILADELPHIA

7th day, the 15th of 4th month, 1769.
*We rode to Philadelphia. My kind Landlady Mary Harvey took me in her Chaise, when Friends seemed generally glad to see me returned safe from so exposing a journey, in which we had travelled about twenty seven hundred miles and had not been hindered above two days in the whole Journey – for which merciful preservation may the great Name be praised, to whom it is due.*

She wrote home on 17th of 4th month, delighted, at last, to receive Isaac's letters reassuring her of his "health and welfare in every Respect" and letters also from other family and friends. She brought him up to date with her travels and finally told him about her fall from her horse, her crushed leg and the ensuing pain:

> ***I should have Mentioned this hapning had not I found it Might Reach thee some other way and proble*** [probably] ***not j[o]ustly Represented – as it was hear*** [here] ***before they could have ye truth from me.***

Her accident had occurred four months previously, on 16th of 12th month, and it would then have taken another two months or so before Isaac learned of it. But at the time of it he had a premonition of something having happened to her.

Rachel then spared a thought for burdening someone back home with her absence from duty at a forthcoming Yearly Meeting in Kendal. She sent her love to a long list of family

> ***also to Cous Anthony Wilson & his wife yt pece of inteligence was very acceptable – if I had bin at home should have thrown in my mite towards furnishing ye hous & if a pair of Blankets wd be accepted Doo give Em a pair at my Request ... I hope to pay a proper Regard to ye many tender cautions Ive Rec'd not to overdo My Self as ye weather is now growing warm – how I may bear that is yet to try. Ive found no hardship with the cold.***

In spite of her friends' concerns, her schedule continued to follow its familiar, unrelenting pattern:

1st day: *I was at three meetings, all large, and favoured with the overshadowing of Divine Good, to the humbling many hearts present*
2nd day: meeting of Ministers and Elders
3rd day: meeting at the Bank
4th day: at Darby
5th day: at Chester
6th day: to Wilmington
7th day: to Duck Creek Monthly Meeting (taken there by *Thomas Cliffords Wife and Son with S Fisher in their Waggon*)

1st day: morning meeting, then Quarterly Meeting in the afternoon
2nd day: meeting of Ministers (*small and dull in the beginning, but rather revived towards the conclusion*)
3rd day at Friends and at George Creek's meeting before going on to Newcastle
4th day: a large, open meeting in the Court House at Newcastle when *the Word of God was preached to the people* and then on to Chester
5th day: meeting at Chester *where Sarah Morris and several more from Philadelphia had acceptable service.*
*We had two Priests at Meeting as we had often, though no opposition; the danger seemed more in favouring than frowning.*
6th day: Monthly Meeting at Chester
7th day: meeting of Ministers and Elders followed by Quarterly Meeting
*... the season very wet, it was small and dull in the fore part, tho' J Pemberton stood up pretty early, yet the Cloud still remained. J Hunt after some time appeared with that if Christ could not work without his Father, how could we expect to do anything of ourselves, and tho' some might have been clothed with the King's Robes and sit upon his throne, yet it was necessary to come to the Gate again. Mary Churchman appeared ... I had also to utter a few expressions how things had been with me ... Dan Stanton also appeared, and Isaac Andrews in supplication ... a few words rested on my mind to request*

*we might all be upon our guard, in making too free with the Ministry in speaking our Sentiments, especially before the youth. Wm Brown, also J Churchman appeared, acknowledging they had received Instruction both secretly and Instrumentally by the hints given.*

John Pemberton was one of a Quaker dynasty: grandson of Phineas Pemberton who came to Pennsylvania in the same year as William Penn (1682) and son of Israel, a wealthy merchant. Israel had three sons, all of whom Rachel met, Israel Jr (and his wife Mary), James and John. Israel, dubbed the "King of the Quakers" and James, who was politically ambitious, were prominent in Pennsylvanian affairs; John, whose mission in life came from a "divine revelation", was one of the most influential Quaker ministers in America and a key player in the process of reform from 1755.

As one account relates:
"The Pemberton home was a nursery of Truth. The atmosphere of it was sweet and fragrant with spiritual religion. The father and mother lived and moved and had their being in the sphere of what Friends called 'the Truth'. There was never any question with them as to which interest in life was paramount. There were large business interests to consider, there were important affairs of the province to direct, but everything had to bend to the call of the Spirit, whose Kingdom was the first concern. Others compromised and adjusted; this family group was accustomed to the practice of surrendering everything else to the clear requirements of inward duty." [61]

Of the others who 'appeared' at this 7th day meeting, John Hunt, John Churchman, his brother-in-law William Brown and Daniel Stanton were all 'weighty Friends' as active preachers and reformers. As previously noted, Rachel had already met many prominent Quakers and non-Quakers and more such names occur throughout the rest of her journal.

On 1st day: at the Bank ... *my Mind was early engaged in supplication. After S Morris appeared with that expression "God is Love and they that dwell in him dwell in Love". She had I thought a good time. I stood up after, clothed with strength to go through what was before me, in manifesting the great Love of God to mankind and in particular to the Inhabitants of that City, which I earnestly craved might have proper place in every mind present John Hunt concluded the Meeting in prayer and humble acknowledgment for the favour received.* Rachel visited a sick Friend and in the afternoon was at Market Street where no one "appeared", afterwards to another Friend, then to *Widow Cotes, she and her daughter being poorly, it appeared to be a House of Mourning; we could not make much stay, the evening Meeting coming on, which was very large and Solemn. I first stood up with "Let him that hath an Ear hear what the Spirit saith unto the churches" ... after Dan'l Stanton appeared with a request to the people to mind the Visitation of Divine Love, which was so mercifully extended that it might ever be with us, as with Jerusalem, when our Dear Lord took up that Lamentation over it; and when he sat down my Mind being afresh engaged, I stood up again with what was upon it and an open time it was. The Meeting ended in thanksgiving and prayer. After had a favourable opportunity at my lodgings. A soldier that had been reached to in the Meeting came to speak to me in an affecting manner: may he hold fast what he hath received is my sincere desire.*

2nd day: Quarterly Meeting

3rd day: Youths meeting when *I had to tell them how I came by my Ministry and the necessity there was to take heed of our Gifts.*

4th day: at meeting at Pine Street *on account of a marriage of a grand daughter of Michael Lightfoot and Benjamin Bury. It was large and favoured with divine goodness, that the Water was indeed made Wine. John Churchman concluded the meeting with prayer. I dined with them when I had to beg the blessing of the everlasting Hills might rest upon them.*

The brevity of this journal entry is typical of Rachel's selflessness, since she ministered powerfully in the meeting as witness a document that has survived in Quaker archives: "A discourse publickly delivered by a female friend from Old England, in the Friends Meeting House in

Pine-street, Philadelphia, on the third day of 5th month, 1769; also a prayer by another Friend, the whole taken down by ... William Darrah; to which is added a preface by the editor".
They continued on to Chester that night.
5th day: to Concord for another Quaker marriage
6th day: Goshen Monthly Meeting – *... pretty large and middling – an early call to diligence attended my mind. I had also to advise to Obedience to Parents, and lay before them the great disadvantage that attended refractory minds.*
7th day: back to Concord for their Select Meeting

1st day: meeting at Middletown in the morning and Concord in the evening
2nd day: Quarterly Meeting *very large and Instructive though close exercise, the Youth many of them Raw, the Ministers shut up in the fore part – towards the conclusion more openness.*
3rd day: at the Youth Meeting *in which things were pertinently spoken to earnestly requesting our trust might be with the Lord alone.*

*After we visited Philip Mendingholes Wife* [possibly Mendenhall], *who was under great depression of Spirit upon whose account our prayers were put up to the God and Father of all our Mercies, yet with great submission with which she seemed a good deal affected. I came away easy and thankful, in that I believed I had done my duty.*

4th day: Youth Meeting at Kennet
*... very large and my mind was enlarged in the ever blessed truth, to set forth the necessity there was for some persons to redouble their Care and Watchfulness as I was sensible some had suffered Loss. The Youth, many of them Raw, yet several happily reached to which it was fresh cause of thankfulness to my Mind in which I had reverently to acknowledge the Goodness of God and his continued Mercies to us, poor unworthy Mortals.*

5th day: Monthly Meeting
*It was long in gathering, and just in our setting down a Storm of wind arose, which unsettled the minds of many by which sensible loss* [a sense of loss] *was sustained and three Friends said a little sweetly, yet*

*made no great alteration in the general feeling, in which state I stood up, having, as I thought, a sense of the State of the Meeting which had place in many minds, that the latter end exceeded the beginning. The Meeting of business in a good degree favoured – there was a Woman received a member that came in by convincement. We dined at Caleb Peases. At this Meeting our valuable Friend S Morris brought me a letter from my Dear Husband and Sister Deborah, which afforded me great satisfaction.*

6th day: at her host's Monthly Meeting which was large
7th day: Select Meeting at the Grove, many Friends from Warrington, Fairfax and Hopewell also attending

1st day: Newgarden Meeting in the morning and the Grove in the evening; both meetings exceedingly large.
2nd day: Quarterly Meeting, again large, lasted until nearly 6 o'clock and she got back to Philadelphia that night.

Rachel had spent four and a half weeks in and around Philadelphia and it was now the middle of fifth month, seven months after reaching America.

She wrote home:

> ***Sarah Morris came to Kennet Last fifth Day & haith bin with us since ... she Brought along thine of ye 23rd 2mo plus one of Eliz of ye same from Sister Deby, Both of which was truly acceptable and aforded Me much Comfort as they conveyed ye agreable account of all your welfare and Every Litle intelegence is pleasing tho I was preserved very quiet & still when Deprived of hearing from any friends for Many Months through one Desapointment or another. Late this Morning had four of thine Dated 10mo 9th, 10mo 28, 11mo 30, 12mo 29 & one from Daughter Rachel Dated 10mo 16 – these all Came to hand since I Began this.***

She was looking forward to meeting her next companion, Sarah Hopkins, at Burlington the next day, ready to be at Yearly Meeting at Long Island on 28th.

> ***I expect ye most Difficult part of ye Journey in Regard to Lodgings ... is gott over, yet this is a Long one I am now going to Enter Upon, but I supose an older Habited Countrey.***
> ***... in this Arduous Undertaking ... I cannot but with Humility Confes Ive Experienced ye fulfilling of ye Gracious promis Even ye hundred fold in this Life – Even of peace & Satisfaction in my Lonly pilgrimage without any hankering Desires after what Ive left behind so as to Desire to be with Em til its Consistant with ye Divine Will. Indeed, Ive often bin in Deep admiration with ye humbling view that, in truth, with God all things are possible. Hard things have bin Maid Esier & ye Bitter Cup sweetened so as to be tolerable pleasant – what haith bin awanting in one Respect haith bin abundantly Maid up in another – Contentment which is indeed a Continual feast and this Ive had plentifuly to Regail My Self with. Ive met with nothing to Exalt or Rais me in mine own opinion; I am to[o] well aquainted with my own weakness and ye fralety*** [frailty] ***yt await humanity to be sett up with Empty Noise; it was Never Pleasant to be so pop[u]lar but haith often Deeply humbled My Mind & caused Me to Drop some tears – with fervent Desires yt I Might be Conducted Safly along to ye Name of him that haith Cald*** [called] ***to that Servis*** …

concluding with her usual love and greetings to the many family, friends and relations

> ***that may inquire after thy truly affectionate and at times Deeply Exercised Wife. Rachel Wilson.***

## Chapter 10

## PHILADELPHIA TO THE FAR NORTH-EAST

18th day of 5th month 1769 (5th day of the week) Rachel left Philadelphia with Thomas Clifford, his wife and son and Hester Fisher and reached Burlington in time for meeting where they met Rachel's new companion Sarah Hopkins.

*Here a young man under sentence of Death for a Rape sent a request that I would pay him a visit which upon considering solidly I found freedom to join in with, several Friends accompanying me, the Jailor and Sheriff both present, I queried with him if he did not think his sentence just, which he acknowledged to me he did but he had never seen his Sin so great as then, and that he did not desire to live, if he could but find mercy with God. I said what was opened in my Mind – and after was engaged to go down upon my knees which the poor creature joined with, tho heavy loaded with Irons. He acknowledged his thankfulness for the visit. It was indeed affecting to see him in that state with his Coffin standing by, shocking to Human Nature – and sorrowful to think that a few minutes indulgence and gratification to self should by any be preferred to lasting peace; sacrificing all but their lustful inclinations till hurried on to their Shame and confusion which frequently ends in destruction of Soul and Body.*

*We also visited the Governor and his Wife, who were both at meeting, with many of the principal Inhabitants; we held a Solemn Season in the Governors house with whom they expressed their satisfaction.*

*On 6th day morning before I left Burlington I went to the Prison again to speak to the Man that had been an accomplice with him that was under sentence of Death, having saved himself by turning Evidence, which seemed to have its effect.*

Burlington was John Woolman's Monthly Meeting but Rachel did not record having met him, either here or on the occasion of her previous visit in 10th month 1768. However the two were well known to each other and there was strong mutual respect between them as borne out by contemporary accounts.

Afterwards the group came to Bordentown where many at meeting were left standing in the rain because of the meeting house being too small so the offer of the Baptists to use their meeting house was accepted. *We dined with John Sikes and his Wife, two innocent honest friends, having been married upwards of 64 years.*

On 7th day Rachel attended meeting at Trenton. It being Court day there, many of the lawyers also attended. On 1st day she visited a sick Friend and attended Stoney Brook Meeting *much crowded with all sorts of People. Finding myself not quite clear we had a meeting appointed at Princetown* [Princeton] *at half past four which was held in the College to pretty good satisfaction, tho' so crowded that a good part stood. The Students behaved well, and several of them came and spoke to me after.*

This meeting was in response to a letter signed the previous day by some fifty of the students requesting Rachel to favour them "with a sermon on Monday next, at whatever time of the day you may please". Among the students were a future Revolutionary War poet (Philip Freneau) and some who would be prominent in the early Republic.[62] (From Rachel's letter home, it would appear that this meeting, in fact, must have been on the 1st day, i.e. the Sunday.) *We dined with Richard Stockton, a lawyer, who with his wife was very kind.*

On 2nd day, meeting was held at Brunswick in the Presbyterian meeting house the people's *hearts being like the thirsty ground that eagerly drank in the Rain.* Two more "large and Edifying" meetings were held on 3rd day – at Woodbridge and Rahway. On 4th day, at Elizabeth Town, the Court House was too small and, in spite of being offered the Presbyterian meeting house, meeting was held out of doors, finding *more freedom out than in* with several *sitting in their Chairs with great solidity. The Mayor of the Place desired, if I came that way back, and found freedom, that I would pay the Baptists a visit at their meeting house, about 8 miles, he hoped there were several in a seeking state; this seemed to be the case with many in these parts, their hearts being prepared to hear the Gospel preached and to receive with gladness.*

They dined en route at an inn and reached New York that evening where they held a "large and comfortable" meeting. On 5th day they crossed over to Long Island and so to Flushing for the Quarterly and Yearly Meetings and for the Select Meeting, these continuing into 6th, 7th, 1st and 2nd days. They lodged with a kind, motherly woman. In a letter home, Rachel brought Isaac up to date as usual and continued:

> ***I cannot write to all My Dear Childer separately ... how their Poor Mother fares in this Remote part of ye world. Im favourd with health having not had one Days Sickness since I Landed or anye Returne of My old Complaint*** [in her breast – see p.17] ***... I cannot but Simpathiz with Doly Under her present trial*** [pregnancy] ***yet I fervently hope shel gett it well over.***

The weather was so warm that Rachel expected to be given lifts for this part of the journey so that she could

> ***Leve My hors behind to Recover – as ye horsis in New England thay apprehend are generaly Better and fitter for that Country.***

On 3rd day they were at Cowneck for another large meeting and spent the night with Friends at Westbury, attending their Monthly Meeting the next day. Two Friends, George Bowne and Joseph Pearsall, arrived from New York ready to accompany them to Rhode Island. Also, John Pemberton joined at this stage of the journey with a concern to visit the yearly meeting here and at Nantucket.

On 5th day, 1st of 6th month, they were at Matendale in the morning and Oyster Bay in the evening where *people flocked much to the meetings* and on 6th day were at Bethpage for a marriage followed by Seugnalaugh in the evening. On 7th day they rode to Brookhaven, near Setauket for a meeting attended by *some tender spirited people, though many Raw and unacquainted with our principles; yet we were enabled to discharge ourselves and come away easy.* Next, they rode 40 miles, having drunk tea at a place called the Old Man, and lodged at an inn overnight where they held a meeting.

They rose early on 1st day and rode 11 miles to meeting at the Court House where:
*Hearing there was a Meeting of those they call'd the Separated* [Separatists] *there was on the road we found a desire to attend, and got there just as they were gathering, but some of their leading Men did not seem free to admit us into their meeting house, so we stood under some Trees close by, and several staid with us, with whom we had an opportunity to declare the way of Life and Salvation. Some of them were much affected, bidding us forward with kindness. ...We got on to our Horses and rode about 3 Miles till we came to another Meeting, where the Priest was preaching. We stop'd our Horses awhile at the Door, then went forward a few steps, hoping we might have pursued our Journey, but soon found it was best to alight and go back; when we came there, they were singing; we staid without till that was over, my mind filling that as they were coming away I step'd in and desired liberty to express a few sentences, which the Priest readily granted, and my mind being filled I was like one that wanted vent. I told them I was come in the Love of God to visit them, having nothing else in view but the honour of God and the good of Souls being opened to lay before them my call to the Ministry.*

*It affected the Priest so that he suffered his temper to rise – and told me if I was going to assert my right to the Ministry, that was inconsistent with the Scriptures, and he must desire me to hold my Peace with some warm* [heated] *expressions. During this time I stood quite still and John Pemberton and David Willis both desiring him to have a little Patience till I had done, and then to make his objections. I then told them if I had said anything inconsistent with the Doctrine of Christ, or his Apostles, I was willing to suffer. He said it was not the time to argue then, so walked out, his hearers deserting him as they wanted to hear me out, that I had a full opportunity to clear myself, and after had a Solemn Season in prayer – the people after bidding us farewell in an affectionate manner, and one of them invited us into a neighbour's house to take some refreshment. As I was pretty much spent, I saw free to go in and take a Glass of Wine.*

In a letter to Isaac, of the people whom she encountered along Long Island, Rachel describes

> ***those yt do not profess with us – Mostly Bigotd presbeterians wear no Meetings haith bin of Lait – and I believe we have left a door open for them that may find ye Lick*** [like] ***Concern to Come after us.***

This was at the time of the 'Great Awakening' referred to later.

They continued on to Southold and, next morning, enjoyed an unexpectedly large meeting at their inn. They then rode to Sterling and took the boat to New London, arriving about 6 o'clock in the evening. The speedy crossing

> ***was but four hours in ye water which they Cald*** [called] ***near thirty Miles; we have bin Much favourd in Crossing ye Waters – I am almost Become a good salor – the forays are Very Numerous in this part of ye world.***

On 3rd day, having started at the Court House, they transferred to the nearby meeting house where Rachel *was opened to lay down the Gospel Ministry and my engagement to visit my Brethren and Sisters. I made a little remark afterwards; John Pemberton stood up and said that though they called themselves Quakers, it was well known we were a peaceable people, and could have no meeting with such as made a practice of disturbing other Societies in their Worship, which that people had done by the account we had heard, in a Ranting manner laying it high* [claiming] *that it was called for at their hands, to testify against such false Worshipers, frequently making so much noise that the Priest could not be heard, and when they were hindered from going in, would at times throw stones against the Doors, for which they were taken up and imprisoned, and some of them whip't – this they seem'd to Glory in as suffering for Christ's sake. I was sorry these measures had been taken, it was only adding fuel to the Fire, it made them still more mad with Zeal of their own arising. Both parties seemed to me wrong, and it was my plan to moderate as much as in my power, the people behaving Civil to us.*

*One of them came and told me she had good unity with me, till I kneeled down. Public prayer being inconsistent with the Doctrine of Scripture, which I desired she would prove, she turned to those expressions, 'pray not as the Pharisees do, but when you pray enter into your closet, and shut the Door, and your Heavenly Father that hears in secret, will reward you aplenty'. I told her I did not apprehend it was a prohibition, neither did I think that to be the Closet of our houses, but the Closet of our hearts and to shutting the door against temptation, so she drop'd the Subject and seemed pretty calm, only telling us the Hardships they had undergone, her Sister being with her, and both their Husbands in prison.*

*After Dinner went to visit them in prison – going along the Street the people flocked after us, which was not so easy to my mind, tho' not in my power to prevent. There were two parsons of the Episcopalians and one young Man a Presbyterian, that were come upon trial: they were all at Meeting; and expressed their satisfaction, and at the prison one of the priests called Grave made some remarks to the prisoners. We sat still; I desired silence which was much wanted on both sides; I had an opportunity to speak what was upon my mind which, when I had done, one asked me what I meant by that if a Man's ways please the Lord he'l make his very enemies to be at Peace with him, to which I gave no answer, wanting not to satisfy that craving disposition after words. The parson took upon himself to explain, which I had rather he had let alone. After this one of them exalted his voice with Glory, Glory to God! I can praise his Name, going over it several times. We finding ourselves easy, bid them farewell; J Pemberton said a little to those of them that seemed more cool.*

*The prisoner that was sick, I thought it was dangerous for him to stay in that close place, that I found freedom to request his being set at liberty; I applied to the Sheriff and some others, and understood the request was granted after our leaving the place, and an account was sent me of it to Newport. One of the priests came down with us to the Boat and bid us affectionately farewell. We came that night to an Inn.*

Rachel's next letter home enlarged upon her journal account:

> ***We had a Meetg at New London this day where we found great openings amongst ye pepol; ye Priest attended our Meetg and behaved with great Regard. Here we mett with those Caled Rogersons or Seventh day Baptists – their Number is not Very Large – I sopose somewear about 40 or 50 – by what I can find. Thayr ye Most Lick what ye persons was in Cumberland – Strictly onest Betwixt Man and Man speaking ye plain Langwish and appears plain – but always Destrusting ye presbeterians in thayr worship – for which they have Suferd Deeply – Both whipings and Imprisonment. We Visited Eight of Em in prison – one of which was sick – My feeling was great Both for ye persequtors and persequted. I Believed Em Both to be in Loving Spirit – and went inabled to Drop some proper hints to Both partys, Especialy J Pemberton – One of ye Men haith sent Me word since I Came here that those in authority have sett the Sick Man at Liberty at My Request that Our Labour haith not bin all in Vain.***

They continued on to Westerly, leaving two of their accompanying Friends to wait for their horses to be brought over from Long Island since the boat had not been large enough to take them all at once.

Next morning, the weekday meeting there was *very small, only 4 Men and 3 Women and 2 Boys that bore our name – several others came in – yet it was painful to see and feel such Lukewarmness and Negligence amongst those that professed with us.*

They rode 40 miles and, by land and water, reached Newport, Rhode Island that night (4th day). They went next to nearby Porstmouth on

5th day for meeting, another large gathering, and returned to Newport on 6th day morning in time for the Ministers and Elders Meeting at 8 o'clock *in which I had some Instinctive hints to drop of which there seemed great occasion for when the answers to the Queries were read. I never observed so much deficiency in attendance of Meetings before in those called Ministers and Elders.* The public meeting for worship followed at 11 and the business meeting at 3. The public meeting on 7th day was large. *We dined with John Docker where we had some service; also in the morning we visited a young woman in decline, her name was Wanton; she seemed much affected with the visit – also her parents.*

On 1st day, there was the meeting of Ministers and Elders at 7 o'clock followed by meeting for worship at 10. On 2nd day there was another meeting of Ministers and Elders at 7, a business meeting at 9, meeting for worship at 11 and a continuation of the business meeting at 3, *all the meetings being much favoured with the overshadowing of Divine Love.*

On 3rd day Rachel wrote home. Israel Pemberton and his brother had kindly lent two of their horses lest Rachel and her companion should not find suitable ones in New England. To Isaac she wrote:

> ***I am well Mountd; it go[e]s Exceding Safe and Ese*** [easy] ***–I hope these hints will not be Desagreable to thee – thou's anxiously Concerned for My welfare ... My Mind haith bin kept quick steadily Eyeing ye pointings out of Best Wisdom. Their Yearly Meetg Ended hear Last night ... the Largist I think I was Ever at ... the whole having bin Conducted to general Satisfaction. ... My Voice continuing Strong and My Natural Strength not failing tho ye Servis Lyes Close upon Me ... Am grown a little W[h]iter Both with Being so much Exposed to ye Wind and Sun and with Constant Exercise of Mind that I supose I Look a good deal older than when I Left My own Habitation but thats a trifal as I am so Much favourd with health ... This***

> ***part of the country do[e]s not want for good acomadations as fare as Ive yet seen – its much Different from ye South.***

In writing to his wife, John Pemberton commented:

"Friend Wilson likes brother Israel's horse well" and "the yearly meeting here ... is thought to have been the largest meeting known for many years; the house here is very large, but could not contain the people by a great number. Great numbers not professing with us attended and behaved with sobriety and solid attention in the general, and Friend Wilson was favoured to speak to them with clearness and Divine authority ... I was a little spent last night with the long meetings we have had from day to day, beginning generally at 7 in the morning, and little intermission till night." Rachel, he noted, was "favoured with a strong constitution." [63] In a later letter home, Rachel remarked on how much she benefited from John's company and how "he grows in his gift" [of ministry].

During dinner she received a message from one of the Assembly Men, the Assembly being then in session, desiring her to pay them a visit in the House *which gave a damp to my Spirits, and I thought it was time to be gone* for she did not feel 'called' to comply: *I had not my Commission from Man neither could I go at Man's bidding,* she explained in her journal.

They left the island and journeyed to a Friend's house at Tiverton for the night. George Bowne and Joseph Pearsall left for home while John Pemberton and Walter Franklin stayed with Rachel. They attended a large meeting at Tiverton on 4th day followed by an afternoon meeting at Little Compton *which was large, but more close, things having got amongst them, that had divided in Israel and scattered in Jacob.* They stayed with another Friend that night and, in the morning (5th day), visited a sick Friend at Acox before reaching Center in the afternoon where the meeting overflowed the meeting house and on to Acushnet for the night. On 6th day they rode to Newtown for another crowded meeting. 7th day was Rochester for a "small yet comfortable" meeting and then to Long Plain for the night.

*Meeting on first day Morning was large, but not much favoured, it being very Hot, and the people without not very quiet.* A similar overcrowding situation arose at Queshiner, the Quaker meeting house having to be abandoned in favour of the Presbyterian one *and a precious Meeting we had. I being much spent we got a draft of Rum and Water at a Tavern near.*

Another hot, crowded meeting greeted them at Apponagansett on 2nd day; afterwards Rachel visited a Friend who had breast cancer. On 3rd day, the intention had been to go on board the boat for Nantucket, but the weather was too dull and hazy with no wind until about 8 o'clock on 4th day when the tide was against them and it was unwise to venture through Woodashole, so the captain cast anchor at Elizabeth Island. Here, several of the company went on shore to pick strawberries. Following the turning of the tide, they got safely through, thanks to a small breeze and, with the wind increasing, wondered if they would reach Nantucket that night. Their captain was cautious of acting without deferring to Rachel. In passing Martha's Vineyard in which only one Quaker family lived and, in weighing the matter carefully, Rachel *had more freedom to stop than to go forward in the night.*

*... we were upwards of twenty passengers, that if we were confined to the Sloop it would be very inconvenient, and I believed it would be best for us to go on shore. The Wind being fair, the Captain's Son in Law seemed desirous to go forward, and made some of the Passengers a little uneasy alledging the Wind might be against us in the Morning and we might lay there some time. I had no fear of that sort upon my mind, as my trust was in Him at whose command the Wind and Seas obey, and mine Eye single to his bidding which I always found answered in every respect, though reason is sometimes like to get in as at this time it was suggested now if they all stay through thee, and anything but well should happen, what a reflection that will be to the great Cause thou art engaged in – but, keeping still, my mind was supported – I said Thou knows O Lord, I have but one view, thy Glory and the good of Souls – and fear fled from me. Our Captain as soon*

*as we got near the Land, advised two of the hands to set him on shore in the Boat, before the Sloop could get to a proper Anchor and as the evening was approaching there was no time to spare* [waste] *in collecting the Inhabitants together, as I found an Inclination to sit with them which proved useful. In the morning* [5th day] *we got early on board and having a good Wind in our favour got safe to Nantucket about 11 o'clock.*

They visited some sick Friends and then on 6th day it was Nantucket Yearly Meeting – "pretty large". A Congregationalist minister who later became president of Yale College, Reverend Ezra Stiles, was in the crowd attending the meeting. His diary records that he heard Rachel, "an eminent Quaker Preacher lately come from Westmoreland in England" and that "she spoke above an hour" and was "a pious sensible woman".[64] In the evening they visited a Friend who had been stricken with blindness and *scarcely got her mind reconciled to her condition.* 7th day was the ministers' and elders' meeting followed by a public meeting.

There were two large meetings on 1st day, the adjourned ministers' and elders' meeting on 2nd day and another public meeting and *we visited three sick Friends this evening, being in hopes we might have been at Liberty to have left the Island early next morning, but my mind was weighed down under apprehension not knowing the cause yet earnestly desiring I might stay till the end of my coming was answered. In the evening the thing was cleared up, a difference having subsisted for many years – a Committee was appointed from the Quarterly Meeting in order to get the parties concerned to submit to refer it, which they had endeavoured for without desired success – finding my mind engaged to join them with my Companion and John Pemberton, and truth favouring our labour was not in vain – they all agreed, and Arbitration Bonds were drawn up and signed to our admiration and thankfulness, for which the great Name be praised.*

~~~~~~~~~~~~~~~~~~
~~~~~~~~~~~~~~~~~~

In many ways, the story of Quaker Nantucket appears as a microcosm of the wider history of American Quakerism: its rise and decline, its dominance of several major populations and commerce in its heyday, the ever-present internal power struggles and subsequent schisms and an almost self-destructive process of discipline and disownment of all Friends who strayed from the Quaker line.[65] In 1708 there were 75 adult members. This grew to 1,173 by 1758 and the Great Meetinghouse, in its finally enlarged form, could hold 2,000 people – a majority of the island's population. By the time of Rachel's visit, some 4,500 (about half of the island's total population) were still Friends. In the first part of the eighteenth century, it was the centre of the world whaling industry with Quakers having a near monopoly.

In 1754, four Friends had been "placed under dealing" (i.e. under the disciplinary procedure) for overstocking the island's common land with sheep (to the detriment of other commoners under the system of allocation that all were expected to follow). It was unheard of for a Meeting to bring commercial affairs within its jurisdiction, but, on this occasion, the common good had been deemed to provide proper grounds for this. Also, the normal disciplinary procedure (of careful examination of and deliberation over Friends' disputes with each other and the opportunity to mend one's ways and to formally apologise so as to avoid disownment) had not been followed. Three Friends had been disowned and bad feelings, including accusations of individuals' ulterior motives, had run high ever since. The authority to make the decision had been confirmed by Quarterly Meeting (QM) on Rhode Island in 1755; that, in due course, had been referred to New England Yearly Meeting (YM), meeting in closed session so as to exclude Nantucketers, and finally, as a last resort, to Meeting for Sufferings in London – the ultimate authority.

London's decision, in 1759, was brought by messenger to another closed session of New England YM and likewise communicated to Rhode Island QM which then, and only then, invited a delegation from Nantucket Monthly Meeting to attend QM three months later.

Both the secrecy afforded to the issue and the enormity of it were unprecedented in Quaker circles. The QM and Nantucket delegations met in closed session for four days – probably the longest QM on record.

London's decision was that it was not expedient for a Monthly Meeting to decide on property rights and land titles, that the disowned Members should be reinstated and that the Meeting should stay out of such matters in the future. An attempt to have the decision set aside failed and the 'Commons Case' rumbled on through the greater trials and tribulations of the seven years Anglo-French war (1756-63). Those Friends who had been overstocking the common land had continued to do so with impunity. Rachel, in company with John Pemberton, now arrived in 1769 with the clear purpose of settling the matter once and for all. The Committee referred to in Rachel's journal reached a multipart compromise between the interested parties. A new reconciliation grew out of Rachel's skilful, spirit-led counselling. Once again, her journal is a typical understatement of a major achievement.

However, it was fully acknowledged by the Quaker Moses Brown, member of the Rhode Island Assembly, a great philanthropist and the benefactor of Brown University, who wrote:

"To the credit of Rachel Wilson, and the influence of her Divine Master, this settlement was made, for it was through her wise and discreet management and influence, she prevailed on Stephen Hopkins [four times Governor of Rhode Island, Chief Justice, and a signer of the Declaration of Independence] and me to go and attend to the business. It was my lot to examine the record, and, in doing so, a worthy man, then a Minister, Elihu Coleman, was cleared of the charge made against him, which fully paid me for my trouble and care in the business at the time, which I mention to the memory of Rachel Wilson, as without her favoured influence as an instrument, the work would not have been effected. She was indeed a wise and favoured Minister, and an apostle of usefulness to me." [66]

(As an aside, it has been said of Stephen Hopkins (born 1707) that, after William Penn, no other Quaker in American history achieved such a distinguished political career or contributed so much to the development of America's national life. At 25 he went to the General Assembly, he received judicial training and reached the highest judicial place in Rhode Island, he was chosen for inter-colonial service in 1746, was a delegate during the "French and Indian War" to the colonial Congresses, including 1754 when Benjamin Franklin advocated a plan of union, he became Governor in 1755 and, as early as 1756, he saw (as Patrick Henry did also) the unconstitutionality of taxation without representation. Papers that he wrote in 1764 were part of the creative foundation of American history; he taught the colonists to think in terms of their country. Then, only four years after Rachel's visit, he was disowned for owning one slave whom he refused to free.) [67]

~~~~~~~~~~~~~~~~~~~

Continuing Rachel's journal:
*We expected we might have been at Liberty to have left the Island but when we got up in the Morning* [3rd day] *the wind was against us, and the other business fell to our Lot. There had been a disagreeable affair amongst them which had caused great warmth* [heat], *and was also become the Quarterly Meeting's business, tho' imprudently introduced, that had occasioned great dispute. A Friend that had visited them, requested a Certificate if they could do it with freedom, but rather to omit it than occasion division amongst themselves, which if it had been regarded would have preserved from much trouble, for some had taken great offence at what he had declared, and others were Zealous for a Certificate, that an open breach was made. The enemy being never awanting to improve every opportunity for the exaltation of his Kingdom, and laying waste the work of God, that we found it our place to enquire into the Matter, and endeavoured to stop any further progress in it, as it would neither tend to the honour of Society, nor the peace of individuals to go much further and a certificate for the Friend seemed rather out of date then that if they*
~~~~~~~~~~~~~~~~~~~

*could be brought to acknowledge that both parties had missed it, and beg of the Quarterly Meeting to pass it, [as] appeared best, which was in a good measure affected, and they hoped it would be teaching to them for the future having got these troublesome matters settled by the assistance of Divine Wisdom which was sensibly experienced.*

During the 1760's, Nantucket Meeting's application of Quaker discipline was draconian. Migration of local Quakers to other places was rigorously resisted (in order to preserve the local Quaker population) and marrying out was condemned, leading to large scale disownment of transgressors. Rachel does not specify the nature of the division that had arisen in this particular case, but the "certificate" presumably related either to a transfer of membership from one Quaker area to another or to a Quaker's marriage to a non-Quaker.

She had time to write a letter, one piece at a time, over six days:

> ***It joust occours to my mind maybe Doly May be near her time and if so no wonder if I am a litl more thoughtful tho I hope shel Do well.***

(Daughter Dorothy's, Hannah, in fact had been born on 5th mo 22nd – four weeks before this letter.)

> ***Sarah Barney is now by Me, a frd that traveled with Jane Crosfield who Desires to be Rememberd to her & Thos Gawthrope and Many more inquire after Em in these parts ... My Strength and Voice holds out ... Ive not bin qasy*** [queasy] ***in what I Eate and Drink and Cyder I own ... aggreas with Me well that Ive No Desire after Malt Liquer.***

Sarah Barney, a prominent Quaker minister, worked tirelessly for the rights of women Friends and, from 1761, for the good reputation of Nantucket Meeting.

Rachel and her companions finally left Nantucket on 5th day morning, reaching Woodashole, back on the mainland, about 5 o'clock, where they held a meeting in the Town Tavern. Fortunately, spring so far this year had been uncommonly cool, which suited Rachel well, but that was about to change.

On 6th day they rode to Falmouth for meeting for worship and then to a Friend's house for Quarterly Meeting at Sandwich; they stayed there for the Select Meeting and meeting for worship before riding 4 miles to their lodging for the night and then 15 miles on 1st day morning for meeting for worship at Yarmouth. It was a small meeting house, crowded and very hot. They rode 19 miles to their lodgings where their host had only been a Friend for about eighteen months, having previously been a Baptist minister *and was still a little tinged, I thought.*

On 2nd day, they journeyed 22 miles to Plymouth for morning meeting *the day being hot, I was much spent and sunk with what was before me ... a few hours sleep refreshed me, and with the ease of riding in a Chair we got there in time, had the meeting in the Courthouse the people behaved remarkably well: Truth favouring to the astonishment of some, and Edification of others in pure Gospel Love.*

Next they travelled to Pembroke for meeting on 3rd day followed by 20 miles to an inn for the night. On 4th day they rode 11 miles to Boston for breakfast in time for a meeting arranged for 11 o'clock to which many of the inhabitants came; they had an "open time" with them and many thanked Rachel and told her how inspiring they had found her.

The crowded meetings here (and almost everywhere else on this part of Rachel's religious visit), sometimes necessitating the hiring of large halls, were a sign of the times. There was a hunger and thirst among the people for spiritual enlightenment. Much advance publicity was given to the visit to America of this evangelical English female preacher. The 'Boston Gazette' reporting on her as an eminent preacher among Friends observed "Her discourse was nervous, pertinent and solemn; in which, as in the whole of her deportment, she clearly displayed the most lively imagination, a singular penetration, and most of that general benevolence, which is the distinguishing characteristic of the true Christian." [68] Rachel was met all the way with requests from city and town leaders, from other sects, from student organisations and others for her to make time to address their citizens, congregations and groups.

~~~~~~~~~~~~~~~~~~~~

In part this was a product of the 'Great Awakening' [69] – a rapid and dramatic revivalism that swept through New England and the Middle Colonies from the 1740's. Communities and the established churches were divided into anti-revivalist, Old Lights/Old Side, and revivalist, New Lights/New Side, among the Congregationalists/Presbyterians respectively. The ensuing evangelical fervour envisioned a 'new birth' through God's grace. The state-driven church system eventually disintegrated, largely because the taxation system could not favour one faction over another. A vast range of religious options was on offer from itinerant preachers. People's eagerness to go and hear them, as they debated which form of worship to adopt, created a new environment of religious liberty. Indirectly, this opened up more freedom for Quaker travelling ministers, especially women since in many churches women were debarred from being preachers, and also drew large general public audiences to them. One of the best known preachers was the charismatic, ordained Anglican George Whitefield who was noted for his stirring, invigorating style and preaching in the open air. Rachel gained a similar reputation, her eloquence being compared to his; Whitefield himself commented how deeply impressed he had been when hearing Rachel preach in Bristol, England in 1764. In all the main churches outside Quakerism, women preachers were a rarity or did not exist.

It is extraordinary to think that, only 100 years before Rachel's visit, the Puritan authorities in Boston saw Quakers as such a threat that they fined ships' captains who brought Quakers into the province and made it illegal for Quakers to be there. In particular, they dreaded women Quaker missionaries, confiscating their pamphlets and other
~~~~~~~~~~~~~~~~~~~~

property and searching them for marks that might identify them as witches. There was a real fear that their heresy and sedition were contagious and would spread; local inhabitants had to undertake what may best be described as a form of self-imposed quarantine and stay clear of these women.

Although Quakers were accepted and held office in high places in several of the colonies from these early years, Boston was the outstanding exception. Persecution here was extreme and the 'Boston Martyrs' have as important a place in Quaker history as do the Quakers who suffered extensive persecution in England and in other parts of the world. It was yet another example in history of the persecuted having turned into even worse persecutors, for it was the descendants of persecuted Puritans who had come to settle in the colonies and who were now in power.

The same was true of New Amsterdam (to become New York in 1664). Holland was the forerunner of religious toleration in Europe and provided a haven for early Quakers. In New Amsterdam, however, the tolerant Dutch turned intolerant and persecution of Quakers there almost mirrored that in Boston. In the 17th century, Quaker persecution was also widespread and severe in Virginia.

The two first Quaker missionaries to Boston were Mary Fisher and Anne Austin in 1656. They were imprisoned for five weeks, the windows were boarded up so that no one could speak with them and they were denied food. They would have died there had not a member of another church taken pity on them and paid the jailer to take them food. They were transported back to England under strict orders that no one speak to them.

Similar transportations of other Quakers followed, but those who felt the compelling call of God to go to New England responded unhesitatingly. A Mary Clark who came to Boston to warn persecutors against their cruelties was punished with twenty stripes on her naked back and imprisoned for twelve weeks in winter. There is a long list of others who likewise suffered.

History recounts: "Weak women and old men were kept without food or fires, beaten and abused; some had their ears cut off, and others their tongues bored with hot irons. Even this did not satisfy the persecutors, and in October 1658, an act was passed against 'a pernicious sect (commonly called Quakers)', giving power to any constable to take up and imprison any persons suspected of being Quakers and condemning them, if the charge proved true, to banishment on pain of death." [70]

Three Quakers were led to the gallows, guarded by two hundred horsemen lest the people tried to rescue them and with drums being beaten so that no one should hear them speak. One of them, Mary Dyer, in response to her son's cry from the crowd, was reprieved after the halter had been placed around her neck, but she felt compelled to return the next year when she, too, was put to death.

One is deeply moved by Rufus M Jones's descriptions of the vicious persecution endured by the early American Quakers. To give but a small selection of the total sufferings:

"Two ... women stripped stark naked and searched in an inhuman manner; twelve ... whippings, most of them with a whip of three cords with knots at the ends; 64 imprisonments ... amounting to 519 weeks; two beaten with pitched ropes, the blows amounting to an hundred and thirty nine; an innocent old man banished from his wife and children, and for returning put in prison for above a year; fines [of £1,000] laid upon the inhabitants for meeting together; five kept fifteen days without food; one laid neck and heels in irons for sixteen hours; one [deeply branded in his right hand after being beaten with 30 stripes]; one chained to a log of wood for the most part of twenty days in winter time; three had their right ears cropped off; one ... had one half of his house and land seized; two ordered [to be] sold as bond servants." [71]

When a banished Quaker, Samuel Shattuck, returned from England bearing King Charles II's mandamus [a writ or command] requiring Governor Endicott to cease the persecutions and to release all imprisoned Quakers, the requirement had to be met. But the reprieve lasted only until the enraged and humiliated governor could bring in new laws "to prevent the intrusion of Quakers". The "Cart and Whip Act, 1661" was every bit as savage as its predecessor. "Any person not giving civil respect by the usual gestures, or by any other means manifesting himself to be a Quaker, shall ... be stripped naked from the middle upwards and be tied to a cart's tail and whipped through the town, and from thence immediately conveyed to the constable of the next town, to the borders of our jurisdiction, and so from constable to constable till they be conveyed through any of the outwardmost towns of our jurisdiction." [72] Women were treated the same as men. Among a long list of sufferings, there was an instance of two men who were whipped through two towns under an ingeniously contrived whip that tore through the flesh.

George Fox's first convert, Elizabeth Hooton, had endured a lifetime of hardship and persecution for truth's sake when, incredibly and by now in her mid 60's, she came to Boston, having walked a large part of the way from Virginia. She carried with her a special licence from the King to build a house in America, but this was rejected. She was, in turn: imprisoned; put in the stocks and again imprisoned; locked in a "close, foul dungeon"; given no food or drink for two days; whipped out of the jurisdiction (in spite of producing the King's licence); tied to a post and given ten lashes with a three-corded whip; given ten more lashes in Watertown; on a cold, frosty morning, tied to a cart and given ten more lashes and taken to woods where she was left, torn and bleeding, before making her own way to the haven of religious toleration in Newport, Rhode Island. Even then, she returned to try to bring the Quaker message to Boston and endured similar consequences: ten stripes at the House of Correction followed by being whipped through three towns and again being left in the woods. She made a third and final attempt on Boston, but was cruelly whipped out of town once more.[73]

100 years before her visit, therefore, Rachel could well have been suspected of being a witch. In all probability, she and her companions would have been arrested, searched for 'signs', inhumanely imprisoned, tortured and banished on pain of death. By contrast, on their return journey (recounted in the next chapter): *We lodged with Benjamin Bagnell, who told me since he lived there, they would scarcely speak to a Friend, and now no place more open which seem'd to comfort the honest old man to see such a change in his time.*

It is interesting to note that the Indians greatly admired the early Quaker martyrs and how this added to the bonds of friendship between them. These bonds continued to develop as Quakers resolutely maintained their testimony to the equality of all human beings and lived with the Indians as neighbours. During the much later wars with the Indians, it was this that saved a large proportion of the settlers from the worst effects of Indian guerrilla war. Quakers also had formed the Friendly Association for Regaining and Preserving Peace with Indians by Pacific Measures, which lasted from 1757 to 1762.

~~~~~~~~~~~~~~~~~~~

Leaving Boston, Rachel and her companions faced another busy schedule over the next seven days (4th day through to 3rd day) as they continued on their way to a range of meetings (for worship, select, discipline, parting, public) at Lynn, Salem, Newbury, Amesbury, Hampton, Kittery and Dover. William Rotch, his wife and sister and Sarah Barney left them at Hampton, having accompanied them this far from Nantucket. They were working their way gradually to the most easterly Quaker settlement on the continent – Merryconeeg (or Merryconeeg Neck), alternatively referred to as Harpswell in one of Rachel's letters. They stopped en route for meeting at Berwick (11 miles) and spent the night at an inn (15 miles). On 5th day, Rachel left her own horse to rest and the one she was now riding fell down with her and she sprained her left arm, making it difficult to hold the bridle. In this condition, she rode 30 miles to Falmouth for meeting in the evening.
~~~~~~~~~~~~~~~~~~~

On 6th day they rode about 3 miles to a river and left their horses *crossing Casco Bay about 18 miles to Morienique* (sic). Only a few Friends were settled in this remote outpost. Rachel saw it as *a poor place inwardly and outwardly. I thought my Spirits were a good deal oppressed whilst I staid; things seemed so much out of order. We lodged with the Widow Eagles and were enabled to discharge ourselves so as to get a little peace.*

Two days later, from Falmouth, Rachel was able to bring Isaac up to date, mentioning among other things, that at Boston they "Behaved Exceeding well that hears [here's] a great Change in ye Behaviour of ye pepol towards frds instead of persequting".

## Chapter 11

## THE FAR NORTH-EAST BACK TO PHILADELPHIA

They made a U-turn at Merryconeeg and set off back towards base in Philadelphia. Their schedule became even more hectic. It was 7th day, the 15th of 7th month and high summer – often unbearably hot and prone to violent thunderstorms. The publicity being given to Rachel's religious visit attracted ever greater attention, especially in these more advanced colonies. They stopped again at Kittery at the end of a day of heavy rain crossing back over the bay *in an open Boat that we were much wet and were a good deal fatigued.* After a good night's rest, they reached the new meeting house at Falmouth in time for first day meeting for worship. On 2nd day they rode 50 miles to Berwick and stopped overnight at Bedford but not without first having a large meeting at short notice at their inn.

Next day they travelled 12 miles to Dover for a very large meeting in the morning and then 22 miles to a Friend for the night. According to Rachel's journal, four priests attended the meeting at Dover where they *behaved well and acknowledged their satisfaction,* but, in a letter home, dated two days prior to Dover, she refers to four priests having come to a meeting at "a place called Cacacha" (possibly between Merryconeeg and Falmouth). Such a discrepancy is understandable, given that she cannot have had time to write up her journal every day.

In the morning, 4th day, they rode 8 miles to Newbury where they met in the Court House, *the people generally flocking in. It was much crowded, yet they behaved well; they seemed to be a tender people in that Town, to whom our visit was acceptable.* They rode another 24 miles that day. Rachel felt a strong pull, or "hint", to re-visit Salem on 5th day, but word had been sent ahead to Boston of her imminent arrival. She resisted the "hint" and decided that they should go forward to Boston, but John Pemberton felt compelled to respond to the call to remain.

So, she arrived in Boston. The meeting at 11 o'clock was actually rather small but another appointed for 5 o'clock was "large and satisfactory".

*Friends of the Town were pressing for a Meeting to be held in the Hall, a large commodious Room, as the Meeting House was quite too small, but my mind being low I durst not venture, and I came away thankful in my mind for the favour received, hoping I might have left the place easy, and ordered things ready to set off next morning. But in the night such a weight came over my mind that I could but sleep little, and it plainly appeared there was a further service for me in Boston. This brought me low that when the Horses came to the Door, I could not go, but sent them back. Visited Friends families in the morning and had a Meeting in the Hall in the evening, which the Great Master was graciously pleased to attend with his presence and tho' very large and hot, and most part stood yet were very quiet. There were most of the people of note in the Town, and behaved with great Civility, some reached to, and acknowledged the Truth. There seems a seeking people at Boston.*

This was at none other than the prestigious Faneuil Hall.

As mentioned in the previous chapter, they lodged with Benjamin Bagnell and he and his wife saw them on their way the next morning (7th day) when they rode 33 miles to Bolton. Rachel had intended going to meeting in Leicester on 1st day but "found" she could not leave until she had stayed for another meeting in Bolton, which "proved satisfactory" and they came away "easy". Friends from Leicester accompanied them to Uxbridge followed by Mendon, the meetings at both places being *favoured with the overshadowing of the divine presence.*

3rd day meeting at Woonsocket in the morning was followed by Smithfield in the afternoon. Rachel felt bound to query with them *what they went to their place of worship for because some, if there was no priest, returned home as if there was nothing to be done. Was it the Priest they came to Worship or Him whose presence fills the Heaven and Earth, and the Heaven of Heavens cannot contain the Majesty of his Glory? If there was nothing to be done without Man whose breath is in his Nostril and to such the Woe was pronounced. Truth gained ground, and we parted with great thankfulness.*

They continued that evening to Providence and found that a petition had been sent from the prisoners whom they had met on their way out from Philadelphia. On 5th day, *Went to visit them in the morning, which they acknowledged thankfulness for.*

*I had several other different requests from other quarters to have Meetings with them. Their meeting house doors were open for me, but I found it necessary to dwell low, and carefully feel after the right way which I trust my Kind Master was pleased to open to my view and I could not join in the requests that were made, nor stay longer in many places than just the Meetings were over, which were generally highly favoured, for which may I ever be thankful and praise the Great Name.*

Their next stop was Taunton, 22 miles, and the crowd was so great that they had to meet outside in the scorching sunshine, some sitting on the ground and others standing, all very attentive and seemingly well satisfied and desiring another meeting while Rachel was there. She wanted to go home and rest that evening at their host's, but as they went through the town where the Court House was, the people were already gathered together and so desirous of a meeting that Rachel was led to sit with them, her heart being warmed with Divine Love. The Court House filled up quickly and Rachel *had full opportunity to deliver the Truth and open Friends' principles to them*, of which many of those present had previously been ignorant.

On 6th day, they went to Freetown Meeting and on 7th day to Swansea. In spite of being wet, the meeting was large. They stayed at Providence for the night. On first day morning they attended meeting at Shantecut followed by Warwick in the afternoon, both being crowded with the greater part of those present being out of doors. They finished the day at Greenwich. There, next morning, *There was a gust of Thunder and Rain, which as the Crowd was great was somewhat difficult for a while, one or two fainting – but my mind was preserved very still, and the Storm ceased, and we were enabled to preach the Gospel in Power and demonstration. We dined with our Friend Thomas Aldrige, had a melting season. One of the New Lights Ministers came after to ask me some questions which I answered and we parted in Love.* (See previous chapter for the 'Great Awakening' and 'New Lights' revivalism.)

They continued on to their host where they had a "Salutory Season" with several Friends also coming from Newport. They reached South Kingston on 3rd day where Rachel pointed out the great advantage of silence – also the reason why Friends do not call the Bible the Word of God. Later they reached James Ferry's Meeting and thoroughly enjoyed meeting a lively ninety years old Friend. On 4th day morning they attended meeting at Richmond followed by Hopkinton.

They set off early on 5th day for Quarterly Meeting at "Patuxent" (Pawcatuck or Westerley), breakfasting en route at an inn and enjoying a conversation with an elderly man there. This Quarterly Meeting was significant because it had formally expressed its concern over the wrongfulness of slaveholding, appointed a large committee to visit Quakers who held slaves and passed its concern up to Yearly Meeting. It was reported that in one quarterly meeting area, one individual Quaker, in the course of visiting Quaker slaveholders, had met with the owners of no fewer than 1,100 slaves in total.

They called at New London, dined at Hope Ferry, drank tea near Sea Brook Ferry and finally reached their lodging after having ridden 43 miles. On 6th day they rode a further 32 miles to Newhaven where the upper room of the Court House had been hired for a meeting at half past three.

*The Inhabitants came so fully that the upper room was so crowded, tho' very still, that after I had stood a while I was seized in such a manner that I could scarcely speak. The windows were so crowded no air could come in, that I was obliged to tell them if they would not stand before them, I must sit down; one man immediately stood up, and desired we would go into the Low Room, which was much larger and more Airy as there were many more than could get in. I found freedom to join with it and stood upon a Table.*

They rode another 10 miles to an inn for the night and spent 7th day travelling: Fairfield, Newark, Stamford and Hornneck, some 42 miles in all. At meeting at Purchase on 1st day they met many Friends, it being the last day of their Quarterly Meeting. The number attending was so great that the Quaker stillness was somewhat lacking. Next day they had a pleasant meeting in the orchard of a local Friend's house *which made it more satisfactory as some hundreds attended.* In the afternoon they had a further meeting at a place near Bedford in a barn where, once again, many people gathered at short notice. A Baptist preacher attended both meetings having passed the word around his neighbours.

On 3rd day they came to Peach Pond with the Baptists and several others also coming. They reached New Milford that night and spent the next two days there or at Oblong. Friends who had been travelling with them went their various ways, mostly to New England but one to North Carolina. *There is a fine Body of Friends settled here* and they had meetings on both days; the first was "long in gathering" but the second was "large and satisfactory".

6th day started with meeting at nearby Nine Partners which was so overcrowded that one of the joists gave way, yet thankfully did no damage, although it happened just as the meeting was gathering which, needless to say, caused some disturbance. Once again, quite a lot of people had to remain out of doors. Two more short journeys took them to Oswego on 7th day for a large meeting and to Amawalk for first day meeting where local Friends made provision both inside and out of doors for the large number attending. 2nd day at Chappaqua was “close and hot” making the overflowing meeting “hard work” but they came away easy having done what seemed to be their duty. They were back at Purchase on 3rd day for yet another very large meeting.

A violent thunderstorm made them a little late for a pre-arranged meeting at White Plains that afternoon and the place was soon filled. The weather being so hot, Rachel was “much spent”. They had a “religious opportunity” that evening at their host’s where his sister was unable to get out to meeting because of a paralytic stroke. On 4th day they reached Westchester, having stopped on the way for meeting at Mamaroneck and on 5th day, New York, via meeting at Kingsbridge, the second leg of the journey being by courtesy of a local Friend in his chaise.

In her journal, Rachel only very occasionally admits how tiring it was – how “spent” she felt – to have this unremitting succession of mostly large meetings, many of them open to the public or even organised specifically as public occasions, in the oppressively hot weather, quite unlike the hills of northern England. It is hardly surprising that, in this part of her religious visit, she made only fairly cryptic entries in her journal and only brief mention of her own ministry. As an example:
*we had a precious meeting, dined with William Franklin ... On seventh day, had a Meeting at Newark at the Court House; amongst the Presbyterians they appeared a little Raw at first. Truth favouring, many were reached to, and came and acknowledged their thankfulness for the opportunity.*

In fact, this must have been the day that she spoke to a packed and appreciative public meeting at Beekman’s Precinct. Unknown to her, one of the audience recorded what she was saying which he later published as a pamphlet (see appendix):

"A discourse delivered
on Saturday, the 10th day of August, 1769
at the FRIENDS Meeting House in Beakman's Precinct,
Dutches County in the Province of New York
by the celebrated Rachel Wilson
(one of the People called Quakers)
to a numerous audience of different persuasions,
taken in short hand from the mouth of the speaker by one of the audience."

There is a discrepancy here since 10th August was a 5th day (i.e. Thursday). A week later, on 5th, 6th and 7th days she was in New York, Newark and Rahway – places all very close to each other. The 'auditor' may have written "Saturday, the 19th day of August, 1769" which was then misprinted as "10th" and the "Friends Meeting House" may have been the local Court House recorded by Rachel with the Presbyterians she refers to being what the pamphlet describes as "a numerous audience of different persuasions". Alternatively, the location may have been the enlarged Oblong Friends Meeting House, built in 1764, where Rachel was on 10th August. What is beyond dispute, however, is that there cannot have been more than one "celebrated Rachel Wilson" delivering a public sermon like this one at the same time as her visit.

By way of apology, the 'auditor' explains in his introductory 'advertisement to the reader':

"The publisher of the following Discourse, being only an accidental Auditor, when it was delivered, and entirely unknown to the Author, would not have taken the Liberty to publish it without her Consent, if he had either an Opportunity of asking it, or a Doubt, in case he had asked it, that it would have been refused. But being fully persuaded that the same Spirit of Piety and Benevolence, by which the Words were conceived and uttered for the Benefit of the Hearers, would have induced the Preacher, if she had been applied to, to consent to the Publication, and thereby make the Benefit more extensive, he

therefore concludes, she will not be displeased with, but rather approve of, the Publication of her Discourse.
... The Publisher may, by some, be thought blameable for this exposing of an extempore Discourse, delivered without Note, or any regard to grammatical Niceties of expression.
... The Language is indeed plain, and the Words, such as are in common Use, intelligible to the meanest Capacity ... The Sentiments in the following Discourse are just and important; the Language expresses those Sentiments with Clearness, Strength and Solemnity, and as they seem to flow with Sincerity and Warmth from the Heart, will be likely to reach the Hearer."

During her whole religious visit, Rachel, as on this occasion, sensed the frequent occasions when "many were reached" by her ministry.

Afterwards, she and her companions dined at an inn and then came to Rahway for Quarterly Meeting attended by many Friends from different places. The very hot weather and the "very troublesome" mosquitoes ("muskettoes" in Rachel's journal) made it a "close exercise". The Meeting for elders "was but low".

On 1st day, there were two public meetings, one at Rahway and the other at Woodbridge. They had a further meeting there next morning when Rachel was moved *to break forth upon the subject of true Love as a proper Badge of a Gospel Minister*. She related that *there were several there, who have treated Friends very ill in their Sermons, one who had said Quakerism was as dangerous to the Soul as poison to the Body*. The Meeting for Discipline followed and afterwards they were joined at dinner by the Mayor of Elizabeth Town who had waited for them and they "had a solacing season together".

She had been trying in vain to find a way of despatching her next letter home ever since starting it in Westchester:

***West Chester 8mo 17th 1769***

***My Dear Husband***

***Recd thine of ye 28 of ye 4 Month ... ye perusal whereof aforded Me much Comfort ... we have had hott wether since My Last from Falmouth and Boston. Ive mostly bin in a hott Bath Swetting so freely I belive haith bin of servis yt I find no Bad Efects from it ... I expect to Reach Newyork to Night ... I was interrupted yesterday from writing by frds who Came from Newyork to meet us – ye meeting of Westchester and Kingsbridge was much favored with ye overshadowing of Divine good that when I got hear ... and Reflected how we had got along ... Both by water and Land My Mind was Coverd with Sweetness and humble Gratitude. I can now inform thee Ive Recd thine of ye 23 of ye 6 month which conveys the agreable intelegence of your Continued welfare and Dolys safe Delivery – news indeed very acceptable.*** [Daughter Dorothy's baby, Hannah, born 22nd 5th month 1769]

Having crossed over to Rahway, New Jersey, she was resigned to her letter probably not being able to be despatched until Philadelphia. Like her journal, there is no mention in it of the public meeting at Beekman's Precinct.

On 3rd day, Select Meeting at Woodbridge was followed by a public meeting, after which they moved on to Plainfield for meeting, held mostly under trees so as to accommodate everyone who came.

On 4th day they continued on to Morristown for a meeting at 2 o'clock at the Court House only to find that the Baptists had arranged one there for 4 o'clock. Rachel's meeting was well attended and was still going on when the Baptists arrived but they "made no destruction" and the one or two priests "behaved well". They spent the night with Friends at Minden where they attended meeting the following morning before travelling on to Hardwick, some 25 miles away. They went to meeting on 6th day and then dined with Jacob Wilson before riding another 25 miles until a storm blew up, forcing them to go to an inn for the night. Next morning, 7th day, they were at meeting at Ridgewood, after having breakfasted with Friends on the way, *which was large and open tho' my mind was very low in our sitting down, but Truth arose and the fear of Man vanished, and a precious opportunity we had – the subject was 'It is shown unto thee, O Man,! What thou should do; do justly, Love, Mercy, and walk humbly with thy God'.*

They crossed the Delaware River into Pennsylvania, had a "religious opportunity" with a local Friend and, with darkness approaching, were obliged, once again, to lodge at an inn. They rose early, had breakfast with two Friends and were at both of the local meetings, composed mostly of Friends, being *favoured with the overshadowing of Divine Good to the strengthening and establishing in Righteousness.* They rode on to a Friend near Plumstead ready for meeting there next morning (2nd day), followed by a large meeting at Buckingham – *the best Meeting House in the County.* They lodged with a "valuable" Friend whose wife was paralysed after a stroke "yet sweet in spirit". They had meetings with Friends at Wrightstown and Marisfield on 3rd day and at the Falls on 4th day, including Quarterly Meeting and their Select Meeting *in which many profitable hints were drop't.*

A local Friend described this meeting and these "hints": [74]

"In a Quarterly meeting of ministers and elders held at the Falls in Bucks county, Pennsylvania, 8th month 30th, 1769, our dear Friend Rachel Wilson, had an open encouraging time. She first addressed ministers, using a familiar proverb, 'strike while the iron is hot,' which she applied to their observing the right time for standing up; reminding them also of the fruitless labour attending striking when the heat was gone out; and in particular, she exhorted those who were young in the ministry, that they might not let in the reasoned, and think, because such and such friends were at meeting, they had best smother or withhold their little exercises. She said she had often been helped by a few words, dropped in the simplicity, in the forepart of a meeting; and that it was often like opening a door to further service;

but some, she said, when they had something to offer, kept it to themselves; chewed it and chewed it, till they had got all the substance out, and perhaps just at the close of a meeting, when they found themselves uneasy with letting the right time slip, had stood up, and like spit it out, when it was of no use to any body else.

"She observed to the elders, that the snuffers, under the law, were to be made of the same beaten gold with the lamps; and enlarged on the use of the snuffers, – that oftentimes without them, the tallow, the life of the candle, would be in danger of wasting; – that they were of great service when skilfully used to take off all superfluous matter: and remarked when it was done with judgment, how much brighter the lamp or candle burned; but cautioned against too frequently using them; for she had seen the disadvantage attending it, especially as some people were seldom easy, unless they were snuffing."

They passed the night here "very agreeably" as well as having a large and satisfactory meeting the following day.

*The Meeting for Discipline was held after, in which I had to visit the Men, with a particular request not to give place to a rending dividing Spirit, which I feared was secretly Lurking and which, if given way to, was in danger of doing great harm. Truth favouring, I came away thankful and was easy to leave the Youth's Meeting to be at Bristol.*

Discovering from some Friends here that the vessel from Philadelphia had not yet gone, she wrote another short letter home:

> ***... I find it my plaice singly to Look to that which Makes for peace ... to get forward with what was before Me, Every Circumstance Contributing to Confirm Me that my stepings along was in the ordering of Divine wisdom ye Reflection whereof is Caus of thankfulness. The ingagement indeed haith bin Close Exercise Both to Body and Mind but he that haith Cald into the servis is abundantly Suficient to fitt and qualifie for Every Days work – tho My knees haith bin many times Nearly to Smite one against***

***another Under a sense of My own weakness when I see such flocking to Meetings with pepol of all Denominations ...***

*On sixth day morning had a religious opportunity in the family, which was very affecting as it opened on my mind, as if some unexpected trial was hanging over me which I expressed as carefully as I could to procure peace to my mind, as William Buckley's Wife was with Child I was fearful of its sinking too deep in her mind which I found after there was need of, as his former Wife had died of her first Child.*

Meeting after was large and they enjoyed meeting a Friend who was over from England. Next morning they left Bristol and visited a distressed family before going to a crowded meeting for worship at Middletown, many having to gather outside. It was a "precious occasion" with Rachel's cousin Grace Wilson and several of Grace's children also there, together with her brother Anthony. They ended the day at North Wales, some 20 miles distant. On 1st day they were joined at meeting by many from Philadelphia making it far larger than expected. They stayed with another local Friend that night before making for Plymouth on 2nd day where meeting was "but middling". 3rd day saw them at New Providence followed by covering a few more miles to a meeting in a school house in the place where they were to lodge. Next day they carried on to Exeter – another very large meeting – and to Reading where meeting was held in the Court House attended also by many local inhabitants even though this was principally a Dutch neighbourhood.

On 5th day they were at Maidencreek. They returned to Reading that night and next morning crossed the Schuykill River in heavy rain to reach Robeson Meeting – *Divine favour extended to the truly seeking souls, the afflicted were comforted and the lukewarm stirred up to more diligence.* A violent storm developed and many trees came down in the wind and rain. They rode 12 miles and took shelter for the night with a kind Friend, his wife and mother who all accompanied them next morning as far as Nantmeal on their way to their next stop which was Pikeland.

On 1$^{st}$ day they attended their hosts' meeting at Upland – *very large and attended by the overshadowing of Divine Love to the Baptising our hearts together.* On 2$^{nd}$ day they were at the Valley meeting; 3$^{rd}$ day at Radnor followed by Newtown; 4$^{th}$ day at Springfield and then Hartford; 5$^{th}$ day back again at Radnor. There was an old couple here whose combined ages totalled 155 years and who still rode their horses to meeting.

In company with a local Friend *We had to tell some present their actions had been such as called for repentance and deep humiliation before God who had not yet forsaken them but was favouring with a fresh visitation, but if not regarded, we were fearful it might be the last.*

Monthly Meeting followed and was very long in gathering and things were *but low amongst them in respect to Discipline.* Afterwards they met an *innocent, sweet spirited man* of 90 whose daughter and granddaughter were both poorly whom they visited, very much to the old man's comfort.

On 6th day, meeting was at Merion, Philadelphia – *very large and a conceived call was extended to arouse the careless and stir up the Lukewarm.*

They spent another 13 days either in or around Philadelphia:

Haddonfield; Evesham; Mount Holly; Sheremount; Upper Springfield; Old Springfield; Burlington; Rancocas; Morristown; Haddonfield; The Bank; Market Street and Philadelphia itself. 7$^{th}$ day (23$^{rd}$ of 9$^{th}$ month) was Yearly meeting and also the select meeting where Rachel met many friends from different parts, including Sarah Janney who Rachel was *truly glad to meet in that pure Love that nearly* [closely] *unites us.*

A local Friend recounted: [75]

"In the Yearly Meeting of ministers and elders held at Philadelphia, in the 9th month, 1769, at the opening of the meeting she rose and began with these words, 'If I have a right sense in this meeting, there is a withholding more than is meet, by which the work is retarded, individuals suffer, and the general body are sensible of the loss.'"

The same Friend also recalled:

"In the several meetings, she appeared divers times; and once, when she was about to express something relative to herself, she signified she was led from her own concern to speak about our friend John Woolman, who was under a concern to visit some of the islands. She addressed him with much sympathy, and ardently wished the good hand might be with him; and enable him to divide [divine?] the word aright, to the honour of the great name, the comfort of those among whom he had to labour, and his own lasting peace. And for his encouragement, she testified, that she steadily eyed her great Master from day to day, she had been in no lack of any thing; but he had been altogether sufficient."

The Friend recalled again Rachel's advice to those too fond of snuffing and continued:

"She also remarked, it was much easier to take away the light than to give it; and further said, she had been comforted with every communication in the several meetings, that had been in the line of the truth, and that none had ever been in her way that had been in the life, and that she was free to say, she had not opened her mouth by way of reflection on any.

"Towards the conclusion, she signified she had as much need as any other to live near the Truth; and requested the prayers of her friends for her preservation and help, for she expected to meet with trials and exercises if she should live. In the concluding women's meeting for business, she was led to speak very encouragingly respecting the attendance of religious meetings; and said she had not abundance of this world's wealth, yet sufficient and enough; and that her outward affairs had never suffered by attending meetings; and further she had this testimony for herself, that she never, since she knew the truth, neglected going to meeting, unless prevented by sickness in her family, or on account of the care of infants, which she allowed was sometimes a reasonable excuse."

Later that day
*A subscription was put forward for the assistance of some poor Friends which I took some pains to get accomplished; it succeeded so well that upwards of one hundred pounds was collected.*

John Woolman was also at this Yearly Meeting. As mentioned earlier, he and Rachel held each other in high regard. Rachel had been at Burlington, the location of Woolman's monthly meeting, in 10th month 1768, again in 5th month 1769 and was also at Mount Holly, Woolman's local meeting, in 9th month 1769 so could have met him on any of these occasions, but neither of their journals makes any reference to when they met.

In a letter to Rachel written in 1772 when he visited the Wilson home in Kendal, Woolman acknowledges God's love, in the improved social climate for Friends, which enabled them to preach the Gospel without hindrance and the responsibility thus laid upon them and rejoiced in the "opportunity" to meet the family and "feeling a sweetness in my mind towards thee". His letter concludes: "I feel that pure love toward thee, in which there is freedom. I look at that precious gift bestowed on thee, with Awfulness, before him who gave it, and feel a care that we may be so separated [set apart] to the gospel of Christ, that those who proceed [depart] from the Spirit of this world may have no place among us."

Not only was Woolman tireless in his work among his fellow Quakers to abolish slavery but also he adhered unswervingly to his simple living. He revered creation. For example, as already noted in earlier chapters, he insisted during his voyage to England (in 1772) on travelling in the steerage in the ship so as to fulfil his belief in the equality of all men and then refused to associate himself with the cruelties suffered by the horses and the post boys in operating the new stage coach services, choosing instead to travel on foot.

His simple lifestyle convinced him that he should wear only undyed clothing, partly because some dyes relied on slave labour for their production, partly because the run-off from the dyeing processes contaminated the soil and watercourses and partly because Friends should not get drawn into worldly vanity in the way that they chose to dress. He made a stand against worldly pretensions in other ways also. There are several examples of his requesting his hosts to replace the luxurious family silver place settings, brought out when entertaining him as one of their guests, with plain, everyday utensils. As previously mentioned, when on his travels, if his host owned slaves, he would insist on paying for their hospitality rather than freely receive something that might have been provided through slave labour.

In all these situations, his approach to his fellow Friends always was one of gentleness and tact, so that while he was direct and unambiguous in what he had to say, he did this without causing offence. Indeed, he gained respect from many wealthy Friends as a result. When in England, he called at Isaac's and Rachel's home (although she was away on another religious visit) and saw the Wilsons' shearman dyer business at first hand, with the dyed products spread out in the open to dry and the waste being washed out untreated. He wrote a tactful reproach even to Rachel.

"Beloved Friend,

When I followed the trade of a Taylor I had a Feeling of that which pleased the proud Mind in People, and growing uneasy was strengthened to leave off that which was superfluous in my Trade: the Pride of People being gratified in some part of the Business thou followest, and feel a Concern in pure Love to endeavour thus to inform thee of it. Christ our Leader is worthy of being followed in his Leadings at all Times, the Enemy gets many on his side; O that we may not be divided between the Two, but may be wholly on the Side of Christ!

In true Love to you all I remain thy Friend.
JW"

But this was four years into the future. Returning to 24th of 9th month 1769:

1st day they were at large meetings at Pine Street, the Bank and Market Street. They attended a succession of meetings on 2nd, 3rd and 4th days, including the elders and ministers meeting, when Rachel informed them that it looked as if her service on the Continent was nearly over and she hoped that they would feel free to give her a few lines to recognise it. Needless to say, her request was readily granted. Then came the public meeting for worship; the meeting for Discipline where all the Quarterly Meeting reports came in; receiving epistles from London, Rhode Island, Long Island, North Carolina, Virginia and Maryland and making responses to each of them.

From here, on 27th of 9th month Rachel wrote her last letter home, but, as is evident from Isaac's marginal note, it was destined not to arrive until "7 days after my Dear's return home", nearly three months later.

> ***I now Expect about 5 weeks will sett Me at Liberty. Ive a Litl to do in ye Jerseys and Down into Maryland to their [Y]Early Meeting at Choptank and Little Creek ... some time in ye 11 month I expect to imbark upon ye pensilvania packet ... May god of his infinit Mercy bless and preserve you in ye hol[l]ow of his hand, in the Earnest Breathing of My Dear Childer in My [ ] and thy truly affectionat and simpathizing wife.***
> ***Rachel Wilson***

Rachel went on board the *Pennsylvania Pacquet* to 'feel out' how things were there. *Ann Moore and Sarah Janney and some other with me where my mind was sweetly covered with a sense of Divine Goodness which I could not but express with thankfulness. Ann had also to tell us she found nothing but peace which was very satisfactory and Sarah Janney appeared in supplication which seemed to me a renewed evidence of its being my place to return in her.*

On 5th day, Rachel's 'certificate' (the endorsement of the satisfactory accomplishment of her religious visit to America) was signed at a "precious meeting".

One can visualise this meeting in Philadelphia's main meeting house, overflowing with Friends who have travelled to bid her farewell. Rachel is there in their midst filled with the strong sense of her ever present "inner guide", of the "merciful goodness, graciously favoured in opening the way of Life and Salvation" and of "the humbling and baptizing our Spirits together" which form the constant experience that radiates from her through her journal.

One can imagine her looking into the faces of many, many Friends whom she met during her travels and recalling all the others who lived too far away to get to Philadelphia. In her journal, she gives the names of more than 600 of these people: nearly all of them were Friends but a few of them were prominent public figures from outside.

Over 100 of these, plus Rachel herself, made their way into the pages of American Quaker history. One cannot neatly categorise them into different spheres of activity or influence because several overlap, such as Quaker merchants who were also ministers or key political figures. A rough analysis shows around 30 Quaker ministers, 50 Quakers prominent in other activities, some purely as wealthy merchants but many more as holders of important Quaker positions or active in social issues (notably anti-slavery) and nearly 20 who were, or had been, governors, assemblymen, councillors or legislators.

In addition, no fewer than 15 Monthly, Quarterly or Yearly Meetings produced certificates of appreciation of Rachel, bearing signatures ranging in number from 60 to 120, and she received numerous very affectionate, personal letters from those who had accompanied her on various stages of her journey or who had been her overnight hosts and hostesses.[76]

*I had to give my testimony to the harmony in which we had travelled together, all those whose Company I had been favoured with that I never had Cause to be uneasy or think they were in my way, neither had I opened my Mouth slightly on anyone which was then cause of thankfulness to my Mind.*

Although Rachel did not live long enough to witness the future conduct and outcome of the Revolutionary War as news of it reached England, Isaac would have heard it all. He would have known the names of the American Friends who featured in his beloved wife's journal and have felt shock and grief at those who suffered extensively for Truth and, especially, for pacifism at the hands of the revolutionaries. Samuel Fisher (see p.47) and all three Pemberton brothers suffered while two aged and infirm Friends, John Hunt and Thomas Gilpin, died in exile in Virginia. John Hunt had started as an English Quaker minister, like Rachel, and died as a result of an unsuccessful amputation of a leg that became infected whilst in exile. A third, Israel Pemberton, became much weakened and died shortly after return from exile. John Roberts (together with another Friend) was executed for treason. Many of Rachel's Friends, especially the wealthier ones, suffered disproportionate distraints upon their property for resisting the payment of war taxes and for refusing formally to swear or affirm allegiance to the new political regime.

Rachel was there before all of this, at the end of what may be described as the golden age of Quakerism in America.

## Chapter 12

## EGG HARBOURS, THIRD HAVEN AND FAREWELL

Notwithstanding the recognition of her momentous journey as embodied in her 'certificate', Rachel still continued for another six weeks, visiting the Jerseys and Maryland (as mentioned in her last letter) before she finally set sail for England.

Early on 6th day, the 29th of 9th month, she and her companions headed for Barnegat some 35 miles distant, stopping off at Friends at Little Egg Harbour on the way. Next morning, they attended meeting there, followed by Egg Harbour in the afternoon – *both favoured with Good.* The mosquitoes were very troublesome that night. On 1st day they rose early and crossed the river, their host taking them round the head of the Marsh in his boat while their horses were *got over the Marsh with some difficulty.* They reached Upper Great Egg Harbour where there was a small meeting house, unable to contain all the people who came. There was another large meeting after this at Great Egg Harbour. On 2nd day, they crossed Great Egg Harbour River to reach Monthly Meeting at Cape May.

*Many came over the River that the House did not hold them, and I thought it close heavy work; in that Meeting there seemed something that hindered the pure running of Shiloh's Streams. I had some thoughts of another meeting that evening, at the other meeting house, about 8 miles; a way had been made for it, but the Monthly Meeting held so long I drop't it.*

A Friend then took them in his wagon to Greenwich *as what we had rode on could not be got over the River.* They parted with the kind Friends who had accompanied them thus far and lodged with another Friend that night. They rose early next morning and rode 40 miles through the woods to New England Town where a meeting had been appointed amongst the Presbyterians. Both priest and people attended and Rachel opened to them "the way of life and satisfaction in the power and demonstration of the Spirit", with which many seemed "affected".

On 4th day they visited their host's sister, a widow, and her children. *He that hath graciously promised to be a helper to the Widow, and a Father to the Fatherless was there, and his Love was tasted that is better than Wine.*

They crossed the Cohansey River to a large meeting at Greenwich. Next day (5th) they went to meeting at Alloways Creek. A Friend and his wife from Philadelphia were with them who, they learned, had buried three children in just a few weeks. On 6th day they were at Salem for another large and "much favoured" meeting ending in prayer and praise. They crossed the Delaware River at Pinestock Ferry to reach Newcastle, Delaware where they were re-united with their horses.

On 7th day they rode the 26 miles to Nottingham where *the dinner being long in getting ready, we read several passages in my Journal.* Next they visited "worthy Friend", John Churchman, and his wife who was confined to her bedroom, yet "very sensible"; and they had "a sweet refreshing season together". In the morning they went to meeting at East Nottingham which again was large and somewhat slow to gather, being "too much outward", but things revived and they had a "heavenly Meeting". They rode five miles to meeting at West Nottingham in the afternoon where only half of those attending could get into the meeting house yet the people were very still and *a precious opportunity it was; the little provision being blessed, the whole multitude was satisfied and we came away thankful praising the great Giver who thus plentifully favoured his poor dependant children with Bread in due Season.*

On 2nd day they moved on to Little Britain for another large meeting attended by many neighbours and feeling the same strong presence of God in their midst. They crossed the Susquehanna River, more than a mile wide, on horseback to reach their host for the night. On 3rd day they were at Deer Creek where they found a seeking people; on 4th day at Bush River they had to transfer from the undersized meeting house to the house of a local Friend *the people flocking so to meeting.* They reached the Falls on 5th day for another large meeting to which several Friends from Deer Creek also came. Rachel, understandably, was "a little spent".

*In the morning,* [6th day] *I was not easy to leave the family till all the Negroes were called in, to whom favour was extended, and I came away easy to Gunpowder, 12 miles.* Here again, the meeting house overflowed. In the evening, they had a "solemn season" at table with their hosts, *the family and Negroes being called in, we had to press to more diligence as there seemed too much remissness in coming up in their duty to God and the way of Truth departed from in Dress and address, which were closely spoke to.*

On 7th day, meeting was at the small meeting house at Palapsee, five miles away, where many people had to stand outside, "yet a deep stillness enfolded them". Rachel felt moved in her heart to have a meeting at nearby Baltimore Town and made this known to the meeting, whereupon a lawyer who was present said that he had applied for the Presbyterian meeting house and that this had been freely granted. The inhabitants came and "behaved well", giving Rachel ample opportunity to open the way of Quakerism to them, to preach Christ's word of God and the universality of his love to the children of men.

*In the evening, one Man came and asked a few questions about the Universality of God's Grain which I answered, but I never met with any so strong before for Election and Reprobation, tho' he reasoned cool, and when he bid me farewell, seemed very Loving & wished me a prosperous Journey.*

On 1st day, they reached Elkridge (12 miles) in good time for meeting; on 2nd Sandy Spring; on 3rd Indian Spring; on 4th Patuxent for their meeting followed by West River. On 5th day their plan had been to cross Herring Creek but Rachel felt called to remain and a meeting was arranged at very short notice, "yet large for the place". Sarah Janney, who had, once again, been accompanying Rachel, now had to return home. On 6th day the weather was much too foggy to cross the bay in a local Friend's (Philip Chew's) sloop so they made an early start at 4.00 am on 7th day to attempt the crossing. However, the slight wind died away so Joseph Pemberton's horses were instead put on the ferry rowing boat which took them over to Kent Island and then returned to the rest of the party – Rachel, John Morris and Robert Pleasants. The three of them and their horses transferred from Philip Chew's boat to the ferry and were rowed to land, arriving about half past three. It was a blessing, Rachel noted, that the weather was calm enough to enable all of this. They landed at one John Camp's place called the Bay Side and rode on 18 miles to Joseph Bartlett's for the night. The others whom they had left behind (Philip Thomas and his wife, Joseph Pemberton and several others), were rowed to Chew Island, that evening.

Unfortunately, they missed the first part of Yearly Meeting at Third Haven which had started earlier that day. They arrived after the Select Meeting had finished on 1st day and then moved into the large, public meeting for worship. *Sarah Morris first appeared; then it fell to my Lot to set forth the great advantage that attended true and saving Faith, and how necessary for everyone to be acquainted with the Great Master's presence; attending to the strengthening and establishing of them in Righteousness. It ended in prayer and Praises.*

*On second day [there was] a Meeting for Worship at 11 to which the Parson and most of his hearers came, and many went away that could not get in.* The Parson appeared again at a meeting on 3rd day, the numbers so great that, once again, many could not get in, yet the meeting was *well favoured with the overshadowing of Good.* During these two days there were various meetings, including for elders and for discipline. The main subject one day was silence and the other day was *the expression: 'if ye live after the flesh, Ye shall die, but if by the Spirit you mortify the deeds of the Body, then shall ye live'*. They departed and crossed the Choptank River to spend the night at Friends close by.

They rode 28 miles on 4th day in time for a meeting in a Friend's house where they met some Nicholites who seemed well satisfied with what they heard. On 5th day they rode to Lewistown, 21 miles away, and on 6th day continued to Mothers Hill, 37 miles. Here they attended a meeting that overflowed the capacity of the house and met some more Nicholites. Rachel was a little tired, but a good night's sleep revived her. Before departing on 7th day, one of the Nicholites arrived and wanted a conversation with her, but did not want to delay them.

*I found freedom to sit down with him, several Friends being present; he seemed in a good frame of mind, not wanting to cavil but really desirous of information; pointing out the difference betwixt us and them, telling us they have been led to the Spirit, that taught them to forsake sin and every evil way, and to wear their cloth[e]s plain and coarse, & to answer the real use, to keep them warm and cover their nakedness, and not to indulge pride and vanity; for which they were become a despised People, yet upon the ancient foundation upon which Quakerism was first established. We heard him patiently and answered his Questions with regard to Discipline, which had been one of their chief objections in regard to joining Friends; but now, he owned they saw more the necessity for some necessary Rules as they had run into great extravagancies which he says was a Delusion. We parted friendly and came to Dover, 5 Miles.*

The Nicholites, started by the powerful preacher Joseph Nichols, eventually became a localised sect based mainly on the eastern shore of Maryland, their tenets being much as described here to Rachel. It is possible that they had also been inspired by John Woolman's insistence on wearing plain, undyed clothing but, going further than Woolman, they adopted a uniformity of materials in their dress code.

Like the Quakers, they made slave-owning a disownable offence (in 1780).[77]

After breakfast here, they went to Little Creek for their Yearly Meeting, returning to Dover that night. In the morning (1st day) it was the Select Meeting followed by a large public meeting for worship. They journeyed on to Duck Creek on 2nd day. Next day they rode the 30 miles to Newcastle and spent time with a couple who had long been poorly. They crossed the Delaware River and continued another 10 miles to their lodging for the night. On 4th day, 1st of 11th month, at meeting at Pilesgrove, they met up again with Rachel's companion, Sarah Hopkins, where they were delighted to see each other. They went to meeting at Upper Greenwich on 5th day and at Woodbury on 6th day.

*The time of my going on board drawing near, on 7th day in the morning put up my cloth[e]s, and went to the Select Meeting at 11, in which we were highly favoured with the sweet income of Divine Love as a fresh confirmation that the Steps I had taken were in Divine Wisdom.*

There was a very sad occasion that afternoon when they attended the burial of William Brown's grandchild. They visited one or two Friends, including Widow Wilson's family and a young Friend looking forward to marriage.

On 1st day they crossed the Delaware to Newtown for a meeting that was held once a month and which was large. In the company of many other Friends, they visited a sick Friend at the ferry house before re-crossing the river for an evening meeting and continued to visit Friends on 2nd day. Before leaving the dinner table, a Friend came in wanting a little conversation with Rachel. He explained that he had doubts about the vessel as fear had attended his mind about her.

*I said would not thou have me go in her? telling him what was my reasons for going in Her, that no other had ever appeared to be my place. He said as to Captain Faulkner there is no man that I had rather go with, and if he behaved as he had done, he will always be full of Passengers. This conversation affected my mind, tho' I had no Count to doubt from my own feelings but the conclusion was right, yet this sunk my Spirit so that* [seven named Friends] *and several others came on Board, where Divine Mercy was evidently manifested for our help, and the Relief of my sorely distressed and tossed mind – as the enemy is never awanting to lay hold on every opportunity to distract and disrupt the still running of Shiloh's Streams; but thanks be to God, his power is limitless. I was unexpectedly relieved and my Spirit set at Liberty.*

On 3rd day, the Youths Meeting was already fully gathered when Rachel arrived. She found it gratifying how that, over the course of her religious visit, young Friends had displayed an uncommon eagerness to come to her meetings. She dined with a local Friend and then attended the 'Negroes Meeting' in the afternoon which proved to be the largest for many years. Several 'appeared'.

Active right up to the end, she attended meetings at Frankford and Fairhill on 4th day, the latter being so crowded that she joined those outside the meeting house. Mary Pemberton took Rachel by chariot to Abel James, who was in a poor state of health and had decided to accompany Rachel back to England, leaving behind his wife and several children. *It was a little moving and the farewell truly solemn.* Great numbers came to Rachel's lodgings that evening to wish her well.

On 5th day, she was due on board at Chester. She had a truly "solemn meeting" at Providence, many more Friends coming to say good bye to the remarkable Quaker minister who had been in their country for the last thirteen months. They wanted to arrange a final public meeting, but Rachel sensed she should decline:

*I found my mind dipped into supplication in which our prayers were unitedly put up for preservation, both by Sea and Land, and that the many favours and mercies might be remembered and the gracious End answered to the Salvation of our Souls.*
*After this solemn Farewell, we came on Board the Pennsylvania Pacquet, Captain Faulkner and some hundreds accompanying us to the Water Side.*

Several Friends came on board, including some who had been particularly supportive to Rachel during her visit *and we had a sweet taste of Divine Love together before we parted.*

When Jane Crosfield parted at the end of her religious visit in 1761, Friends had sent her on her way with the customary complete outfit, one might say, for her voyage, including a "Pewter chamber pott". Friends made parting gifts to Rachel of an even more impressive supply of provisions: a sheep; 2 pigs; 3 dozen ducks/chickens; tripe; tongues; ham; butter; cheese; eggs; vegetables; pickles; spices; rice; barley; fresh and preserved fruits; jams; currants; raisins; cranberries; tea; coffee; chocolate; sugars; candy; liquorice; a gallon each of best brandy, rum and British brandy; dozens of bottles of wine, cider and ale and even "tobacco, pipes etc"! However, as noted on the outward voyage, passengers had to supply their own provisions, it was the normal custom and practice for the captain and ship's officers to share in them and, moreover, this was a Quaker family business. Rachel's main luggage comprised her saddle, two trunks with clothes and a long box of curiosities.[78]

As already mentioned, there were many tributes to Rachel as the time came for her to leave America. There was one from a poet who wrote "... that like a Woolman or a Wilson shines ..." and there was another poem, written by John Drinker, a Friend in Philadelphia Yearly Meeting who was one of those who "became conspicuous for their piety and service to the Society".[79]

He introduced his poem "A minister of the Gospel among the people called Quakers. After having visited most, if not all, the widely extended colonies in North America, in the space of about one year, with such persevering constancy and unwearied industry as is scarcely credible for a woman, she embarked on her return to her husband and family, residing at Kendal in England, in the beginning of the 11th month 1769."

A FAREWELL TO RACHEL WILSON

Happy the humble soul that lives to God,
Refin'd from sensual dross, pursues the way,
The only blessed way, – true pleasure's road –
Leading thro' time's thick night, to endless day.

In humble hope, let honest hearts unite,
That the great harvest's Lord may yet endow
More faithful lab'rers, with immortal might,
And willing minds the Master's work to do.

Rachel, the field is wide, the harvest great,
Noble the purpose of thy embassy:
Stupid the mind that does not feel the weight
Of potent love which operates in thee.

Wean'd from the love of life and earthly things,
Obedient to the soul-redeeming power,
Borne o'er the deep on evangelic wings,
A welcome envoy to this western shore.

The straying mind descends from barren heights,
Soft melody vibrating in the ear,
And in the lowly verdant vale delights
The gospel music of thy voice to hear.

Thus the good Shepherd tunes his rural reed,
The stragglers of his flock are gather'd near;
Charm'd with his voice they in his presence feed,
Safe from the beast of prey, and void of fear.

*Rachel Wilson*

Cloth'd with the love that makes the lily white,
Thy fervent labours, Wilson, have been bless'd,
Or this FAREWELL had never seen the light,
Nor thus a fellow worm had thee addressed.

And is thy task fulfilled? Must thou depart?
Go, then; – and may angelic peace be thine:
Absence cannot erase thee from my heart,
For time to come, if time to come be mine.

Divinely fitted for a sacred use,
As such, 'tis sure no flattery to commend,
A vessel honor'd in thy master's house'
As such I but salute thee, as a friend.

Favor'd of God, Farewell! And to thy shore,
(Bless'd with celestial calm, tho' billows foam),
May gales propitious waft thee safely o'er,
Endeared Rachel, to thy native home.

## Chapter 13

## RETURN HOME
## AND TESTIMONY TO A REMARKABLE LIFE

Evening of 5th day, 9th of 11th month 1769: it was foggy so they did not get far. Rachel slept well that night *with great sweetness upon my mind.*

Next morning the wind and tide were both favourable. They quickly passed places that Rachel had come to know – Wilmington and Newcastle – before anchoring at Reedy Island, the captain being fearful of venturing in the night. At 4.00 am (6th day), they set sail, it was pleasant and Rachel wrote some letters. 7th day the water was smooth. *I kept well in my health, and under sweet composure of mind, for which favour my Spirit is deeply bowed in humble gratitude, whilst penning this.*

The pilot boat left them and they sailed out of Delaware Bay in fair weather. It became squally in the night, giving a good deal of motion to the vessel and several of the little Quaker group were seasick, but, being 1st day, they still held a meeting for worship and welcomed all those on board who were able to join them. Her companions for this voyage were Abel James, Isaac Stroud, John Montgomery and Nancy [Montgomery]. The strong winds carried them along at 7 – 8 knots, increasing even more during the night of 3rd day, so much so that *The sea broke over the Vessel fast, which was affecting, washing several Hen Coops loose and throwing things into a little confusion both above and below. About 2 o'clock it abated and remained North and North West 4th and 5th day though we sailed fast.*

Rachel was feeling better by 1st day and they held another meeting for worship. Now the wind changed to an unfavourable quarter and it was three days before it swung round to the south. By 5th day it was blowing a gale from the southwest and they flew along at 10 – 11 knots for three days *but O, how was I sunk at times with fears and doubts yet I had nothing to look back at with pain; when the most distressed I had not to believe I had left America before the Work was done for which I was sent. This gave me a little sleep, being well satisfied that He that had been with me was able to support to the end* and they had a "comfortable opportunity" in her cabin.

The wind abated on 2nd day and it was almost calm on 3rd day. An easterly wind on 4th, 5th and 6th days meant that they made little progress until 7th day when it veered round to the west and the weather was clear and pleasant. *Yet my mind was covered with many needless doubts and fears; I know not that ever I experienced more weight of Darkness, all which I kept to myself. That evening we sat in Silence a while, but was quite closed up. Afterwards I desired John Montgomery to read a Chapter in the Bible, he choosing the Place, it proved to be the Epistle of Paul to the Hebrews.*

Next morning was meeting for worship as usual and Rachel was soon restored – *light afresh sprung up and the darkness vanished.* On 2nd day, they spoke to a passing brig bound from Cork to Jamaica, enabling the captain to confirm that his bearings were correct to within one degree, namely that Scilly bore "E.N.E. 70 Leagues". He checked his bearings with other passing brigs the next two days – the first going from "Santa Crock" [probably a Santa Cruz – one of many in the world – rather than Santa Croce, Italy] to Dunkirk (*70 days out who informed us they had spoke with a Vessel 6 days before and had been relieved with Provisions*) and the second from London to the Coast of Africa, who confirmed that, east-north-east, The Lizard was 62 leagues away. It sounds as if this first vessel had been at sea much longer than planned and had been running perilously short of provisions, highlighting, once again, one of the many hazards attending global seafaring, powered only by the wind.

5th day there was nothing of note. 6th day, a little after 7 in the morning, they sighted the Island of Jersey very clearly about 2 leagues distant, followed soon after by Guernsey and *to our surprise we found we were between these Islands, upon which the Vessel was tacked about and it being a clear morning after the Sun was up, and the Wind blowing fresh at South, we weathered the Island of Guernsey without any difficulty, and got safe from among the Islands and into the Channel again. On seventh day we got a sight of Dover, the wind hushed and we were near the Rocks, which gave great anxiety for a few hours. During this trial, my mind was engaged in supplication, by which my fears were dispersed. The Wind sprung up in our favour in a short time and we reached the Downs about 2 o'clock on first day morning and landed at Deal about 4 to our Joy and thankfulness.*

They got some refreshment and then, *with Abel James, Isaac Stroud, John Montgomery and Nancy* set off overland towards London, leaving the ship to follow her course via the Thames estuary. They took the post chaise 16 miles to Canterbury for meeting before travelling another 30 miles, or so, to an inn for the night.

On 2nd day, 11th of 12th month 1769 they reached London *where Friends seemed glad to see me, and we had thankfully to partake of his Love and Life giving Presence together in the Morning at Meeting.* Rachel delivered her 'certificate' and many others given her from America, these being read to the meeting. In the afternoon she attended two weeks Meeting where she saw many of her Quaker friends.

Her ship reached London that night; on 3rd day she collected her belongings. She was thankful that *all circumstances contributed to expedite my return to my Dear Husband and Children.* She left London the same evening, accompanied by four London Friends, and lodged at the coaching inn at "Alban" – not "St. Albans" since Quakers do not acknowledge sainthoods.

Early next morning, as her London Friends returned home, *the Coach called on us and we reached Kendal in safety on 15th* [of 12th month 1769] *my Dear Husband meeting me at Lancaster ... that great was the thankfulness that filled both our minds under a sense of the many preservations both by Sea and Land. I found my Dear Children favoured with Health. My Husband had not had one day's sickness during my absence nor I whilst on the Continent of America.*

In a letter to her friend Eliza Fisher, Rachel described her homecoming: "... We got safe to Lancaster about 2 on [7th] day following, where my dear husband met us, in perfect health – only the joy upon the occasion had like to have been too much for him, which he soon recovered & we got safe to our own habitation about 7, where I found all my children & family well". She sent her dear love to all of the Fisher family, the Moretons, Pembertons, Morris's, Benezets "& any others that may inquire".

She lived another five years, dying when she was only 55.

It is clear from her letters that her great love was to be with her family and that she wove this into her devoted life of service to God. When she left England, she had nine children but returned home to just eight, her invalid son, Anthony aged 18, having died while she was on her outward voyage. A new granddaughter, Deborah's daughter Rachel, had been born just two weeks after she left home and was now seventeen months old. Dorothy's son Isaac was that much older as well – now four – and she saw her newest grandchild, Dorothy's Hannah, now seven months old, for the first time. Only the month before Rachel left, Dorothy had given birth to twins who both died that same month, hence Rachel's anxiety, while in America, over how Dorothy's next pregnancy was proceeding. In later years, John was born in 1773 (but survived only until 1775) followed by a baby girl (another Rachel), born in July 1774, but, tragically, Dorothy herself died that same month, aged just 32, leaving four children aged 8, 4, 10 months and the new-born baby.

Rachel endured a long and potentially serious illness in 1774; a pain in her right side, according to letters that she wrote, had become so severe as to keep her from riding. Was it a recurrence of her "old complaint" – the pain in her breast mentioned in her journal before leaving England? Remarkably, she was in excellent health for the whole of her time in America and one wonders whether the English climate or even pollution from the family business's dyeing process adjacent to the home in Kendal may have contributed to her condition. However, she was well enough to undertake another religious visit, this time to London, in 1st month of 1775. A 19th century publication describes this visit and Rachel's final illness: [80]

"She was a loving wife, an affectionate parent, a kind & helpful neighbour, tenderly sympathising with the afflicted, and frequent in visiting the sick, in which visits she was very serviceable; often administering comfort to the drooping, distressed mind.

"In the course of her religious duty she came to London about the first month 1775 ... She entered into her service with great humility, visited most of the Friends' Meetings in the city, and finding her mind concerned for the inhabitants of Gravesend, (having had two meetings with them when she embarked for America,) she went again to visit them. She was gladly received, and held two meetings in the Town Hall, where through divine favour, she was helped through her service to her own peace, and the comfort of many present. She afterwards attended several weekday meetings, in the last of which, at Devonshire House, she was clothed with divine love, in an encouraging testimony to the honest hearted.

"The next day, being 4th of Second mo. she was taken ill & was confined wholly to her chamber, and mostly to her bed for six weeks; during which time she was favoured with quietness of mind; expressed her resignation either to live or to die; and requested her husband, who attended upon her a great part of the time, that he would tell their children, that it was her great desire that they, above every consideration, mind the one thing needful, which having been her care, was her unspeakable consolation."

The last words she was heard to say were, 'Good Tidings.'

Isaac's letter of 18.3.1775 to their children reads:

"The two last letters I wrote would make you apprehensive of and look for the account I have now to transmit viz. the affecting intelligence of your dear mother being removed from us about one o'clock this morning. For about twenty-four hours of the time, after I wrote last, she was very light-headed, almost without intermission. This was a distressing dispensation to me & tended to fill my mind with thankfulness when I perceived her drawing away & becoming still, which happened about three hours before she drew her last, which she did very quietly." [81]

This was at the home of her close friend, Richard Chester. After a special meeting for worship at Devonshire House, she was buried in London at Bunhill Fields, the site of some 12,000 Quaker burials (many of them victims of the great plague), including Edward Burrough, Richard Hubberthorne, George Whitehead, Stephen Crisp and George Fox.

Isaac, 5 years Rachel's senior, survived her by 10 years, dying when he was 70.

Rachel, like others before her, travelled the full length of the American colonies wherever there were Quakers. She and her companions struggled through the deep snows of winter, swam their horses over dangerously flooded rivers, were given lifts in Friends' 'chariots' and endured the oppressive heat, humidity, storms and mosquitoes of summer.

She went to the remotest outposts of Quakerism, often passing through no sizeable place for days or even weeks on end (and getting seriously lost at least once); she had hectic schedules when she was at overflowing meetings, many with public engagements, day after day with often up to three meetings in a day, she visited the sick, attended weddings and funerals, met prisoners under death sentences, resolved internal conflicts in meetings and in individual families, came face to face with Quaker slave ownership and in all of this made time to write her journal and letters.

She was at every kind of meeting – yearly, quarterly, monthly, preparative, for discipline, select, ministers and elders, 'negroes', youths, women's, as well as at the main public meetings for worship, at public engagements and at informal meetings in the homes of Friends, one or more meetings arising on nearly every day of every week. Throughout it all, she received immeasurably kind hospitality from the Friends with whom she lodged where she had many "comfortable seasons" and "melting seasons" together and found herself "engaged in supplication at the Table".

In the pages of her three tiny notebooks, Rachel more than amply wrote her own testimony to the grace of God in her extraordinarily full life, led wholly in the Light. Her preaching, her superhuman energy, her deep Quaker witness, her complete dedication to God's calling and her abundant warmth and love inspired all who met her. Through her, Quakers individually and in their meetings, local inhabitants at the places she visited, large audiences at public meetings, prisoners, the sick and needy, people in high office and people at chance encounters – all were "reached".

# EPILOGUE

Where does the testimony of Rachel, of John Woolman and of other early Friends lead us? What was Quakerism then? What is Quakerism today? I have this picture in my mind:

There is a navigable channel. It has a strong undertow and it has a maze of surface cross currents. Boats on the surface – thousands of them – are being taken in all directions by these currents. A few boats are being held to the direction of the undertow. The channel is Quakerism. The undertow is God through the teachings and example of Jesus. The cross currents are the forces diverting Quakers – the 'boats' – from their true course.

That there are these cross currents, this maze of diversity, across the whole of the Religious Society of Friends (Quakers) in Britain is manifested in the pages of 'the Friend'. How strong the undertow is in Britain, I do not know. To me it often feels more like the Gulf Stream and the threat that global warming poses to the future of that vital organ of life on earth: it may just dissipate altogether.

If we cease to accept God and Christ as the heart of Quakerism then we become simply a 'society of friends' – excellent and whole but not 'religious' and not 'Quaker'. There's nothing religious left and nothing left to quake about.

In a letter to 'the Friend' in 2009, a Friend wrote:

"In the end, diversity will kill off Quakers as a religious society. We have neglected our roots, which are being strangled by the growth of the other plants that we have allowed in. Roots neglected die and the signs are all there."

Quakers no longer have to be 'convinced' in order to gain membership, as witness 'members' who are openly atheist, agnostic, pagan, dual faith, Muslim – the list extends to well over a dozen and is increasing. In part it arises from a claim that one should be open to new light from whatever source it may come. But the context of this 'advice' (or Quaker 'discipline') is that "Light refers not just to new ideas but to the different aspects of 'The one true Light that lights everyone who comes into the world'" [82]

American Quakerism went through a process of reformation spanning the time that Rachel was there. It was driven by a thorough application of the Quaker 'discipline' that had grown from the seed – the radical, direct experience of God that was discovered by the first Quakers. It achieved a solidarity and identity of witness; it was true to the essence of Quakerism.

In the two centuries that followed, American Quakerism, through evolution and schisms, developed into four main strands. In England, after the very roughly definable periods of being 'quietist' during the 18$^{th}$ century, evangelical during the 19$^{th}$ and of liberal theology during the 20$^{th}$, the Society of Friends is still ostensibly a single body (with one or two very minor splinter groups), but invaded with 'diversity'.

In Rachel's time, slavery was a burning issue for Quakers, especially in America. For me, the burning issue for our Society today is the essence of Quakerism itself. Rachel was constantly alert to identifying those who 'professed' with Friends (and those who did not). Professing with Friends meant accepting and experiencing Quakerism in its purest sense – what the first Friends sought and then found as truth. These days, many seem not to 'profess' with Friends.

At the heart of Quakerism is the meeting for worship. For the first generation of Friends, it has been described in this vignette, drawn from their journals:

"However plain and marked with toil these Friends might be, and however imminent the danger of persecution might be, in 'the meeting' on First day morning they felt themselves in heavenly places. They were moved and animated, quickened and possessed with a common faith that God was with them in their meeting, and that they were admitted behind the veil into the holy of holies. The silence was intense, for it was living and dynamic, and they believed that there in the hush, in their humble group, the Great God of the Universe was preparing a mouthpiece for His word, and that when the seal of silence was broken and utterance should come, it would be the prophetic word of the Lord. There were tears of joy and rapture on many faces as they sat in stillness, and a tremulous movement often swept over the company, making the name of 'Quaker' not altogether inappropriate. The meeting ... was the time when many individuals were merged and baptized into a living group, with a common consciousness of a divine Presence, and the utterances which were given were expected to be 'in the common life,' and it was an occasion of profound feeling, of lofty joy, and of real refreshing." [83]

The travelling Quaker ministers, like Rachel, were "divinely sent messengers".

Things, of course, always need to move on and the way for that is encapsulated by W.C. Braithwaite (my grandfather) when he wrote:

"The past is pregnant with lessons for the present, not indeed by prescribing ready-made solutions for our modern problems, but by showing the spirit of dedication and adventure in which these problems must be faced. We lose its inspiration when we think of it as some far-off age untroubled by the spiritual doubts and difficulties that beset us; closer examination shows that it was crowded with its own perplexities and fateful issues, through which those could walk most worthily who fronted the dawn in glad surrender to its light." [84]

Quakers need a vision for the 21st century; they need enlightenment; they need the service of powerful ministry from people of Rachel's calibre. Britain Yearly Meeting in 2006 charged Meeting for Sufferings with taking on "a visionary and prophetic role for the life of the Yearly Meeting, to draw our whole community together, to work for a better world" and "to become a crucible for sharing and testing all the work".[85]

In taking on their new responsibilities, Meeting for Sufferings declared: "We understand that a crucible is a melting pot. Reactions take place, and something different emerges. Being a crucible means that Meeting for Sufferings should become a vehicle for transformation, of ourselves and of the Society as a whole. There should be room for exciting change. Meeting for Sufferings should offer spiritual leadings. We should seek the leadings of God, and ask how God is working among us."

Again, my grandfather wrote: "In identifying religion on the one hand with personal communion with God and on the other with a life of practical righteousness, Friends were closely associating themselves with the spirit of primitive Christianity and with the type of religion that we call prophetic and 'charismatic', by contrast with the priestly and institutional type. ... Quakerism has always been distinctly 'prophetic' in character." [86] To quote a present-day Friend: "British Quakerism has diluted its Christian heritage to the point where, often nowadays, to become a member of the Society, one has simply to say 'I feel at home'. But a balanced spirituality, within any healthy faith, depends on three sources: scriptural revelation, church tradition /church community, and – of prime importance for Friends – personal experience of the Divine presence."

The leadings of God have been wonderfully manifested in Quakers' lives and sufferings of the past and in their determined pursuit of social justice and pacifism where their influence has been disproportionately great.

Friends today tend to avoid the language of most Christian churches when talking about Christ – the 'Christ who lived and died for us all'. But it was Quakers' direct experience of God and their realisation that 'Christ is come to teach his people himself' that led many hundreds of them to suffer persecution, to devote their lives to 'gospel ministry', to being world leaders in removing social evils and to die for Quakerism. It is that past which is our lesson for the present.

# APPENDIX *(See pp131-3)*

## Text of "Discourse" delivered in New York, 1769

On the Duties and Importance of Religion, the unspeakable Advantages arising from it, and the great Danger of Evil.
Addressed to
Children and Servants, People in General, and Preachers of the Gospel.

ISAIAH, XL, Chap. 6 and 8 Verses.

*The voice said cry: And he said what shall I cry? All Flesh is Grass, and all the Goodliness thereof as the Flower of the Field. The Grass withereth, the Flower fadeth: But the Word of our God shall stand for ever.*

The soul that has its thoughts fix'd upon God, - firmly relying upon god for help, upon its Maker for protection and countenance, thro' all the changes of this mortal life, is certainly happy beyond any finite comprehension. The divine image, when grafted in the soul, utterly excludes all vain and ostentatious thoughts of our own sufficiency; a confidence in which would be inconsistent with the character of a christian, as well as repugnant to the express command of God, given to the prophet, *to debase the creature, and exalt the Creator.*

My mind has been not a little affected, while sitting in this meeting, - How unfit the very best of us are, to render our Maker meet and acceptable service, appears from that express command given to the prophet Isaiah, where the Lord says, *cry*; the prophet answers, *what shall I cry?* Cry *that all flesh is grass, and all the goodliness thereof is as the flower of the field. The grass withereth and the flower fadeth: But the word of the Lord endureth for ever.* That all flesh is grass, and the goodliness thereof, is an awful truth: How short is the interval between the cradle and the tomb! If so, as most certainly it is, ought we not, my friends, to try diligently, - to try the sincerity of our faith, while here below; and live in a holy and reverential fear of that God, who, when he sees fit, can make the stoutest heart tremble? The fear of the Lord is the beginning of Wisdom. The soul that truly relies upon God for help, let me say it, and that from a blessed experience, it will find a present help in time of trouble. I know it, and therefore I can speak it. That love which passeth all understanding, and was so manifestly displayed in the redemption of mankind, has lost none of its efficacy; God is the same, yesterday, to day, and for ever; and if we sincerely look unto him for aid, renouncing all sufficiency of our own, and set our faces Sion ward (for there is no enjoyment here – to expect any thing else but disappointment, is to deceive ourselves – to think of real happiness, in a state of finite existence, is mere delusion,) I say, if we earnestly look up to him, who is able and willing to save to the uttermost, we shall have that comfortable assurance, that one day or other, sooner or later, we shall be uninterruptedly happy: Sooner or later, my dear friends, we must *all* die: Death when he comes, will make no distinction, he will shew no difference, but where his errand is, there will he execute it. How have we seen an affectionate husband removed from an affectionate wife, and affectionate wife from an affectionate husband! Methinks here may be some who may be ready to say, 'ah! Such may be my case, and how soon God only knows; yet I am not without hope, that my melancholy would, in some measure, be alleviated by the dutifulness of my children.' I wou'd it were so; and I am concerned to speak to you, youths, - that you would hear the commandment of the Lord, and render all due obedience to your parents, - that your days may be long in the land, which the Lord your God hath given you; let your readiness to obey, and your eagerness to execute their reasonable commands, be as a staff to their age, and as balm to their declining nature. Methinks the language of some parents has affected me very much; to hear them lament how disobedient and refractory their children are. That since the time they had first the reins in their own Hands, and removed from under their governance, they have despis'd their counsels, and wou'd none of their reproof; and that their commands were enforced, till their children were constrained to an absolute compliance therewith; with what reluctance they obey'd, and how tardy they were in performing so reasonable a service.

O! That youth would seriously consider, and render to their parents, the tribute of obedience; for this is well pleasing to the Lord; It will be for their present, as well as future welfare. The wise man saith, *My son hear the instruction of thy father, and forsake not the law of thy mother, for they shall be an ornament of grace unto thy head, and chains about thy neck. The tribute of obedience is better that all burnt offerings and sacrifices;* The Lord saith of the house of the Rechabites, *Because ye have obeyed the commandment of Jonadab, your father, and kept all his precepts, and done according unto all that he hath commanded you: Therefore, thus saith the Lord of hosts, the God of Israel, Jonadab, the son of Rechab, shall not want a man to stand before me for ever.*

This promise was in consequence of their obedience; and will not this same blessing descend upon the obedient, even in this our day? My dear friends, God is the same, yesterday, to day, and for ever. And oh! That his grace may be influential on all of us, 'to will and to do of his good pleasure'; on the other hand, where a child is stubborn and refractory to its Parents; such disobedience not only brings down with it the judgments of the Lord, but never can admit peace of mind in this Life; much less can it afford you any reasonable hopes of happiness hereafter; for, 'there is no peace saith my God to the wicked.' 'He that honoureth me, I will honour; and he that despiseth me, shall be lightly esteem'd:' Nay, such is the Almighty's just abhorrence of disobedient children, that as a punishment to such, we read, 'The eye that mocketh his Father, and despiseth to obey his Mother, the Ravens of the valley shall pick it out, and the young Eagles shall eat it'; whereas a life spent in a way conformable to the will and pleasure of the Almighty, will insure to us peace here, and obtain the plaudit of *well done*, when time shall be no more. How earnestly do I wish, that every youth, not only those who are more immediately under the tuition of their parents, but those who are arrived to mature years, would consider this. My dear friends, to live in rebellion is living in open defiance to God and his laws. There is no real, solid contentment to be had, but by living a life agreeable to the will of our heavenly father; who has promised, 'that those who honour him, he will honour, and those that despise him, shall be lightly esteemed;' and whoever thou art, who art any ways stubborn, obstinate and perverse to thy parents, let me tell thee, - Thou can'st never experience any real happiness, but from an entire subjection to the will of God. 'Children obey your parents in the Lord,' saith the apostle, 'for this is well pleasing to God.' O! How many youths are there, (I make no doubt, tho' I hope none within the audience of my voice,) who when their parents have rebuked them for their good, tho' with the expressions of the utmost tenderness, have slighted or despised the reproof? How unseasonable have they reckoned the admonition! 'I don't like to come till my present amusements are over,' think they, 'whatever be the consequence, I'll not quit my diversions till I see fit; my companions like it best, they will perhaps deride me, if I leave 'em, therefore I am determined to enjoy the pleasures of sin for a season, come what will.' If such is the case, as we have too much reason to fear it frequently is, the fault does not lie in your tutors, but in yourselves. Tho' I have known many to blame others, when indeed the fault was really in themselves. O consider the shortness of life, and the certainty of death. 'All flesh is grass, and the goodliness thereof is as the flower of the field, the grass withereth, and the flower fadeth, but the goodness of God endureth for ever.' One day or other, we 'must all appear before the awful judge of quick and dead, to answer for the deeds done in the body, whether they be good or whether they be evil,' and O! That we may learn, every one of us, 'so to number our days, that we may apply our hearts unto wisdom;' then let us turn inwards, and narrowly examine our ways, scrutinize thoroughly our own hearts, and see if every thing is right within; let us deny ourselves every gratification that wou'd, otherwise, divert our thoughts from that which is our highest good. It is much to be wish'd, that all who really love their children, would endeavour, by all the means in their power, to cultivate morals, and secure for them their immortal interests; to bring them up in the nurture and admonition of the Lord, (like one that I heard of, who, on his deathbed, very affectionately exhorted his children to make his God their God) and then you will have great reason to expect in them an useful and unblamable conduct, through the whole course of their lives; thus by endeavouring to conduct their minds into an early knowledge of Christ, what a reciprocal advantage will it be from the one to the other? Every thing wou'd go on with that good harmony and understanding that it would visibly carry its own reward along with it; there would be no more eye-servants, as men-pleasers, but all in singleness of heart, as unto Christ, serving God, from the heart, every one cheerfully and willingly performing his duty, in the station whereunto it had pleased God to call them, and servants would become really valuable to their masters and mistresses. If God was in truth made the ultimate end of all our aims, the first and the last of each day's thoughts, what manner of persons shou'd we then be, in all holy conversation and godliness? None would be chargeable with purloining, or breach of trust in affairs committed to their management, but every thing would be done in such a manner, as consists with knowing that one day we must give an account.

Many I know are apt to complain, and say, the fault lies sometimes in their masters and mistresses; I grant it, but this is not a case so general as the contrary; I should rather suppose, good servants would make good masters. I would not be misunderstood, as laying the stress wholly upon children and servants; but I would be understood thus, that while all act agreeably to their respective characters, and confidently within their duty, every thing they take in hand will undoubtedly prosper; they will have joy in this life, and a comfortable assurance of a better one to come; for the God of heaven delights in such, they will die in his favour, and have a plaudit of 'Well done thou good and faithful servant, thou hast been faithful over a little, thou shalt be made ruler over much.' And nor, my friends, I would speak to you all in an unlimited sense: Let us get as well through this world as we can, that we may arrive at those enjoyments in store for us, which will yield a full and complete satisfaction. What can we think of the pleasures of this world, but that they are below the care of us who are born to so great expectation? 'All flesh is grass, and the goodliness thereof is the flower of the field.' Thus must we think of innocent delights; *they* are frail, transitory, and uncertain: *We* are immortal. – The Pleasures of this life, should not divert our attention from the *one thing needful*; these are unworthy objects of our desires; fit to be used, but too mean to be courted; proper for our diversion, but never good enough to become our business.

Let us, my brethren, earnestly set about the great work of our salvation while it is day. O! Listen to that small still voice that whispers peace to the conscience! Don't let us refuse to obey the Lord any longer, or great will be our condemnation: To live disrespectful and unmindful of an earthly parent, is certainly a temper of mind very different from that of a Christian; and how much greater want of gratitude does it argue, to live unmindful of that being, by whom we live and move, and have every blessing we enjoy? Shall I forget the God of my salvation? Shall I render him no expressions of thankfulness? Yes, and my life shall speak his praise in the language of devout obedience. My dear friends, it is very improbable I shall ever have an opportunity of seeing you, or any of you, again.: Cleave unto the Lord, and serve him with a perfect heart and willing mind, lest the Lord of hosts should swear in his wrath, that such abusers of his long-sufferings shall never enter into rest. – Evil habits are soon apt to get rooted and ingrain'd in the disposition; by that means we contract as it were a familiarity with sin, and with Solomon's fools, learn to make a mock of it, till by degrees our consciences are hardened, and not to be touch'd by any soft impression: My fear is, that many of you, by a long course of wickedness have so accustomed yourselves to that which is sinful, that evil habits have grown insensibly upon you: Evil habits steal imperceptibly upon us; to the truth of this, experience daily witness. With how much pain and uneasiness do men bring themselves to do the things, which in a little time, they glory and take pride in, or at least grow easy and contented under; and so become like those of whom it is said, they have drunken up iniquity, as the ox drinketh up water.

My friends, the moment you give yourselves up to sin, you give yourselves out of your own power; you lay restraint upon reason, and set the passions free: Upon the whole, there is great reason to fear, that sin, if once we indulge it, should get the better of and destroy our resolution of repentance; and, Oh my friends! I wish you would reason calmly upon these things. Enter into this debate with your own hearts, and consider what danger you are in a few moments cannot be too much to spend in so weighty an affair; and whenever you retire to these cool thoughts, may the father of mercies influence those moments of your life, upon which all eternity depends: Most people are apt to say ' I have now such and such business to do, and will not bestow a serious thought upon religious matters until the morrow;' – when, alas! We know not whether we shall ever see the light of another day. O! Who all that love their own souls, would seek the Lord, while happily he may be found; before the day comes, when the heavens being as brass, and the earth as iron, shall be wrapped up like a scroll: We have had repeated warnings, and that again and again, to repentance, to depart from sin, and Satan that grand and potent adversary of mankind. Let us return unto our divine Lord, in whom is no variableness nor shadow of turning; he is an undivided fountain, thither let us repair: He giveth unto all men liberally, and upbraideth not; many and manifold are the blessings that God has in store for them that fear him. He who has fixed in his mind a just notion of God, will find his way to peace, be the darkness about him ever so thick. It is a great misfortune for a person to know much of religion, and little of God; such a person's religion must either be his plague or his contempt; it must appear to him either ridiculous or terrible; and let him take it which way he will, he will find terror in it at last. It is in vain therefore to seek for satisfaction till we know God; till we can witness to our hearts, that we know him in whom we have trusted: this will make our religion become an holy and reverential fear, unmixed with terror and confusion; it will make our knowledge in religious matters become a wisdom unto salvation, and preserve to us that true freedom of mind, to which, as well the scoffers of age, as the superstitious, are mere strangers.

And further, friends! Don't let us entertain wrong notions of God; that is, don't let us consider him in his attribute of justice only, not his darling one, that of mercy; but let us consider him as a God, who himself hath said, 'I will visit the iniquities of the fathers upon the children, unto the third and fourth generation of them that hate me, and will shew mercy unto thousands of them that love me and keep my commandments.' There are too many, now a days, who forget the plain parts of scripture, (of which there are enough for every man to profit withal) and from a want of understanding the more obscure ones, are too apt to think irreverently of the Deity, and so grow entirely negligent with respect to the great work of their salvation. – But, my friends, the word of God is plain to every man who has the light to reason, 'that without holiness, no man shall see the Lord;' this is the foundation of all religion. Surely no one need be at a stand how to act with respect to God, his neighbour and himself. God has promised his assistance to all who endeavour to serve him; and surely there can be no difficulty in understanding this. When we read, that all who in any manner, injure their neighbours and fellow creatures, shall perish everlastingly;

we perceive that crimes and punishments are so inseparably connected, that, being conscious of the crimes, we see no way to escape the punishment.

But, when on the other hand, we consider, 'that unto whomsoever much is given, of him shall much be required;' we are too apt to infer from thence, that unto whomsoever little is given, of him shall little be required; and so conclude that all our imperfections, of what kind soever, are well secured; and so we think, whoever errs, be it for want of understanding, of the outward means of knowledge, or through passion and prejudices, that such want the light, and are to be considered as those to whom little is given. I say, my friends, this is one way the lukewarm have to lull their consciences to sleep, as it were: But full conscience returns, and proves that they have the light, in many instances in which they have been great offenders. – Surely, the state of such people plainly answers to our Lord's likening the kingdom of Heaven to a man's travelling into a far country, who called his own servants, and delivered unto them his goods: And to one he gave five talents, to another two and to another one; to every man according to his particular ability, and straightway took his journey. Then he that had received the five talents, went and traded with the same, and by prudent management made them another five talents. And he that had received two, gained also another two. But he that had received one, went and hid his Lord's talent. And when their Lord came to reckon with them, he that had received five talents, came and said, "Lord thou deliveredst unto me five talents; behold I have gained beside them five talents more". His Lord said, "well done thou good and faithful servant; thou has been faithful over a few things, I will make thee ruler over many things: enter thou into the joy of thy Lord." He that had received two talents gained beside them other two: He likewise had the answer of, "Well done thou good and faithful servant, thou hast been faithful over a little, I will make thee ruler over much." But the other came, we are told, saying, "Lord, behold here is thy pound, which I have kept laid up in a napkin: For I feared thee, because thou art an austere man: Thou takest up that thou laidst not down, and reapest that thou didst not sow." But his Lord's reply was, "Out of thine own mouth will I judge thee, thou wicked servant; thou knewest that I was an austere man, taking up that I laid not down, and reaping that I did not sow; wherefore then gavest not thou my money unto the bank, that at my coming I might have required mine own with usury." Here then we see is no excuse; - it is in vain to plead ignorance, 'for there is given unto every man, to profit withal.' No one shall be condemned by a law he knew nothing of; every one shall stand or fall by the light that was given him; it being true of every action, what the apostle has affirmed of alms-giving, 'It shall be accepted according to that a man hath, and not according to that he hath not.' Upon the whole, my friends, it appears from scripture, that every man hath the light of reason to direct him, knowing thus much, 'That without holiness no man shall see the Lord'. And since morality is founded upon that reason which is a common gift to mankind, every man must answer for the use of his reason: And therefore where reason shews him the difference of good and evil, if he chooses the evil, he is without excuse. And since there is given unto every one to profit withal, let us instantly set about improving the talents that God has given us; nay, even tho' it were but one, for it shall be accepted according to that a man hath, and not according to that he hath not: Neither let us, my friends, look with envy on those above us, who may be endowed with greater gifts than we; or contemptuously on those below us; but let each act up to the light of reason, which we have given us, and we shall do well. 'Tis an old received maxim, in my country, that *evil thinkers are generally evil doers*: And the case is so general indeed, every where, that methinks there needs not much be said to prove it. I could wish, that all the difference amongst us, was only, which should live a life most consistent with the character of a Christian.

I am concerned to admonish each and every of you, to seek the Lord while he may be found. 'Let the wicked forsake his ways, and the unrighteous man his thoughts, and let him return unto the Lord, and he will have mercy upon him, and to our God, for he will abundantly pardon him.' But then, my friends, we are not to plead any merit in ourselves, nor stand up, and, with a self-sufficient temper, think to vindicate or justify ourselves for our own righteousness, which is as filthy rags, and can stand us in no stead before the eyes of a perfectly pure and holy God. Oh friends! The day is coming, when all that is on the earth shall be as stubble: Then the scoffers, who mock at sin, and make their game of the serious and devout – those, who, instead of giving all diligence to make their calling and election sure, have trampled upon the frequent admonitions given them to a better life – will wish they had employed their time to a better purpose. But it will be too late! For when once the master of the house has shut the door, in vain we shall stand without and knock. Alas! Are we not stupid? Are we not senseless to the last degree, to live thus in open rebellion against the best of beings, when, for ought we know, the next minute we may be called, we may be summoned to appear, all guilty as we are, before an injured God, in whose presence no impure thing can enter? 'Every man's work shall be made manifest, for the day shall declare it.' There is no other way to secure to ourselves the favour of the Lord, but by a timely repentance; and repentance is the gift of God: Ask it of God, saying, *we are unworthy servants*, and he will give it to you; he will send none away that thus come unto him, nay, he delights in such; don't let thy sins, tho' heinous as they may be, retard thee one moment from supplicating for mercy. Christ says, 'I came not to call the righteous, but sinners to repentance'; He came to seek and to save that which was lost; for as he saith himself, 'what man of you, having an hundred sheep, if he lose one of them, doth not leave the ninety and nine in the wilderness, and go after that which is lost, until he find it? And when he hath found it, he layeth it on his shoulders, rejoicing. And when he cometh home, he calleth together his friends and neighbours, saying unto them, rejoice with me, for I have found my sheep which was lost. I say unto you, that likewise joy shall be in Heaven, over one sinner that repenteth, more than over ninety and nine just persons who need no repentance.' So we see here is a promise of life everlasting, provided we repent: We have only to repent, and live. Oh! Then, 'let the wicked forsake his ways, and the unrighteous man his thoughts, and let him return unto the Lord, and he will have mercy upon him, and to our God, for he will abundantly pardon him.'

The very end and design of Christ's coming, was to abolish sin, and bring in a new and complete satisfaction, a new and sufficient righteousness; which he did by offering himself a ransom for sinners, and suffering in their stead, 'that we might be made the righteous of God in him.'

O! That there was, from this moment, 'a death unto sin, and a new life unto righteousness.' – Finally, my brethren, since Christ Jesus has stood in the place of sinners, 'has become sin for us, who knew no sin, that we may be made the righteous of God in him:' Then let there be, from this moment, 'a death unto sin, and a new life unto righteousness.' Let us listen to the apostle's admonition. 'Walk not in chambering [being wanton] and wantonness, in strife and envying, but put ye on the Lord Jesus Christ, and make not provision for the flesh, to fulfil the lusts thereof.' God has given us appetites, and made part of our trial to govern and restrain them within their proper channels; and to indulge these appetites beyond measure, wou'd be the highest ingratitude to our heavenly benefactor. Let us look to the glory and immortality which is placed before us, the everlasting mansions, prepared for those who serve their master in holiness and newness of life, and keep themselves unspotted from the world: Then, let us view the vast variety of temptations which are so apt to fix us down to this world, and interrupt all our hopes of a better.

From these considerations, what more powerful arguments can there be imagined, to prevail with us, to abstain from fleshly lusts, than this; that 'we are strangers and pilgrims on earth, and look for another, even an Heavenly habitation, whose builder and maker is God.' Let us then instantly bid adieu to all unlawful, worldly delights, which are so apt to enslave and captivate the heart of man. Let us instantly set about the great work of our salvation, while it is day, that is, while we have the blessed opportunity. Let us say, with the apostle, 'The world is crucified unto me, and I unto the world.' Let us instantly beg of God, to 'lead us into the way, the truth and the light.' Oh! That his holy spirit may guide you into truth. The scripture saith, 'It is God that worketh in us both to will and to do his good pleasure.' The apostle positively renounceth all sufficiency of his own, he will have no merit imputed to the creature; 'not I' saith he, 'but Christ that dwelleth in me.' All human accomplishments are no more than dross or dung, when compared to the excellency of the knowledge of Jesus Christ. If there was really a thorough change in our natures, if there was really a longing, an earnest longing after God, what universal charity wou'd then abound among all ranks of people? Ministers wou'd have that care and sincere love for their flock, as knowing that one day they must give an account. In short, my friends, were we to consider the great and mighty Being, as he really is, the Alpha and Omega, the first and Last! I say, my friends, were we to make this God our 'God, the First and Last of each day's thought; what manner of persons should we then be in all holy conversation and godliness?' Our lives would be such as would bespeak us 'a peculiar, chosen people, zealous of good works.'

The day is hastening, when that awful doom will take place, - 'He that is holy, let him be holy still; and he that is filthy, let him be filthy still!' This is an alarming thought, and well deserves our attention. Methinks I am concerned to speak it again and again in your ears, that you all earnestly attend to the one thing needful; 'that you press towards the mark of the prize of our high-calling in Christ Jesus.' It will not do to be lukewarm, to be listless and careless in an affair of the utmost consequence, and especially since we know, 'It is appointed unto all men to die.'

Methinks it argues a depravity of understanding, as well as the greatest impiety, to make no provision for another world, whither we are all hastening.

Here is no hiding place. – Give all diligence, I beseech you, to secure to yourselves an interest in Christ, before that day come, when proclamation will be made, *'That time shall be no more.'* 'All flesh is grass, and all the goodliness thereof as the flower of the field. The grass withereth, and the flower fadeth, but the word of the Lord endureth for ever.' This was the prophet's declaration. Every thing relating to human life will cease, the world itself will come to an end.

Be wise then betimes, lest that day come upon you when you think not, and in an hour when you are not aware: O! 'buy the truth, and sell it not;' like the merchant our Lord speaks of, 'who when he had found the costly pearl, the pearl of great price, he immediately sold all that he had,' (he denied himself of every gratification that might otherwise divert his thoughts from that which was his chiefest good) that he might purchase that field where the invaluable pearl lay.

Most men live as though they were never to die.

There is either a total neglect, or a general carelessness, with regard to spiritual things, in every thing they do; but this is certainly bad, - 'tis shocking to the last degree, to live regardless of futurity; to live thus unmindful of that being who has set a day in which he will judge the world! A tribunal, at which every created being must appear, there to answer for the deeds done in the body! And, my friends, I will ask you this plain question: Is not this a matter that well deserves our attention? Is not a consideration sufficient, of itself, to draw our attention from the vain and trifling amusements of this transitory life, and engage ourselves in the pursuit of one thing needful, the pearl of great price, which will visibly carry its own reward along with it? The grave is the land where all things (of temporal concernment) are forgotten; Let us give all diligence to have our lamps trimmed, that if sickness should attack us, and death stare us in the face, we may say, with resignation, cheerfulness and triumph, 'O death! Where is thy sting? O grave! Where is thy victory? All flesh is grass, and all the goodliness thereof as the flower of the field, the grass withereth, and the flower fadeth, but the word of the Lord endureth forever.'

Eternity is at hand, 'behold he that cometh, will come, and will not tarry.' Let our lives be such, that when our Lord comes to reckon with us, we may be able to render him a just and true account. And indeed by conducting ourselves in the path of religion and virtue, and where only true joy is to be found, our lives will be influential of the lives of others: Example is better than precept, it would speak to them thus, 'that you follow us, as we follow God.'

O, that ministers might have watchful care over their flocks! O, that their lives may be a transcript and pattern of what they teach. Finally, my brethren, let me advise you to live and becometh Christians: There would be that harmony, that content and satisfaction, that the world's applause cannot give, nor its censure take away.

God has promised his peace to all who seek it: It is a peace which far surpasseth all human understanding. 'My peace I leave with you, my peace I give unto you; not as the world giveth, give I unto you.'

But then, my dear friends, we can never expect this peace, if we live in a course of wickedness; for, 'there is no peace, saith my God, to the wicked:' 'He that honoureth me, I will honour, and he that despiseth me shall be lightly esteemed.' Neither must we content ourselves with thinking that by departing from the most enormous crimes, God will be thus satisfied. No, this is a mistaken notion: God is not to be mocked; he saith, 'My son, give me thine heart.'

There must be an utter destruction of Amaleck, or God is not satisfied, it is not doing our duty in part, that will avail us; we must give up every thing, every darling sin, that most easily besets us. 'That for the fire to the fire, and that for the hammer to the hammer. God is of purer eyes than to behold iniquity.' He will not dwell in an unclean temple. Let us narrowly inspect into our ways, and scrutinize into our own hearts, and see if every thing be right within; and if so, it will be readily manifested by our lives and conversations. O! my friend, whoever thou art, that is within the audience of my voice, let me intreat thee to make God thy friend; for, after death, comes the judgment in on each of us! I would also, that ministers give all diligence in their callings, for if we fall, we fall not alone. 'Cry aloud, and spare not; tell my people 'their transgressions, and the house of Jacob their sins.' – Our business (as preachers) is to preach repentance to all, without respect to persons, 'whether they will hear, or whether they will forbear.' If we act counter to this, if we, of its hurting our temporal concerns, neglect to preach with that plainness that ought ever to distinguish a gospel minister, - Let me tell thee, whoever thou art, that neglectest to strike at the root of sin, and dost thy duty but in part, thou wilt receive Saul's condemnation; who, notwithstanding his express order from God, was to make an utter destruction of Amaleck, yet spared what was best, agreeable to his own fond inclinations; we read, he saved the best of the sheep and oxen, and Agag.

But, however merciful this may appear, in Saul's sparing Agag, his foolish pity and compassion to the captive king, was ill timed, when God's will was otherwise. I don't want to go through with every proof that could be brought in support of what I have been endeavouring to enforce: Let us only act agreeable to the will and pleasure of our maker, and what he orders to be done, to do it with cheerfulness and alacrity as unto a faithful Creator. I can say truly, that he who thus approves himself, is worthy of all honour. Finally, my brethren, let us instantly sacrifice every darling sin that may seem to stand in our way to glory. Let us give up every thing; - 'that for the fire to the fire, and that for the hammer to the hammer.' Don't be drudges to the Devil any longer. Hard task-masters, sin and Satan are; But our God, whom we serve, is no austere nor hard master. His unbounded mercy hath in this our day lost none of its efficacy; he requireth nothing without giving suitable abilities.

O! that we may all gather the manna, the blessed manna, the which he who eateth, shall even live thereby. Let me utter it in your ears again and again, 'All flesh is grass, and all the goodliness thereof, as the flower of the field; the grass withereth, and the flower fadeth, but the word of the Lord endureth for ever.' Let me exhort every one of you, with a heart full of compassion, that you seek thy Lord while he may be found; and before that time come, when these blessed opportunities, which we now have, for repentance and reconciliation, will be offered no more.

*FINIS.*

# SOURCES AND REFERENCES

## MAIN SOURCES

**Journal**

Rachel Wilson's Journal as copied out by her daughter, Deborah Braithwaite, in "An Account of Rachel Wilson's Religious Visit to Friends in America carefully transcribed from her Manuscript for the Information and Benefit of her Children and her near Relatives". The 'journal pages' quoted in the main text and appendices are those of this transcript. (Page 181 is followed by 192, 182 – 191 having been omitted from the numbering.)


**Braithwaite, William Charles**

Beginnings of Quakerism, The *Macmillan & Co, London 1912*

Second Period of Quakerism, The *Macmillan & Co, London 1919*

**Emmott, Elizabeth Braithwaite**

Short History of Quakerism, A *George H Doran Company, New York, 1923*

Story of Quakerism, The *Headley Brothers, London 1908*

**Fox, George**

Journal of – 'Bi-centenary edition' *Friends Tract Association, London 1891*

Journal of – ed. Norman Penney, Vol. ii *Cambridge University Press, 1911*

**Jones, Rufus M**

Quakers in the American Colonies, The *Macmillan & Co, London 1923*

**Larson, Rebecca**

Daughters of Light *Univ. of North Carolina Press, Chapel Hill, NC 1999*

**Leach, Robert J and Gow, Peter**

Quaker Nantucket *Mill Hill Press, Nantucket, MA 1997*

**Marietta, Jack D**

Reformation of American Quakerism, 1748-1783

*University of Pennsylvania Press, Philadelphia 1984*

**Somervell, John**

Isaac & Rachel Wilson Quakers of Kendal, 1714-85

*Swarthmore Press Ltd, London 1924*

**Whitney, Janet**

John Woolman, Quaker *George G.Harrap & Co Ltd, London 1943*

OTHER SOURCES

**Memoirs.** J. Bevan Braithwaite – A Friend of the 19th Century by his children (principally, Anna Lloyd Braithwaite Thomas)
*Hodder & Stoughton, London 1909*

**Philbrick, Nathaniel** 'Mayflower – A Voyage To War' *Harper Collins*

**G.M.D.Howat** 'Dictionary of World History', Gen. Editor *Nelson, 1973*

**'Quaker Biographies'**, Rachel Wilson by Anna L B Thomas
Friends House Library, London

**Cowley's Miscellany**, Vol. 8 Friends House Library, London

**Friends Miscellany**, Vol. IV Friends House Library, London

**'Piety Promoted'** (testimonies to the lives of 17th & 18th century Friends)
Friends House Library, London

**Britain Yearly Meeting Epistle, 2006**

**Hoare, Edward** – correspondence in *The Friend*

**Martin, Philip** 'Scalping: Fact & Fantasy' Manataka Amer. Indian Council

**Bacon, Margaret Hope** 'The Quiet Rebels' *Pendle Hill Publications, PA*

---

REFERENCES

1 Somervell p.31
2 Memoirs p.3
3 Larson p.145
4 Emmott, Story of Quakerism p.164
5 Jones p.253
6 *Ibid* pp.540-3
7 Whitney p.382
8 *Ibid* p.354
9 Somervell pp.49-50
10 Whitney pp.14-15
11 Braithwaite, Beginnings of Quakerism p.3
12 *Ibid* p.4
13 *Ibid* p.4

[14] *Ibid* p.6
[15] Philbrick p.xvii
[16] Braithwaite, Beginnings of Quakerism p.9
[17] Howat
[18] *Ibid*
[19] Braithwaite, Beginnings of Quakerism p.10
[20] Howat
[21] Braithwaite, Second Period of Quakerism p.6
[22] Fox, Bi-centenary Journal p.11
[23] Whitney p.15
[24] *Ibid* p.15
[25] *Ibid* p.24
[26] *Ibid* p.11
[27] Emmott, Story of Quakerism, quoting Rufus M Jones – paper read at American Five Years Meeting, 1907 p.247
[28] Emmott, Story of Quakerism pp.243-4
[29] *Ibid* p.149
[30] *Ibid* p.155
[31] Jones p.433
[32] Martin
[33] Whitney pp.302-3
[34] *Ibid* pp.301-2
[35] *Ibid* p.162
[36] Marietta pp.6-7
[37] Hoare
[38] Bacon p.167
[39] Emmott, Story of Quakerism p.248
[40] Whitney p.135
[41] *Ibid* p.111
[42] *Ibid* p.118
[43] *Ibid* p.111
[44] Fox, 'Cambridge' Journal p.195
[45] Emmott, Story of Quakerism p.187
[46] Whitney pp.247-8
[47] *Ibid* p.135
[48] *Ibid* p.245
[49] *Ibid* p.257
[50] Leach and Gow pp.101 and 113
[51] Fox, 'Bi-centenary' Journal p.165

[52] Larson p.266
[53] *Ibid* p.206
[54] *Ibid* p.267
[55] *Ibid* p.125
[56] *Ibid* p.237
[57] Howat
[58] Jones p.318
[59] Larson p.265
[60] *Ibid* p.287
[61] Emmott, Short History of Quakerism - Earlier Periods p.51
[62] Larson p.237
[63] Somervell pp.61-2
[64] Larson p.292
[65] Leach and Gow, for all references to the history of Quaker Nantucket
[66] Somervell, quoting Moses Brown p.62
[67] Larson p.259
[68] Larson, quoting the 'Boston Gazette' p.233
[69] Larson p.268
[70] Emmott, Story of Quakerism p.64
[71] Jones pp.91-2
[72] *Ibid* pp.101-2
[73] *Ibid* pp.105-7
[74] Cowley p.219
[75] *Ibid* p.220
[76] Somervell p.64
[77] Whitney p.330
[78] Somervell pp.66-7
[79] Friends Miscellany pp.239-40
[80] 'Piety Promoted'
[81] Somervell pp.104-5
[82] Hoare
[83] Jones pp.137-8
[84] Braithwaite, Second Period of Quakerism – Preface p.v
[85] Britain Yearly Meeting Epistle, 2006
[86] Braithwaite, Beginnings of Quakerism pp.523-4

# GLOSSARY

## Quaker terminology

**Meeting:** (1) a Quaker meeting for worship; (2) the congregation of Friends who meet at a particular place for worship or for business.

**Monthly Meeting:** (in the UK a Local or Preparative Meeting) the local meeting serving a defined geographical area.

**Quarterly Meeting:** (in the UK a Monthly or Area Meeting) a geographical grouping of Monthly (Local) Meetings.

**Yearly Meeting:** a wider grouping of Quarterly Meetings, e.g. by state (in the UK the whole country) and of the individuals in membership of the Society of Friends as a whole; the Society's ultimate decision-making, constitutional body.

**Business Meeting:** Quaker policy and business dealt with at meetings for worship for business held, typically, monthly, quarterly or yearly within the meeting structure and serving local, regional and national or international agendas as appropriate.

**Meeting for Sufferings:** originally the meeting for keeping track of Friends suffering imprisonment, deportation, enslavement, fines, distraint on their property etc in the course of adhering to Quaker principles and for procuring relief and refuge for their dependents. (In due course, in the UK, it became a meeting of appointed representatives from geographical meetings responsible for implementing YM decisions and reviewing YM's core purposes between one YM and the next.)

**elders:** Individual Quakers appointed to be responsible as a group for the nurture of the spiritual life of Meetings in their area or region and of the individuals in those Meetings.

**ministry:** a Friend's response to a personal calling from God to stand (to **appear**) and give vocal ministry in a meeting for worship. (See also 'Gospel' below.) *v.i.* to **minister**; *n.* **minister:** mainly dating back to the $17^{th}$ – $19^{th}$ centuries, a Quaker formally recognised by the Meeting as having the gift of ministry and, typically, undertaking extensive visits to other Meetings, locally, nationally or abroad, hence

**religious visit** (also **travelling in the ministry):** such visits, often frequent and demanding and supported by a **certificate** of support from the minister's Meeting.

**Select Meeting:** a meeting of elders and ministers.

**discipline:** the adherence to Quaker principles; **meetings for discipline** arranged for the counselling of those not adhering and for recommending action in relation to those refusing correction (after being placed under **dealing**), e.g. **disownment**.

**epistle:** a letter approved at and issued by a Yearly Meeting, often 'to all Friends everywhere', reflecting the matters considered by and experiences of Friends who attended.

**opportunity:** any informal or spontaneous time of worship and quiet enabling communication and communion among those who made the opportunity for it. Similarly, **solemn season/melting season**.

**gospel**, in conjunction with **order, labour, love, ministry**: A return to the everlasting gospel as experienced and preached by the apostles, but subsequently lost – this formed the foundation of Quakerism with its rejection of ecclesiastical obedience, religious profession and holy orders. The first Quaker meetings for worship were of people who received this gospel, gathering together in Christ's name to wait and feel his presence as their living teacher, leader, ruler, counsellor and 'orderer' and to see **the Light (**an eternal, mutually binding relationship with God), through which they became **convinced** of the truth; hence the call to bring one's life wholly within the 'gospel order' (i.e. the right relationship of every part of creation, however small, to every other part and to the Creator) through 'gospel labour', 'gospel love', 'gospel ministry' (preaching) etc. Quaker ministers preached not only in regular meetings for worship but also in specially appointed public meetings and in family homes and they gave personal counselling.

**convincement:** originally a normal condition of Membership of the Society of Friends. Later, children automatically became **'birthright'** Members while newcomers were admitted on the strength of their convincement.

**first day – seventh day:** Sunday – Saturday

**first month – twelfth month:** January – December

**other terms**

**chair:** a vehicle, wheeled or carried, for one person

**chaise:** a light, open carriage for one or more persons

**chariot:** a light, four-wheeled carriage with back seats and box

**creek:** *US* a small river or brook; (*UK* a small inlet, bay or tidal estuary)

**Shiloh:** (1) the Messiah *(Gen.49.10),* (2) ancient biblical city, capital of Israel before Jerusalem and where the tabernacle was kept. **Shiloh's streams:** "… a river the streams whereof shall make glad the city of God, the holy place of the tabernacles of the most High" *(Ps 46.4)*; the head of the river is the heart of God, its channel is Christ *(from a biblical commentary).*

INDEX

See pages 206-215 for lists of places and people's names appearing in the Journal

# JOURNAL CHRONOLOGY ETC.

List of places and people in date order

List of places A – Z

List of people A – Z

All the places in the journal are included in the main text and in this index.

Only some of the names of people recorded in the journal are included in the main text, but all the names are included in this index.

Where the spelling of places or people in the journal is known to be incorrect, the correct spelling has been substituted in the main text (but not in direct quotations) and in this index.

LIST OF PLACES AND PEOPLE IN CHRONOLOGICAL ORDER

h=husband w=wife s=son/s d=daughter/s ch=children f=family

| Journal page | Day 1-7 | Date Day | Date Mo. | Place | Col-ony | Names in journal | |
|---|---|---|---|---|---|---|---|
| 3 | 4 | [25] | 7 | Kendal | Engl | | |
| 3 | 4 | [25] | 7 | Lancaster | Engl | | |
| 3 | 4 | [25] | 7 | Warrington | Engl | Fothergill,Sam'l | Gough,John |
| 3 | 4 | [25] | 7 | Warrington | Engl | Whitwell,cous. | |
| 3 | 5 | 28 | 7 | Middlewich | Engl | Fallows,Joshua | |
| 3 | 5 | 28 | 7 | Talkothill | Engl | | |
| 3 | 5 | 28 | 7 | Litchfield | Engl | | |
| 3 | 6 | 29 | 7 | Coventry | Engl | | |
| 3 | 6 | 29 | 7 | Stowe | Engl | | |
| 3 | 6 | 29 | 7 | Dunstable | Engl | | |
| 3 | 6 | 29 | 7 | London | Engl | Chester,Rich'd | Row,Jos |
| 3 | 6 | 29 | 7 | London | Engl | Fisher,Sam'l | Wagstaff,Thos |
| 3 | 7 | 30 | 7 | London | Engl | Falconer,Capt. | Bell,Mary |
| 3 | 7 | 30 | 7 | London | Engl | Plumstead,Widow | Bell,Rob't |
| 3 | **1** | 31 | 7 | London Gracech'chSt | Engl | Bevan,Timothy | |
| 4 | 2 | 1 | 8 | London | Engl | Wright,John | |
| 4 | 3 | 2 | 8 | London DevHse | Engl | | |
| 4 | 3 | 2 | 8 | London Bromley | Engl | | |
| 4 | 4 | 3 | 8 | London Gracech'chSt | Engl | | |
| 5 | 5 | 4 | 8 | London Park | Engl | Sharples,Isaac | |
| 5 | 6 | 5 | 8 | London Gracech'chSt | Engl | | |
| 6 | 7 | 6 | 8 | London Tottenham | Engl | Sharples,Isaac | Barclay,John |
| 6 | 7 | 6 | 8 | London Tottenham | Engl | Mildred,Daniel | |
| 6 | **1** | 7 | 8 | London Tottenham | Engl | Wardle,Eliz | |
| 6 | 2 | 8 | 8 | London Plaistow | Engl | Wardle,Eliz | Chester, R +w |
| 6 | 2 | 8 | 8 | London Plaistow | Engl | Foster,cous.Jane | Hunt,John |
| 6 | 2 | 8 | 8 | London | Engl | Townsend,John | Cockfield,Zach |
| 7 | 3 | 9 | 8 | London Peel | Engl | Townsend,Jas | |
| 8 | 4 | 10 | 8 | London Wandsworth | Engl | Bell,Mary | Chester,P |
| 8 | 4 | 10 | 8 | London Wandsworth | Engl | Hester,Gray w | Lunn,Widow |
| 8 | 4 | 10 | 8 | London Gracech'chSt | Engl | Sharples,Isaac | Bevan,Timothy |
| 8 | 4 | 10 | 8 | London Gracech'chSt | Engl | Hill,Jas | Townsend,J |
| 9 | 5 | 11 | 8 | London Park | Engl | | |
| 10 | 6 | 12 | 8 | London | Engl | Sharples,I | |
| 10-12 | 7-4 | 13-17 | 8 | Gravesend | Engl | Chester, R +w+s+d | Blakeby,Wm |
| | | | | | | Chester,P | Talwin,E |

| Journal page | Day 1-7 | Date Day | Date Mo. | Place | Col-ony | Names in journal | |
|---|---|---|---|---|---|---|---|
| 12-17 | 5-4 | 18-24 | 8 | Downs, The | Engl | Mildred,D | Buck,Jas |
| | | | | | | Coleman,Wm | Fisher,Sam'l |
| | | | | | | Lambert,Widow | Lambert,Rebecca |
| | | | | | | Elgar,Jacob or Jos | |
| 18 | 5 | 25 | 8 | Dungeness | Engl | Law,Rich'd | Ravis,Thos |
| from 18 | 6 | 26 | 8 | Voyage | | Coleman,Wm | Fisher,Sam'l |
| to 27 | 4 | 12 | 10 | including 7 **"1st days"** | | Buck,Jas | |
| 27 | 5 | 13 | 10 | Capes of Delaware | | | |
| 27 | 6-7 | 14-15 | 10 | "little progress" | | | |
| 28 | **1** | 16 | 10 | Newcastle | DE | Fisher,S | Buck,J |
| 28 | **1** | 16 | 10 | Newcastle | DE | Shipley,Eliz | White,Esther |
| 28 | **1** | 16 | 10 | Wilmington | DE | Harvey,Widow | |
| 29 | 2 | 17 | 10 | Chester | PA | Shipley,Eliz | Fisher,S |
| 29 | 2 | 17 | 10 | Chester | PA | Fisher,Thos | Meredith,P |
| 29 | 2 | 17 | 10 | Philadelphia | PA | Fisher,Josh | Churchman,John |
| 29 | 2 | 17 | 10 | Philadelphia | PA | Stanton,Daniel | Pemberton,John |
| 30 | 3 | 18 | 10 | Philadelphia | PA | Pemberton,John | Stanton,D |
| 30 | 3 | 18 | 10 | Philadelphia | PA | Churchman,J +w | |
| 30 | 4 | 19 | 10 | Philadelphia | PA | Colesworth,Mary | Yarnold,Mordicai |
| 30 | 4 | 19 | 10 | Philadelphia | PA | Pemberton,Israel | Fisher,S |
| 31 | 4 | 19 | 10 | Philadelphia | PA | Churchman,J | Fisher,Esther |
| 31 | 5 | 20 | 10 | Bristol | PA | Ince,Benj | Percy,John |
| 31 | 5 | 20 | 10 | Bristol | PA | Williams,Encon +w | |
| 31 | 6 | 21 | 10 | Allentown | NJ | | |
| 31 | 6 | 21 | 10 | Freehold | NJ | Reed,Chas (judge) | Pemberton,Israel |
| 31 | 7 | 22 | 10 | Shrewsbury | NJ | Stardale,Jos | |
| 32 | **1** | 23 | 10 | Shrewsbury | NJ | | |
| 32 | 2 | 24 | 10 | Shrewsbury | NJ | Williams,Wid. +ch | Williams,Elia |
| 32 | 2 | 24 | 10 | Shrewsbury | NJ | Latanico,Rich'd | |
| 32 | 3 | 25 | 10 | Shrewsbury | NJ | Wardle,J+f | |
| 32 | 3 | 25 | 10 | Freehold | NJ | | |
| 33 | 4 | 26 | 10 | Allentown | NJ | Middleton,Amos | Middleton,Thos +w |
| 33 | 5 | 27 | 10 | Crosswicks | NJ | Thornton,Jas | Middleton,Abel |
| 33 | 5 | 27 | 10 | Crosswicks | NJ | Smith,Eliz | Morris,Sarah |
| 33 | 5 | 27 | 10 | Burlington | NJ | Farrington,Hysiah | Smith,Sam'l |
| 34 | 6 | 28 | 10 | Philadelphia | PA | Pemberton,Israel | Benezet,Joyce |
| 34 | 6 | 28 | 10 | Philadelphia | PA | Logan,Wm | |
| 34 | 7 | 29 | 10 | Philadelphia | PA | | |

| Journal page | Day 1-7 | Date Day | Mo. | Place | Colony | Names in journal | |
|---|---|---|---|---|---|---|---|
| 35 | **1** | 30 | 10 | Philadelphia | PA | Pemberton,John | Fisher,Wm |
| 35 | **1** | 30 | 10 | Philadelphia | PA | Pleasants,Sam'l | |
| 35 | 2 | 31 | 10 | Abington | PA | Pemberton,Israel | Fisher,Thos |
| 35 | 2 | 31 | 10 | Abington | PA | Moreton,Sam'l | Morris,Sarah |
| 36 | 2 | 31 | 10 | Abington | PA | Morris,Joshua | Fletcher,Thos |
| 36 | 3 | 1 | 11 | Horsham | PA | Thornton,Jas | Thomas,David |
| 36 | 3 | 1 | 11 | Horsham | PA | Lloyd,John | Wood,Thos |
| 36 | 3 | 1 | 11 | Horsham | PA | Wilson,Cous | |
| 37 | 4 | 2 | 11 | Byberry | PA | Morris,Sarah | Thornton,Jas |
| 38 | 5 | 3 | 11 | Philadelphia | PA | Pemberton,I | Pemberton,Jas |
| 38 | 6 | 4 | 11 | Germantown | PA | Jones,John | |
| 38 | 6 | 4 | 11 | Fairhill | PA | Morris,Eliz | Fisher,Thos |
| 39 | 7 | 5 | 11 | Fairhill | PA | Greenliff,Isaac | Forbes,Hugh |
| 39 | 7 | 5 | 11 | Fairhill | PA | Pemberton,John | |
| 40 | **1** | 6 | 11 | Philadelphia | PA | Rhoads,Sam'l | Warner,Widow |
| 40 | **1** | 6 | 11 | Philadelphia | PA | Warner,Wid. Mthr | |
| 41 | 2 | 7 | 11 | Philadelphia | PA | Logan,Wm | Meredith,Rice |
| 41 | 3 | 8 | 11 | Philadelphia | PA | Kendal,Benj | Fisher,Esther |
| 41 | 4 | 9 | 11 | Philadelphia | PA | Pemberton,Mary | Diehase,Anthony |
| 42 | 4 | 9 | 11 | Philadelphia | PA | Jordan,Jos | Coleman,Wm |
| 42 | 4 | 9 | 11 | Philadelphia | PA | Emlen,Jas+f | Thompson,Joshua |
| 42 | 4 | 9 | 11 | Philadelphia | PA | Reves,Hannah | Morris,Jos |
| 42 | 4 | 9 | 11 | Philadelphia | PA | Stretch,Jos | Holiwell,Thos |
| 43 | 5 | 10 | 11 | en route | PA | Brown,Jas +f | Lloyd,John |
| 43 | 5 | 10 | 11 | en route | PA | Evans,Isaac | |
| 43 | 6 | 11 | 11 | Sadsbury | PA | Taylor,Isaac | Brown,Wm |
| 43 | 6 | 11 | 11 | Sadsbury | PA | Brimstone,Moses | Norton,Benj |
| 43 | 6 | 11 | 11 | Sadsbury | PA | Forbes,Hugh | Sharpless,Benj |
| 43 | 6 | 11 | 11 | Sadsbury | PA | Fisher,T | |
| 43 | 7 | 12 | 11 | Lancaster | PA | Jones,Susannah | Jervis,Sam'l |
| 43 | 7 | 12 | 11 | Lancaster | PA | Whitelock,Isaac | Webb,Jas |
| 44 | 7 | 12 | 11 | Lancaster | PA | Moreton,Sam'l | |
| 44 | **1** | 13 | 11 | Lancaster | PA | Lightfoot,Thos +w | Logan,Wm |
| 44 | **1** | 13 | 11 | Lancaster | PA | Morris,Sarah | |
| 45 | 2 | 14 | 11 | Wrights Ferry | PA | | |
| 45 | 2 | 14 | 11 | York | PA | Matthews,Wm | Horn,Wm |
| 45 | 2 | 14 | 11 | York | PA | Lain,Isaac | |

| Journal page | Day 1-7 | Date Day | Mo. | Place | Col-ony | Names in journal | |
|---|---|---|---|---|---|---|---|
| 45 | 3 | 15 | 11 | York | PA | Morris,Sarah | Fisher,Esther |
| 45 | 3 | 15 | 11 | York | PA | Horn,W | |
| 46 | 4 | 16 | 11 | Newbury | PA | Zane,I | Morris,S |
| 46 | 4 | 16 | 11 | Newbury | PA | Hutton,Jos | Penrose,Wm |
| 46 | 4 | 16 | 11 | Warrington | PA | Mortland,S | Guest,John |
| 47 | 5 | 17 | 11 | Warrington | PA | | |
| 47 | 6 | 18 | 11 | Huntington | PA | Wiseman,Nic | Delap +f |
| 47 | 7 | 19 | 11 | en route | PA | | |
| 47 | **1** | 20 | 11 | Menallen | PA | | |
| 48 | 2 | 21 | 11 | Pipe Creek | MD | Kendrick,Sam'l | Pidgeon,Wm |
| 48 | 2 | 21 | 11 | Pipe Creek | MD | Farquhar,Wm | |
| 49 | 3 | 22 | 11 | Pipe Creek | MD | Holland,Rich'd | Moore,Ann |
| 49 | 3 | 22 | 11 | Pipe Creek | MD | Whitelock,Isaac | |
| 49 | 4 | 23 | 11 | Bush Creek | MD | Plummer,Thos | |
| 50 | 4 | 23 | 11 | Frederickstown | MD | Parsons,Widow | |
| 50 | 5 | 24 | 11 | Frederickstown | MD | | |
| 50 | 6 | 25 | 11 | Leesburgh | VA | Moore,Ann | Janney,Jos |
| 51 | 7 | 26 | 11 | Fairfax | VA | Janney,Sarah | Morris,S |
| 52 | **1** | 27 | 11 | Fairfax | VA | Hough,John | |
| 52 | 2 | 28 | 11 | Goose Creek | VA | Janney,Jacob | Hough,John |
| 52 | 2 | 28 | 11 | Goose Creek | VA | Morris,S | Fisher,T |
| 53 | 3 | 29 | 11 | Gap,The | VA | | |
| 53 | 3 | 29 | 11 | Shouden | VA | Pleasants,Sam'l | |
| 53 | 4 | 30 | 11 | Winchester | VA | Joliffe,Wm +w | |
| 54 | 5 | 1 | 12 | en route | VA | Jostle,Rich'd | Steer,Jos |
| 54 | 6 | 2 | 12 | Back Creek | VA | Pugh,John | Joliffe,Wm +w |
| 55 | 7 | 3 | 12 | Middle Creek | VA | Joliffe,Wm | Janney,Sarah |
| 55 | **1** | 4 | 12 | Middle Creek | VA | | |
| 55 | 2 | 5 | 12 | Middle Creek | VA | Brown,David | |
| 56 | 3 | 6 | 12 | Crooked Run | VA | Haines,Rob't | |
| 56 | 4 | 7 | 12 | Crook | VA | McCoy,Andrew | |
| 56 | 4 | 7 | 12 | Stowerstown | VA | Houseman,Philip | |
| 56 | 5 | 8 | 12 | Milentown | VA | Hawkins,Jos | |
| 56 | 6-7 | 9-10 | 12 | Smiths Creek | VA | Allen,Jackson | |
| 57 | 1 | 11 | 12 | en route | VA | Moore,Thos | Miller,John |
| 57 | 2 | 12 | 12 | Staunton Town | VA | Graton,John | Allen,Jackson |
| 57 | 2 | 12 | 12 | Staunton Town | VA | Moore,Reuben | |
| 58 | 3 | 13 | 12 | Rockfish Gap | VA | Williams,Rich'd | |
| 58 | 4 | 14 | 12 | en route | VA | Stogton,Thos | |

| Journal page | Day 1-7 | Date Day | Mo. | Place | Col-ony | Names in journal | |
|---|---|---|---|---|---|---|---|
| 59 | 5 | 15 | 12 | en route | VA | | |
| 60 | 6 | 16 | 12 | en route | VA | Woods,Sam'l | |
| 61 | 7 | 17 | 12 | Court H'se,Amherst | VA | Harrison,Batty | |
| 62 | **1** | 18 | 12 | James River | VA | Child,Jas | Clark,Christopher |
| 63 | 2 | 19 | 12 | en route | VA | Ferritt,Micajah | |
| 63 | 3 | 20 | 12 | New London | VA | Ward,Capt's +w | |
| 64 | 4 | 21 | 12 | en route | VA | Ward,Capt | Gilbert,Sam'l |
| 64 | 5 | 22 | 12 | en route | VA | Gilbert,S +f | |
| 64 | 6 | 23 | 12 | Staunton River | VA | Ferritt,Micajah | Moreton,Sam'l |
| 64 | 6 | 23 | 12 | Staunton River | VA | Collins,Jos | |
| 65 | 7 | 24 | 12 | Banister River | VA | Ekells,Wm | |
| 65 | **1** | 25 | 12 | en route | VA | Kirby,Rich'd | |
| 65 | 2 | 26 | 12 | en route | VA | Paine,Wm | |
| 66 | 3 | 27 | 12 | Dan River | VA | Paine,Wm | |
| 66 | 3 | 27 | 12 | Hogins Creek | NC | Shuttlefield,Rob +s | Ferritt,Micajah |
| 66 | 3 | 27 | 12 | Hogins Creek | NC | Moreton,Sam'l | |
| 66 | 4 | 28 | 12 | Hogins Creek | NC | | |
| 67 | 4 | 28 | 12 | Haw River | NC | | |
| 68 | 5 | 29 | 12 | Ready Fork | NC | | |
| 69 | 5 | 29 | 12 | New Garden Settlmt | NC | Balinger,Hy | Hunt,Eleanor |
| 69 | 6 | 30 | 12 | New Garden Settlmt | NC | Unthank,Jos's w | Peel,John +w |
| 69 | 6 | 30 | 12 | New Garden Settlmt | NC | Hunt,Widow | |
| 69 | 7 | 31 | 12 | New Garden Settlmt | NC | | |
| 69 | **1** | 1 | 1 | New Garden Settlmt | NC | | |
| 69 | 2 | 2 | 1 | Deep River | NC | | |
| 70 | 3 | 3 | 1 | en route | NC | Hunt,Wm +w | Mendenhall,Jas |
| 70 | 3 | 3 | 1 | en route | NC | Mendenhall,Mord. | Reynolds,Wm |
| 71 | 4 | 4 | 1 | Centre | NC | Dicks,Peter | |
| 71 | 5 | 5 | 1 | Providence | NC | Hind,Jacob | Pigot,Jeremiah |
| 71 | 6 | 6 | 1 | Rocky River | NC | Pigott,Wm | |
| 71 | 7 | 7 | 1 | Cane Creek | NC | | |
| 72 | **1** | 8 | 1 | Cane Creek | NC | Chamney,Anthony | Hanfield,Wm |
| 73 | 2 | 9 | 1 | Hawfield | NC | Thompson,Jas | |
| 73 | 3 | 10 | 1 | Hillsborough | NC | Lumley,Wm | |
| 73 | 4 | 11 | 1 | Spring Meeting | NC | | |
| 73 | 5 | 12 | 1 | Deep River | NC | Tyson,Cornelius | |
| 74 | 6 | 13 | 1 | Holly Spring | NC | Pigot,Wm | Pike,Abigail |
| 74 | 6 | 13 | 1 | Holly Spring | NC | Carter,John | Thompson,Dan'l |
| 74 | 7 | 14 | 1 | en route | NC | Cox,Thos | |

| Journal page | Day 1-7 | Date Day | Mo. | Place | Colony | Names in journal | |
|---|---|---|---|---|---|---|---|
| 75 | **1** | 15 | 1 | en route | NC | Cox,John | |
| 75 | 2 | 16 | 1 | en route | NC | Vister,David | Bronston,Lewis |
| 75 | 2 | 16 | 1 | en route | NC | Carpenter,John | |
| 75 | 3 | 17 | 1 | Hedge Cook Creek | SC | Tyson,Cornelius | Tyson,Benj |
| 76 | 3 | 17 | 1 | Peedee River | SC | Hailey,Wm | |
| 76 | 4 | 18 | 1 | Hedge Cook Creek | SC | Hailey,Wm | |
| 76 | 5-6 | 19-20 | 1 | en route | SC | Hailey,Wm +s | |
| 76 | 7 | 21 | 1 | Wateree | SC | Wiley,Widow | |
| 77 | **1** | 22 | 1 | Wateree | SC | Kershaw,Jos | |
| 77 | 2-3 | 23-24 | 1 | Wateree | SC | | |
| 77 | 4 | 25 | 1 | Bush River | SC | Kershaw,Jos | Milhouse,Sam'l |
| 77 | 4 | 25 | 1 | Bush River | SC | Wiley,Widow | Gant,Zebulon |
| 77 | 4 | 25 | 1 | Bush River | SC | Pidgeon,Isaac +w | Kelly,Mary |
| 78 | 5-7 | 26-28 | 1 | en route | SC | Kelly,Sam'l | Steadham,Mary |
| 78 | **1** | 29 | 1 | en route | SC | Pearson,Benj | Cannon,Sam'l |
| 78 | 2-3 | 30-31 | 1 | en route | SC | Webb,David | Gant,Zebulon +w |
| 78 | | | | | SC | Willy,Wm | Pidgeon,Sarah |
| 79 | 4 | 1 | 2 | en route | SC | Wilnas, | |
| 79 | 5 | 2 | 2 | Charleston | SC | Wilson (merchant) | Fisher,Josh +ss |
| 79 | 5 | 2 | 2 | Charleston | SC | Coram,John +w | |
| 79 | 6-7 | 3-4 | 2 | Charleston | SC | Johnson,Widow | |
| 80 | **1** | 5 | 2 | Charleston | SC | Veile,Jos | |
| 81 | 2 | 6 | 2 | Charleston | SC | Laurens,Hy Col. | Myers,Philip +f |
| 81 | 2 | 6 | 2 | Charleston | SC | Pickles,Capt. | Ragg,Widow +ch |
| 83 | 3 | 7 | 2 | Charleston | SC | Hopton,Wm+f | Gordon,Widow |
| 84 | 4 | 8 | 2 | Moncks Corner | SC | Short,Thos | Pickles,Capt. |
| 84 | 5 | 9 | 2 | Nelsons Ferry | SC | Witton,- | |
| 84 | 5 | 9 | 2 | Santee Swamp | SC | | |
| 84 | 6 | 10 | 2 | en route | SC | Wiley,Widow | |
| 85 | 7 | 11 | 2 | Links Creek | SC | | |
| 85 | **1** | 12 | 2 | Peedee River | SC | Millhouse,Sam'l | Russell,Sam'l |
| 85 | 2-3 | 13-14 | 2 | en route | SC | McCoy,- (or Malay) | |
| 85 | 4 | 15 | 2 | Cross Creek | NC | Hadley,Thos | |
| 85 | 5 | 16 | 2 | Duns Creek | NC | Grove,Thos +w | Lyon,Rich'd |
| 86 | 5 | 16 | 2 | Cross Creek | NC | Rowan,Rob't | Horn,Hy |
| 86 | 6 | 17 | 28 | Cape [Fear] River | NC | Smith,Colonel | |
| 86 | 6 | 17 | 28 | Simmiter Ferry | NC | | |
| 86 | 7 | 18 | 2 | en route | NC | Lemon,Dunken | |

| Journal page | Day 1-7 | Date Day | Mo. | Place | Colony | Names in journal | |
|---|---|---|---|---|---|---|---|
| 86 | **1** | 19 | 2 | Tar River | NC | Horn,Hy | |
| 87 | 2 | 20 | 2 | Rich Square | NC | Locke,John | Gray,Jos |
| 87 | 2 | 20 | 2 | Rich Square | NC | Peel,John | Horn,Hy |
| 88 | 3 | 21 | 2 | Rich Square | NC | Peel,John | Duke,John's wife |
| 88 | 3 | 21 | 2 | Rich Square | NC | White,Thos w | |
| 88 | 4 | 22 | 2 | Chowan | NC | Shepherd,Stephen | Capland,Thos +f |
| 88 | 5 | 23 | 2 | Little River | NC | Nicholson,Thos | |
| 89 | 6-7 | 24-25 | 2 | Little River | NC | Horn,Hy | |
| 90 | **1** | 26 | 2 | Little River | NC | Nicholson,Thos +f | |
| 91 | 2 | 27 | 2 | Simmonds Creek | NC | Morris,Aaron | |
| 91 | 3 | 28 | 2 | Newbegun Creek | NC | Abberton,Widow | Jordan,Rob't |
| 91 | 3 | 28 | 2 | Newbegun Creek | NC | Morris,John | |
| 91 | 4 | 1 | 3 | en route | NC | Trueblood,Alan | |
| 92 | 5 | 2 | 3 | Old Neck | NC | Nixon,Francis | Newby,Thos |
| 92 | 5 | 2 | 3 | Perquimens River | NC | | |
| 92 | 5 | 2 | 3 | Edenton | NC | | |
| 93 | 6 | 3 | 3 | en route | NC | Nixon,Francis | Nixon,Eliz +f |
| 93 | 6 | 3 | 3 | en route | NC | Payton,C | |
| 93 | 7 | 4 | 3 | Wells | NC | Newby,Thos +w | |
| 93 | **1** | 5 | 3 | Pine Wood | NC | Providence,- +w | |
| 94 | 2 | 6 | 3 | Somerton | VA | Newby,Thos | Jordan,Pleasant |
| 94 | 2 | 6 | 3 | en route | VA | Porter,John +f | |
| 95 | 3 | 7 | 3 | Nansemond | VA | Scott,Jos | Abrams,Rob't |
| 95 | 4 | 8 | 3 | Western Branch | VA | Scott,Jos | Lawrence,J +f |
| 95 | 4 | 8 | 3 | Western Branch | VA | Jordan,Joshua +f | |
| 95 | 5 | 9 | 3 | Suffolk | VA | Cranby,Josiah | |
| 95 | 5-6 | 9-10 | 3 | Bucks Creek | VA | Gibson,Geo | Jordan,Rob't |
| 95 | 7 | 11 | 3 | Chuckatuck | VA | Jordan,Josh | |
| 96 | **1** | 12 | 3 | Western Branch | VA | Scott,Widow | Watkins,Wm |
| 96 | 2 | 13 | 3 | Black Creek | VA | Draper,Thos | Lightfoot,T |
| 96 | 2 | 13 | 3 | Black Creek | VA | Stanton,Jos | |
| 96 | 3 | 14 | 3 | en route | VA | Retford,Thos | |
| 96 | 4 | 15 | 3 | Blackwater | VA | Hargroves,Jos | Bailey,Anselm |
| 97 | 5 | 16 | 3 | Burleigh | VA | Kin...,Widow | |
| 97 | 6 | 17 | 3 | en route | VA | Chappel,Agnes | Ninnicut,Rob't |
| 98 | 7 | 18 | 3 | Petersburgh | VA | Stabler,David | |
| 98 | **1** | 19 | 3 | Petersburgh | VA | | |
| 98 | 2 | 20 | 3 | Gravelly Run | VA | Butler,Wm | Stabler,Edward |

| Journal page | Day 1-7 | Date Day | Mo. | Place | Col-ony | Names in journal | |
|---|---|---|---|---|---|---|---|
| 98-99 | 3-4 | 21-22 | 3 | Curles | VA | Pleasants,John +s | |
| 99 | 5 | 23 | 3 | Winecock | VA | Crew,John | |
| 99 | 5 | 23 | 3 | Cobbles Ferry | VA | | |
| 99 | 6 | 24 | 3 | Skimino | VA | Bates,Jas | |
| 99 | 6 | 24 | 3 | Williamsburg | VA | Stabler,Edward | |
| 100 | 7 | 25 | 3 | Black Creek | VA | Stabler,Edward+w | Pleasants,Rob't |
| 100 | 7 | 25 | 3 | Black Creek | VA | Ellison,Rob't | |
| 100 | **1** | 26 | 3 | Swamp, The | VA | Johnson,David | |
| 100 | 2 | 27 | 3 | Picquinocque | VA | Pleasants,John | |
| 101 | 3 | 28 | 3 | Richmond | VA | Hutchins,Morgan | Pleasants,Rob't |
| 101 | 3 | 28 | 3 | Richmond | VA | Store,Joshua | Ellis,Geo |
| 101 | 4 | 29 | 3 | Genita | VA | Watkins,Wm | |
| 101 | 5 | 30 | 3 | Fork Creek | VA | | |
| 102 | 5 | 30 | 3 | Camp Creek | VA | Moore,Chas | |
| 102 | 6 | 31 | 3 | en route | VA | Douglas,John | Clark,Francis |
| 102 | 6 | 31 | 3 | en route | VA | Henry,Patrick | |
| 103 | 7 | 1 | 4 | Cedar Creek | VA | Bossell,John | Harris,John |
| 103 | **1** | 2 | 4 | Cedar Creek | VA | Harris,John's father | |
| 103 | 2 | 3 | 4 | Caroline | VA | | |
| 104 | 2 | 3 | 4 | en route | VA | | |
| 104 | 3 | 4 | 4 | Port Royal | VA | | |
| 104 | 3 | 4 | 4 | Rapahanack River | VA | | |
| 104 | 3 | 4 | 4 | Potomack River | MD | | |
| 104 | 4 | 5 | 4 | en route | MD | Plummer,Widow | |
| 104 | 5 | 6 | 4 | West River | MD | Thomas,Philip | Thomas,Wm |
| 104 | 5 | 6 | 4 | Hill Delight | MD | | |
| 104 | 6 | 7 | 4 | Annapolis | MD | | |
| 104 | 6 | 7 | 4 | Chesapeake Bay | MD | Janney,Sarah | |
| 105 | 7 | 8 | 4 | Chester River | MD | Lightfoot,T +w | Morris,Eliz |
| 105 | 7 | 8 | 4 | Chester River | MD | Fisher,Grace | |
| 105 | **1** | 9 | 4 | Chester River | MD | | |
| 106 | 2 | 10 | 4 | Chester River | MD | Moreton,S | George,Rob't |
| 106 | 3 | 11 | 4 | Chestertown | MD | Wilkins,Thos+w | |
| 106 | 4 | 12 | 4 | Cicle | MD | Lamb,Josh | Browning,Nixton |
| 106 | 4 | 12 | 4 | Cicle | MD | Fisher,Sam'l | Fisher,Esther |
| 107 | 5 | 13 | 4 | Sassafras | MD | Store,Isaac | |
| 107 | 6 | 14 | 4 | Wilmington | DE | | |
| 107 | 7 | 15 | 4 | Philadelphia | PA | Harvey,Mary | |
| 107 | **1** | 16 | 4 | Philadelphia | PA | Moreton,Sam'l | |

| Journal page | Day 1-7 | Date Day | Mo. | Place | Colony | Names in journal | |
|---|---|---|---|---|---|---|---|
| 107 | 2-3 | 17-18 | 4 | Philadelphia | PA | | |
| 108 | 4 | 19 | 4 | Darby | PA | Hoskins,Jos | |
| 108 | 5 | 20 | 4 | Chester | PA | | |
| 108 | 5 | 20 | 4 | Wilmington | DE | | |
| 108 | 6-7 | 21-22 | 4 | Duck Creek | DE | Clifford,Thos w+s | Fisher,Esther |
| 108 | **1** | 23 | 4 | Duck Creek | DE | | |
| 109 | 2 | 24 | 4 | Duck Creek | DE | Store,Isaac | |
| 109 | 3 | 25 | 4 | Newcastle | DE | Wilson,David+w | Sweet,Benj |
| 109 | 4 | 26 | 4 | Chester | PA | Tinner,Doctor | Hoskins,Jos |
| 109 | 5 | 27 | 4 | Chester | PA | Morris,Sarah | Hoskins,J |
| 110 | 6 | 28 | 4 | Chester | PA | Clifford,Thos | |
| 110 | 7 | 29 | 4 | Chester | PA | Pemberton,J | Hunt,J |
| 110 | 7 | 29 | 4 | Chester | PA | Churchman,Mary | Stanton,Dan'l |
| 111 | 7 | 29 | 4 | Chester | PA | Andrews,Isaac | Brown,Wm |
| 111 | 7 | 29 | 4 | Chester | PA | Churchman,J | Haines,Reuben |
| 111 | 7 | 29 | 4 | Chester | PA | Morris,S | Jacobs,Jos |
| 111 | **1** | 30 | 4 | Philadelphia | PA | Morris,S | Hunt,John |
| 111 | **1** | 30 | 4 | Philadelphia | PA | Sampson,Sam'l | |
| 112 | **1** | 30 | 4 | Philadelphia | PA | Cotes,Widow | Stanton,Dan'l |
| 112 | **1** | 30 | 4 | Philadelphia | PA | Elliot,Jos | Dishley,David |
| 113 | 2 | 1 | 5 | Philadelphia | PA | Jones,Rebecca | Churchman,J |
| 113 | 2 | 1 | 5 | Philadelphia | PA | Pemberton,Isr'l+w | Morris,S |
| 113 | 2 | 1 | 5 | Philadelphia | PA | Morris,Doctor | Wishaw,Widow |
| 114 | 3 | 2 | 5 | Philadelphia | PA | Cotes,Widow | Langdale,Mary |
| 114 | 3 | 2 | 5 | Philadelphia | PA | Roberts,Hugh | Bacon,David+f |
| 114 | 3 | 2 | 5 | Philadelphia | PA | Bury,Benj | Churchman,J |
| 114 | 3 | 2 | 5 | Philadelphia | PA | Emlen,Job&Sam'l | Lightfoot,Michael |
| 115 | 4 | 3 | 5 | Chester | PA | Greenleaf,Isaac | Logan,Hannah |
| 115 | 4 | 3 | 5 | Chester | PA | Fisher,Sam'l | Hoskins,Jos |
| 115 | 5 | 4 | 5 | Concord | PA | Moore,Jas | Newland,Ann |
| 115 | 5 | 4 | 5 | Concord | PA | Gibbins,Jos | |
| 115 | 6 | 5 | 5 | Goshen | PA | Garrett,Jos f | Ashbridge,Aaron |
| 116 | 7 | 6 | 5 | Concord | PA | Yarnall,Nathan | James,Mary |
| 116 | **1** | 7 | 5 | Middletown | PA | Hill,John | Mason,Geo |
| 117 | 2 | 8 | 5 | Concord | PA | Trimble,Sam'l | Spekeman,Micajah |
| 117 | 3 | 9 | 5 | Concord | PA | Lightfoot,S | Yarnall,Mordecai |
| 117 | 3 | 9 | 5 | Concord | PA | Brinston,John | Mendinghole,P w |
| 117 | 3 | 9 | 5 | Concord | PA | Clark,Eliz | |

| Journal page | Day 1-7 | Date Day | Mo. | Place | Colony | Names in journal | |
|---|---|---|---|---|---|---|---|
| 118 | 4 | 10 | 5 | Kennet | PA | Harvey,Wm | Temple,Thos w |
| 119 | 5 | 11 | 5 | Kennet | PA | Pease,Caleb | Morris,S |
| 119 | 5 | 11 | 5 | Kennet | PA | Paine,Thos | |
| 119 | 6 | 12 | 5 | Philadelphia | PA | Mendinghole,Grfth | Morris,S |
| 119 | 6 | 12 | 5 | Philadelphia | PA | Miller,Warwick | White,Jacob |
| 120 | 7 | 13 | 5 | Philadelphia | PA | Miller,Wm | Pease,Josh |
| 120 | 7 | 13 | 5 | Philadelphia | PA | Mason,Geo | |
| 121 | **1** | 14 | 5 | Philadelphia | PA | Miller,Wm | Pease,Josh |
| 121 | 2 | 15 | 5 | Philadelphia | PA | Woodhard,Thos | Harvey,Wm |
| 121 | 3 | 16 | 5 | Philadelphia | PA | King,Benj | Hoskins,Jos |
| 121 | 3 | 16 | 5 | Philadelphia | PA | Gray,Geo | |
| 121 | 4 | 17 | 5 | Philadelphia | PA | | |
| 121 | 5 | 18 | 5 | Burlington | NJ | Clifford,Thos+w+s | Fisher,Esther |
| 121 | 5 | 18 | 5 | Burlington | NJ | Hopkins,Sarah | Smith,John |
| 124 | 6 | 19 | 5 | Bordentown | NJ | Sykes,John+f | Brooks,Edward+w |
| 124 | 6 | 19 | 5 | Bordentown | NJ | Horner,Isaac+f | |
| 124 | 7 | 20 | 5 | Trenton | NJ | Morris,Wm | Clark,Isaac |
| 124 | 7 | 20 | 5 | Trenton | NJ | Worth,Sam'l | |
| 125 | **1** | 21 | 5 | Stoney Brook | NJ | | |
| 125 | **1** | 21 | 5 | Princeton | NJ | Stockton,Rich'd+w | Horner,Jos |
| 125 | 2 | 22 | 5 | Brunswick | NJ | Shotwell,Jos | |
| 126 | 3 | 23 | 5 | Woodbridge | NJ | Shotwell,Jos | |
| 126 | 3 | 23 | 5 | Rahway | NJ | | |
| 126 | 4 | 24 | 5 | Elizabeth Town | NJ | | |
| 126 | 4 | 24 | 5 | New York | NY | | |
| 127 | 5-7 | 25-27 | 5 | Flushing | NY | | |
| 127 | **1** | 28 | 5 | Flushing | NY | | |
| 127 | 2 | 29 | 5 | Flushing | NY | Carlton,Thos | Bowen,Dinah |
| 128 | 3 | 30 | 5 | Cowneck | NY | Latham,Sam'l | |
| 128 | 3 | 30 | 5 | Westbury | NY | Symonds,Thos | |
| 128 | 4 | 31 | 5 | Westbury | NY | Underhill,Abram | Bowne,Geo |
| 128 | 4 | 31 | 5 | Westbury | NY | Pearsall,Jos | |
| 129 | 5 | 1 | 6 | Matendale | NY | | |
| 129 | 5 | 1 | 6 | Oyster Bay | NY | Cocks,John | Willis,Sam'l |
| 129 | 5 | 1 | 6 | Oyster Bay | NY | Weston,Hy | |
| 129 | 6 | 2 | 6 | Bethpage | NY | | |
| 129 | 6 | 2 | 6 | Seugnalaugh | NY | | |
| 129 | 6 | 2 | 6 | Bethpage | NY | Pemberton,John | Franklin,Walter |
| 129 | 6 | 2 | 6 | Bethpage | NY | Willett,Widow | |

| Journal page | Day 1-7 | Date Day | Mo. | Place | Colony | Names in journal | |
|---|---|---|---|---|---|---|---|
| 129 | 7 | 3 | 6 | Brookhaven | NY | Willett,Rebecca | |
| 130 | 7 | 3 | 6 | Setauket | NY | Hollicut,Rich'd | Staing,Doctor |
| 130 | 7 | 3 | 6 | Setauket | NY | Pemberton,John | |
| 131 | **1** | 4 | 6 | en route | NY | Pemberton,John | Willis,David |
| 131 | **1** | 4 | 6 | en route | NY | Janning,Capt | |
| 133 | **1** | 4 | 6 | Southold | NY | | |
| 133 | 2 | 5 | 6 | Sterling | NY | | |
| 133 | 2 | 5 | 6 | New London | CT | | |
| 134 | 3 | 6 | 6 | en route | CT | Haslam,Widow | Mumford,Jas |
| 134 | 3 | 6 | 6 | en route | CT | Pemberton,John | |
| 137 | 4 | 7 | 6 | Westerley | CT | Bowne,Geo | Pearsall,Jos |
| 138 | 4 | 7 | 6 | Newport | RI | Richardson,Widow | |
| 138 | 5 | 8 | 6 | Portsmouth | RI | Mott,Jacob | Laton,Isaac |
| 139 | 6 | 9 | 6 | Newport | RI | Robinson,Thos f | |
| 139 | 7 | 10 | 6 | Newport | RI | Docker,John | Wanton,- |
| 139 | **1** | 11 | 6 | Newport | RI | | |
| 139 | 2 | 12 | 6 | Newport | RI | Redwood,Wm | Hosier,Giles |
| 140 | 3 | 13 | 6 | Tiverton | RI | Pemberton,John | Hadwin,John |
| 140 | 3 | 13 | 6 | Tiverton | RI | Backer,Abram | Michael,Jas |
| 141 | 4 | 14 | 6 | Little Compton | MA | Gifford,Ephraim | |
| 141 | 5 | 15 | 6 | Center | MA | Mossin,Wm | |
| 142 | 6 | 16 | 6 | Newtown | MA | Mossin,Wm | |
| 142 | 6 | 16 | 6 | Acushnet | MA | Hathaway,Thos | |
| 142 | 7 | 17 | 6 | Rochester | MA | Trip,Sam'l | Davis,Timothy |
| 142 | 7 | 17 | 6 | Long Plain | MA | Davis,Timothy | |
| 143 | **1** | 18 | 6 | Queshiner | MA | Russel,Caleb+f | |
| 143 | 2 | 19 | 6 | Apponagansett | MA | Huss,John-Capt | |
| 144 | 3 | 20 | 6 | Elizabeth Island | MA | Huss,John-Capt | |
| 145 | 4 | 21 | 6 | Martha's Vineyard | MA | Coffin,David | |
| 146 | 5 | 22 | 6 | Nantucket | MA | Rotch,Wm+w+sis. | Barney,Sarah |
| 147 | 6 | 23 | 6 | Nantucket | MA | Pemberton,John | Barney,Sarah |
| 147 | 6 | 23 | 6 | Nantucket | MA | Macy,John | |
| 148 | 7 | 24 | 6 | Nantucket | MA | Pemberton,John | Starbuck,Wm |
| 149 | **1** | 25 | 6 | Nantucket | MA | Pemberton,John | |
| 150-1 | 2-4 | 26-28 | 6 | Nantucket | MA | | |
| 151 | 5 | 29 | 6 | Woodashole | MA | Huss,John-Capt | Bonow,Stephen |
| 151 | 6 | 30 | 6 | Falmouth | MA | Allan,Ebenezer | |
| 152 | 6 | 30 | 6 | Sandwich | MA | | |

| Journal page | Day 1-7 | Date Day | Mo. | Place | Colony | Names in journal | |
|---|---|---|---|---|---|---|---|
| 152 | 7 | 1 | 7 | Sandwich | MA | Wing,John | |
| 152 | 1 | 2 | 7 | Yarmouth | MA | Allan,Ebenezer | Ury,John |
| 153 | 2 | 3 | 7 | Plymouth | MA | Rowland,Wm | |
| 153 | 3 | 4 | 7 | Pembroke | MA | Dillingham,Mltia+f | |
| 154 | 4 | 5 | 7 | Boston | MA | Bagnall,Benj | |
| 154 | 4 | 5 | 7 | Lynn | MA | Collins,Zach | |
| 154 | 5 | 6 | 7 | Salem | MA | Hacker,Jeremiah | |
| 154 | 6 | 7 | 7 | Newbury | MA | Sawyer,Danl | |
| 154 | 7 | 8 | 7 | Amesbury | MA | | |
| 154 | 7 | 8 | 7 | Hampton | NH | | |
| 154 | 1 | 9 | 7 | Hampton | NH | | |
| 154 | 2 | 10 | 7 | Hampton | NH | Law,Abram | Rotch,Wm+w+sis |
| 154 | 2 | 10 | 7 | Hampton | NH | Barney,Sarah | Hogg,Nathan |
| 154 | 3 | 11 | 7 | Kittery | NH | | |
| 155 | 3 | 11 | 7 | Dover | NH | Easton,Jos | |
| 155 | 4 | 12 | 7 | Berwick | ME | Morrell,Peter | |
| 155 | 5 | 13 | 7 | Falmouth | ME | Winslow,Benj | |
| 156 | 6 | 14 | 7 | Merryconeeg | ME | Eagles,Widow | |
| 156 | 7 | 15 | 7 | en route | ME | Winslow,Benj+s | Neale,Jas+w |
| 156 | 1 | 16 | 7 | Falmouth | ME | | |
| 156 | 2 | 17 | 7 | Bedford | ME | | |
| 157 | 2 | 17 | 7 | Berwick | ME | | |
| 157 | 3 | 18 | 7 | Dover | NH | Easton,Jos | Daw,Abram |
| 157 | 3-4 | 18-19 | 7 | Newbury | MA | | |
| 157 | 5 | 20 | 7 | Boston | MA | Collins,Zach | Pemberton,John |
| 159 | 6 | 21 | 7 | Boston | MA | Bagnall,Benj | Wheeler,Obadiah |
| 159 | 7 | 22 | 7 | Bolton | MA | | |
| 159 | 1 | 23 | 7 | Uxbridge | MA | Wheeler,Obadiah | |
| 160 | 2 | 24 | 7 | Mendon | MA | Aldridge,Caleb | |
| 160 | 3 | 25 | 7 | Woonsocket | RI | Aldridge,Caleb | |
| 161 | 3 | 26 | 7 | Smithfield | RI | Hopkins,Stephen | |
| 161 | 4 | 26 | 7 | Providence | RI | | |
| 161 | 5 | 27 | 7 | Taunton | MA | Harvey,Widow | Shaw,Theophilus |
| 162 | 6 | 28 | 7 | Freetown | MA | Bown,Hy+w+d | |
| 162 | 7 | 29 | 7 | Swansea | MA | | |
| 163 | 7 | 29 | 7 | Providence | RI | | |

| Journal page | Day 1-7 | Date Day | Mo. | Place | Colony | Names in journal | |
|---|---|---|---|---|---|---|---|
| 163 | **1** | 30 | 7 | Shantecut | RI | Potter,Thos | |
| 163 | **1** | 30 | 7 | Warwick | RI | | |
| 163 | **1** | 30 | 7 | Greenwich | RI | Aldrige,Thos | |
| 164 | 2 | 31 | 7 | Greenwich | RI | Hazard,Thos | |
| 164 | 3 | 1 | 8 | South Kingston | RI | Pukem,Peeleck | Davis,Peter |
| 164 | 3 | 1 | 8 | South Kingston | RI | Corladen,Jos | |
| 164 | 3 | 1 | 8 | James Ferry | RI | | |
| 164 | 4 | 2 | 8 | Richmond | RI | | |
| 165 | 4 | 2 | 8 | Hopkinton | RI | Hoxer,Solomon | Collins,John |
| 165 | 5 | 3 | 8 | Pawcatuck | CT | | |
| 165 | 5 | 3 | 8 | New London | CT | | |
| 165 | 5 | 3 | 8 | Hope Ferry | CT | | |
| 165 | 5 | 3 | 8 | Sea Brook Ferry | CT | Leigh,- | |
| 165 | 6 | 4 | 8 | Newhaven | CT | Hazard,Thos | Collins,John |
| 166 | 7 | 5 | 8 | Fairfield | CT | | |
| 166 | 7 | 5 | 8 | Stamford | CT | | |
| 166 | 7 | 5 | 8 | Hornneck | NY | | |
| 166 | **1** | 6 | 8 | Purchase | NY | Nottingham,Sam'l | Clap,John |
| 167 | 2 | 7 | 8 | Bedford (near) | NY | Trip,Anthony | Baker,Ephraim |
| 168 | 3 | 8 | 8 | Peach Pond | NY | Combstock,Thos | Salkeld,G |
| 168 | 4 | 9 | 8 | New Milford | CT | Hazard,Thos | Collins,John |
| 168 | 4 | 9 | 8 | Oblong | NY | Skinner,Jos | Wheeler,Obadiah |
| 168 | 5 | 10 | 8 | Oblong | NY | Ogburn,Jane | Ferris,Benj |
| 168 | 5 | 10 | 8 | Nine Partners | NY | Mott,John | Mott,Jas |
| 169 | 6 | 11 | 8 | Nine Partners | NY | Neale,Aaron | Moore,Andrew |
| 169 | 7 | 12 | 8 | Oswego | NY | Darling,Sam'l | Backer,Sam'l |
| 169 | **1** | 13 | 8 | Amawalk | NY | Weston,Jos | Powles,Moses |
| 170 | 2 | 14 | 8 | Chappaqua | NY | Underhill,Thos+f | Clap,Jas |
| 171 | 3 | 15 | 8 | Purchase | NY | Camwell,John | |
| 171 | 3 | 15 | 8 | White Plains | NY | Burleigh,Edwd | |
| 171 | 4 | 16 | 8 | Mamaroneck | NY | Cornal,John | Neale,Aaron |
| 171 | 4 | 16 | 8 | Westchester | NY | Ogburn,Paul | |
| 171 | 5 | 17 | 8 | Westchester | NY | | |
| 171 | 5 | 17 | 8 | Kingsbridge | NY | Franklin,Walter | |
| 172 | 5 | 17 | 8 | New York | NY | | |
| 173 | 6 | 18 | 8 | New York | NY | Franklin,Wm | |
| 173 | 7 | 19 | 8 | Newark | NJ | | |
| 173 | 7 | 19 | 8 | Rahway | NJ | Shotwell,Jos | |

| Journal page | Day 1-7 | Date Day | Mo. | Place | Colony | Names in journal | |
|---|---|---|---|---|---|---|---|
| 173 | **1** | 20 | 8 | Woodbridge | NJ | | |
| 173 | 2 | 21 | 8 | Woodbridge | NJ | Nottingham,S | |
| 173 | 3 | 22 | 8 | Plainfield | NJ | Hunt,Solomon | Shotwell,John |
| 174 | 4 | 23 | 8 | Morristown | NJ | | |
| 174 | 4 | 23 | 8 | Minden | NJ | Dill,Nicholas | Morris,John |
| 174 | 5 | 24 | 8 | Hardwick | NJ | Horn,H | Randorf,Timothy |
| 174 | 5 | 24 | 8 | Hardwick | NJ | Lundy,Jacob | |
| 175 | 6 | 25 | 8 | Hardwick | NJ | Wilson,Jacob | |
| 175 | 7 | 26 | 8 | Ridgewood | NJ | Large,Rob't | |
| 175 | 7 | 26 | 8 | Delaware River | | Williams,Benj | |
| 175 | **1** | 27 | 8 | en route | PA | Law,Rich'd | Foulk,John |
| 175 | **1** | 27 | 8 | Plumstead | PA | Pennington,Dan'l | |
| 176 | 2 | 28 | 8 | Plumstead | PA | Wilson,Sam'l | Kinsley,Benj d |
| 176 | 2 | 28 | 8 | Buckingham | PA | Ellis,Hugh+w | |
| 176 | 3 | 29 | 8 | Wrightstown | PA | Vere,Rob't | Clifford,Ann |
| 176 | 3 | 29 | 8 | Marisfield | PA | Morris,Hannah | Morris,John |
| 176 | 3 | 29 | 8 | Marisfield | PA | White,Jos | Taylor,Barnard |
| 176 | 4 | 30 | 8 | Falls, The | PA | White,Jos | Stanton,Dan'l |
| 177 | 5 | 31 | 8 | Bristol | PA | Williams,Encon | Moore,Sarah |
| 178 | 6 | 1 | 9 | Bristol | PA | Buckley,Wm | Morris,Sarah |
| 178 | 6 | 1 | 9 | Middletown | PA | Emlen,J | |
| 178 | 7 | 2 | 9 | Middletown | PA | Jones,Rebecca | White,Jos |
| 178 | 7 | 2 | 9 | North Wales | PA | Wilson,Grace+ch | Wilson,Anthony |
| 178 | 7 | 2 | 9 | North Wales | PA | Evans,John | |
| 179 | **1** | 3 | 9 | North Wales | PA | Potts,Jos | Morris,Sarah |
| 179 | **1** | 3 | 9 | Spring Mill | PA | Morris,Deborah | Fisher,Thos |
| 179 | 2 | 4 | 9 | Spring Mill | PA | Hunt,John | Pemberton,John |
| 179 | 2 | 4 | 9 | Plymouth | PA | Pemberton,Israel | Morris,John |
| 179 | 2 | 4 | 9 | Plymouth | PA | Potts,J | Jacobs,Israel |
| 179 | 3 | 5 | 9 | New Providence | PA | Hopson,Francis | Graves,Peter |
| 179 | 3 | 5 | 9 | Exeter | PA | Potter,Widow | |
| 179 | 4 | 6 | 9 | Exeter | PA | Morris,John | |
| 180 | 4 | 6 | 9 | Reading | PA | Hughes,Sam'l | Steer,Jas |
| 180 | 5 | 7 | 9 | Maidencreek | PA | Stow,John | Parvin,Francis |
| 180 | 6 | 8 | 9 | Schuykill River | PA | | |
| 181 | 6 | 8 | 9 | Robeson | PA | Loader,John | |

| Journal page | Day 1-7 | Date Day | Mo. | Place | Colony | Names in journal | |
|---|---|---|---|---|---|---|---|
| 181 | 7 | 9 | 9 | Nantmeal | PA | Potts,Thos+w+mthr | Lightfoot,Susannah |
| 181 | 7 | 9 | 9 | Pikeland | PA | Meredith,Grace | |
| 181 | 7 | 9 | 9 | Pikeland | PA | Lightfoot,Thos +w | |
| 181 | **1** | 10 | 9 | Upland | PA | | |
| 192 | 2 | 11 | 9 | Valley, The | PA | Lightfoot,Thos +w | Walker,Israel |
| 192 | 2 | 11 | 9 | Radnor | PA | Haven,David+sis | Jones,David |
| 192 | 3 | 12 | 9 | Radnor | PA | Thomas,Thos+w | |
| 192 | 3 | 12 | 9 | Newtown | PA | Lewis,Wm | |
| 192 | 4 | 13 | 9 | Springfield | PA | Yarnall,Mordecai | Green,John w |
| 193 | 4 | 13 | 9 | Hartford | PA | Humphries,Chas | Lightfoot,S |
| 193 | 5 | 14 | 9 | Radnor | PA | Jones,Jonathan | Roberts,John |
| 194 | 6 | 15 | 9 | Merion | NJ | George,Jesse+mthr | |
| 194 | 7 | 16 | 9 | Haddonfield | NJ | Hopkins,Sarah | |
| 194 | **1** | 17 | 9 | Evesham | NJ | Morris,Sarah | Andrews,Isaac+w |
| 194 | **1** | 17 | 9 | Mount Holly | NJ | Foster,Wm | |
| 194 | 2 | 18 | 9 | Mount Holly | NJ | Hoskins,Thos | |
| 195 | 2 | 18 | 9 | Sheremount | NJ | | |
| 195 | 2 | 18 | 9 | en route | NJ | Dillwyn,Wm | |
| 195 | 3 | 19 | 9 | Upper Springfield | NJ | Stockton,John | |
| 196 | 3 | 19 | 9 | Old Springfield | NJ | | |
| 196 | 3 | 19 | 9 | Burlington | NJ | Smith,John | |
| 196 | 4 | 20 | 9 | Rancocas | NJ | Stoker,John | |
| 196 | 4 | 20 | 9 | Morristown | NJ | | |
| 197 | 5-6 | 21-22 | 9 | Haddonfield | NJ | Stabler,Edwd | |
| 197 | 7 | 23 | 9 | Philadelphia | PA | Janney,Sarah | Jones,Owen |
| 198 | **1** | 24 | 9 | Bank,The | PA | Morris,John | |
| 198 | 2 | 25 | 9 | Market Street | PA | Pemberton,Israel | |
| 199 | 3 | 26 | 9 | Philadelphia | PA | Wharton,Thos | Janney,Sarah |
| 199 | 4 | 27 | 9 | Philadelphia | PA | Wharton,Jeremiah | Moore,Ann |
| 199 | 5 | 28 | 9 | Philadelphia | PA | Evans,Thos+ch | |
| 201 | 6 | 29 | 9 | Little Egg Harbour | NJ | Noble,Sam'l | G[arnett],Ann |
| 201 | 6 | 29 | 9 | Barnegat | NJ | Ridgeway,Timothy | |
| 201 | 7 | 30 | 9 | Egg Harbour | NJ | Ridgeway,John | |
| 201 | **1** | 1 | 10 | Marsh, The | NJ | Ridgeway,John | |
| 201 | **1** | 1 | 10 | Upper Gt Egg Harbour | NJ | Andrews,Isaac | Thompson,Josh |
| 201 | **1** | 1 | 10 | Great Egg Harbour | NJ | Smith,Noah | |
| 201 | **1** | 1 | 10 | Great Egg Harbour | NJ | | |

| Journal page | Day 1-7 | Date Day | Mo. | Place | Col-ony | Names in journal | |
|---|---|---|---|---|---|---|---|
| 202 | 2 | 2 | 10 | Cape May | NJ | Woman,Widow | Reeves,Benj |
| 202 | 2 | 2 | 10 | Greenwich | NJ | Noble,Sam'l | Evans,Thos+s |
| 202 | 2 | 2 | 10 | Greenwich | NJ | Foster,Wm | Andrews,Isaac |
| 203 | 3 | 3 | 10 | England Town [New] | NJ | Townsend,Isaac | Reeves,Mark |
| 203 | 3 | 3 | 10 | Cohansey River | NJ | Reeves,M sis+ch | |
| 203 | 4 | 4 | 10 | Cohansey River | NJ | | |
| 204 | 4 | 4 | 10 | Greenwich | NJ | Reeves,Benj | Daniel,Jas |
| 204 | 4 | 4 | 10 | Alloways Creek | NJ | Reeves,Mark | Shepherd,Priscilla |
| 204 | 5 | 5 | 10 | Alloways Creek | NJ | Thompson,Josh | Smith,Rich'd |
| 205 | 6 | 6 | 10 | Salem | NJ | Goodwin,Thos | Reeves,Mark |
| 205 | 6 | 6 | 10 | Pinestock Ferry | NJ | Daniel,Amos | Shepherd,Priscilla |
| 205 | 6 | 6 | 10 | Pinestock Ferry | NJ | Burgas,Jas+w+sis | Morris,John |
| 205 | 6 | 6 | 10 | Newcastle | DE | Sweet,Benj s | |
| 205 | 6 | 6 | 10 | Newcastle | DE | | |
| 205 | 7 | 7 | 10 | Nottingham | PA | Sharples,Benj | Churchman,John |
| 205 | 7 | 7 | 10 | East Nottingham | PA | Churchman,Geo | |
| 205 | **1** | 8 | 10 | East Nottingham | PA | | |
| 206 | **1** | 8 | 10 | West Nottingham | PA | Reynolds,Hy | |
| 206 | 2 | 9 | 10 | Little Britain | PA | King,Michael | Rigby,Ian |
| 206 | 2 | 9 | 10 | Susquehanna River | PA | Rigby,Jas s | |
| 207 | 3 | 10 | 10 | Deer Creek | MD | Cox,Wm+w | Pemberton,Jos |
| 207 | 3 | 10 | 10 | Bush River | MD | Wilson,John+w | |
| 207 | 4 | 11 | 10 | Bush River | MD | Webster,Isaac | Wilson,Hy |
| 208 | 5 | 12 | 10 | Falls, The | MD | Wilson,Benj | |
| 208 | 6 | 13 | 10 | Falls, The | MD | Matthews,Oliver | Hopkins,Rich'd |
| 208 | 6 | 13 | 10 | Gunpowder | MD | | |
| 210 | 7 | 14 | 10 | Palapsee | MD | Hopkins,Gervase | |
| 210 | **1** | 15 | 10 | Elkridge | MD | Pierpoint,Hy | Brooke,Roger |
| 210 | 2 | 16 | 10 | Sandy Spring | MD | Thomas,Rich'd | Snowden,Sam'l |
| 211 | 3 | 17 | 10 | Indian Spring | MD | Waters,Sam'l | Stephenson,Dan'l |
| 211 | 3 | 17 | 10 | Patuxent | MD | Plummer,Wm | |
| 211 | 4 | 18 | 10 | Patuxent | MD | | |
| 211 | 4 | 18 | 10 | West River | MD | | |
| 211 | 5 | 19 | 10 | Herring Creek | MD | Chew,- | |
| 212 | 6 | 20 | 10 | en route | MD | Johns,Widow | Janney,Sarah |
| 212 | 6 | 20 | 10 | Kent Island | MD | Thomas,Philip | Chew,Philip |

| Journal page | Day 1-7 | Date Day | Mo. | Place | Colony | Names in journal | |
|---|---|---|---|---|---|---|---|
| 212 | 7 | 21 | 10 | Kent Island | MD | Pemberton,Jos | |
| 212 | 7 | 21 | 10 | Bay, The | MD | Camp,John | Bartlet,Jos |
| 212 | 7 | 21 | 10 | Bay, The | MD | Morris,John | Pleasants,Rob't |
| 213 | 7 | 21 | 10 | Bay, The | MD | Thomas,Philip+w | Pemberton,Jos |
| 213 | 7 | 21 | 10 | Chew Island | MD | Chew,Philip | |
| 213 | 7 | 21 | 10 | Chew Island | MD | | |
| 213 | **1** | 22 | 10 | Third Haven | MD | Morris,Sarah | Fisher,Esther |
| 213 | **1** | 22 | 10 | Third Haven | MD | Sweet,Benj | Bartlet,Jos |
| 214 | 2 | 23 | 10 | Third Haven | MD | Burpson,Benj | Troth,Hy |
| 214 | 3 | 24 | 10 | Choptank River | MD | Edmondson,P+w | |
| 215 | 4 | 25 | 10 | en route | MD | Lightfoot,Thos | |
| 215 | 5 | 26 | 10 | Lewistown | MD | Lightfoot,Wm | Rodney,John |
| 215 | 5 | 26 | 10 | Mothers Hill | DE | Rowlands,Sam'l | |
| 215 | 6 | 27 | 10 | Mothers Hill | DE | Rowlands,Sam'l s | Mifflin,Warner |
| 216 | 7 | 28 | 10 | Little Creek | DE | Vinning,John+w | |
| 217 | **1** | 29 | 10 | Dover | DE | Hanson,Sam'l | |
| 217 | 2 | 30 | 10 | Duck Creek | DE | Sweet,Benj | Hanson,Thos |
| 217 | 3 | 31 | 10 | Newcastle | DE | Fisher,G | |
| 217 | 3 | 31 | 10 | Newcastle | DE | Store,Isaac | Store,Thos+w+bro |
| 217 | 3 | 31 | 10 | Delaware River | | | |
| 218 | 3 | 31 | 10 | Salem | NJ | Goodwin,Thos | |
| 218 | 4 | 1 | 11 | Pilesgrove | NJ | Hopkins,Sarah | Davies,David |
| 218 | 4 | 1 | 11 | Upper Greenwich | NJ | Lipencote,Caleb | |
| 218 | 5 | 2 | 11 | Upper Greenwich | NJ | Lord,Josh | Cooper,Jas |
| 218 | 5 | 2 | 11 | Woodbury | NJ | Cooper,David | |
| 219 | 6 | 3 | 11 | Woodbury | NJ | Pemberton,Israel | Fisher,T |
| 219 | 6 | 3 | 11 | Philadelphia | PA | Gilpin,Thos | Hopkins,John |
| 219 | 7 | 4 | 11 | Philadelphia | PA | Haines,Isaac | Brown,Wm |
| 219 | 7 | 4 | 11 | Newtown | PA | Wilson,Widow | Mott,Sarah |
| 220 | **1** | 5 | 11 | Newtown | PA | Emlen,Sam'l | Cooper,Wm |
| 220 | **1** | 5 | 11 | Philadelphia | PA | Smith,Rich'd | |
| 220 | 2 | 6 | 11 | Philadelphia | PA | Dishley,David | Moreton,John+w |
| 220 | 2 | 6 | 11 | Philadelphia | PA | Mason,Geo | Hunt,John |
| 220 | 2 | 6 | 11 | Philadelphia | PA | Stanton,David | Morris,Sarah |
| 220 | 2 | 6 | 11 | Philadelphia | PA | Pemberton,Isr'l+w | Lightfoot,T+w |
| 221 | 3 | 7 | 11 | Philadelphia | PA | Morris,Widow | |
| 222 | 4 | 8 | 11 | Frankford | PA | Pemberton,Mary | James,Abel |
| 222 | 4 | 8 | 11 | Fairhill | MD | Pemberton,Israel | |

| Journal page | Day 1-7 | Date Day | Mo. | Place | Colony | Names in journal | |
|---|---|---|---|---|---|---|---|
| 223 | 5 | 9 | 11 | Fairhill | MD | Haskins,Jos | Falconer,Capt |
| 223 | 5 | 9 | 11 | Chester | PA | Moreton,Phebe | Fisher,Esther |
| 223 | 5 | 9 | 11 | Chester | PA | Morris,D w | Morris,Sarah |
| 223 | 5 | 9 | 11 | On board boat | | Fisher,Thos&Sarah | Wellbank,Abram |
| 224 | 6-7 | 10-11 | 11 | Delaware Bay | | | |
| from225 | **1** | 12 | 11 | Voyage home | | Montgomery,John | Nancy |
| to 229 | 6 | 8 | 12 | including 4 **"1st days"** | | James,Abel | Stroud,Isaac |
| 229 | 7 | 9 | 12 | Deal | Engl | | |
| 229 | **1** | 10 | 12 | Canterbury | Engl | | |
| 229 | **1** | 10 | 12 | Canterbury | Engl | | |
| 229 | **1** | 10 | 12 | en route | Engl | | |
| 230 | 2 | 11 | 12 | London | Engl | | |
| 230 | 3 | 12 | 12 | St Albans | Engl | Chester,Rich'd+w | Roberts,John+s |
| 230 | 4-5 | 13-14 | 12 | en route | Engl | | |
| 230 | 6 | 15 | 12 | Kendal | Engl | | |

LIST OF PLACES A -Z

LIST OF PEOPLE A - Z

# MAPS

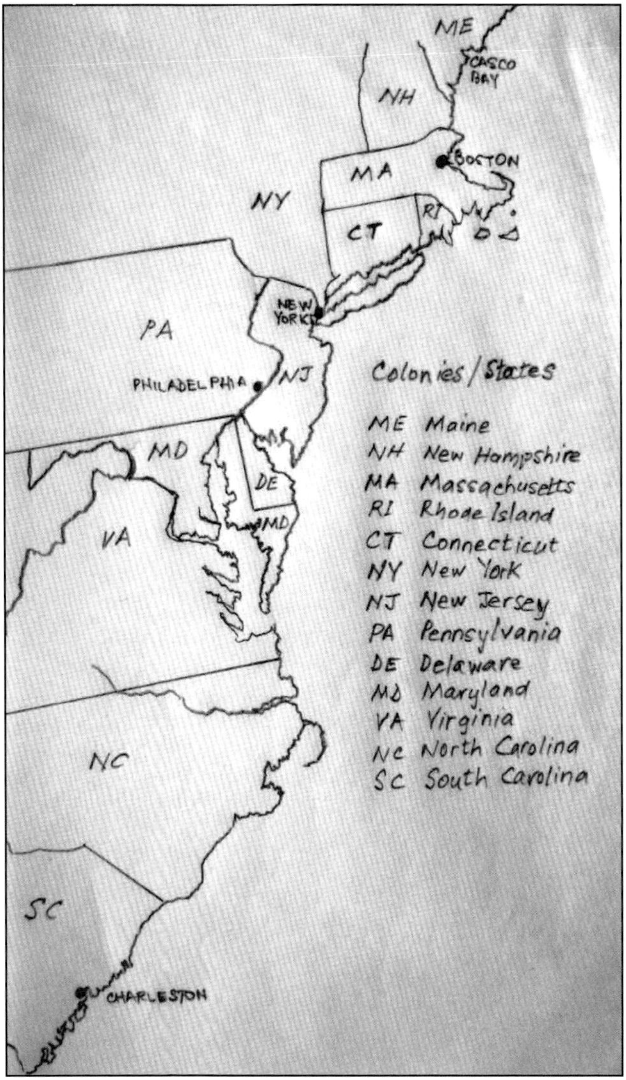
ME
CASCO BAY
NH
BOSTON
MA
NY
RI
CT
NEW YORK
PA
PHILADELPHIA
NJ
MD
DE
MD
VA
NC
SC
CHARLESTON
Colonies/States
ME Maine
NH New Hampshire
MA Massachusetts
RI Rhode Island
CT Connecticut
NY New York
NJ New Jersey
PA Pennsylvania
DE Delaware
MD Maryland
VA Virginia
NC North Carolina
SC South Carolina

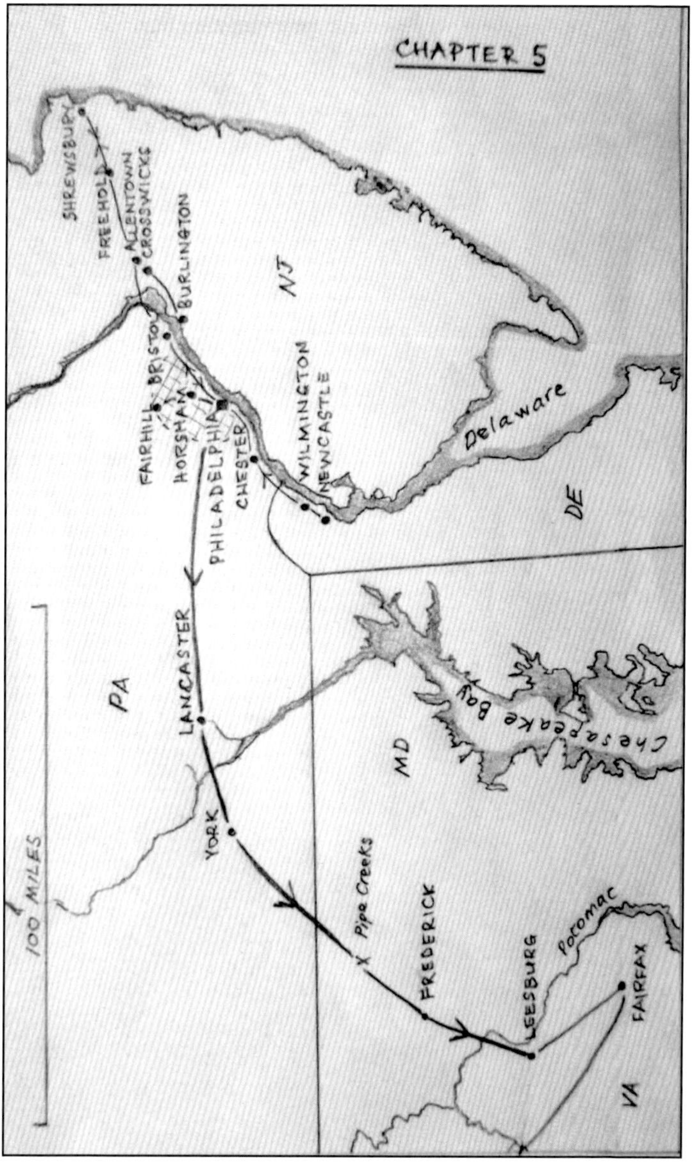
CHAPTER 5
SHREWSBURY
FREEHOLD
ALLENTOWN
CROSSWICKS
BURLINGTON
NJ
BRISTO
FAIRHILL
HORSHAM
PHILADELPHIA
CHESTER
WILMINGTON
NEWCASTLE
Delaware
DE
PA
LANCASTER
MD
Chesapeake Bay
YORK
Pipe Creeks
FREDERICK
Pocomac
LEESBURG
FAIRFAX
VA
100 MILES

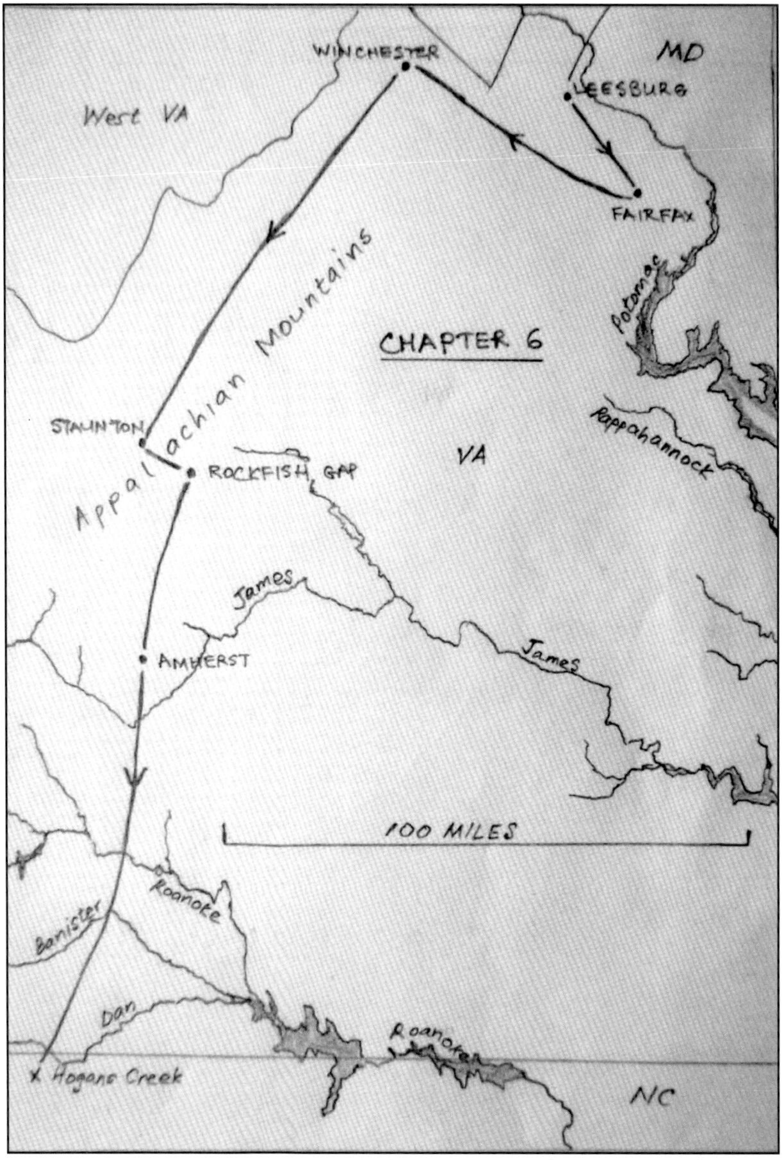
WINCHESTER
MD
LEESBURG
West VA
FAIRFAX
Appalachian Mountains
Potomac
CHAPTER 6
STAUNTON
Rappahannock
VA
ROCKFISH GAP
James
AMHERST
James
100 MILES
Roanoke
Banister
Dan
Roanoke
Hogans Creek
NC

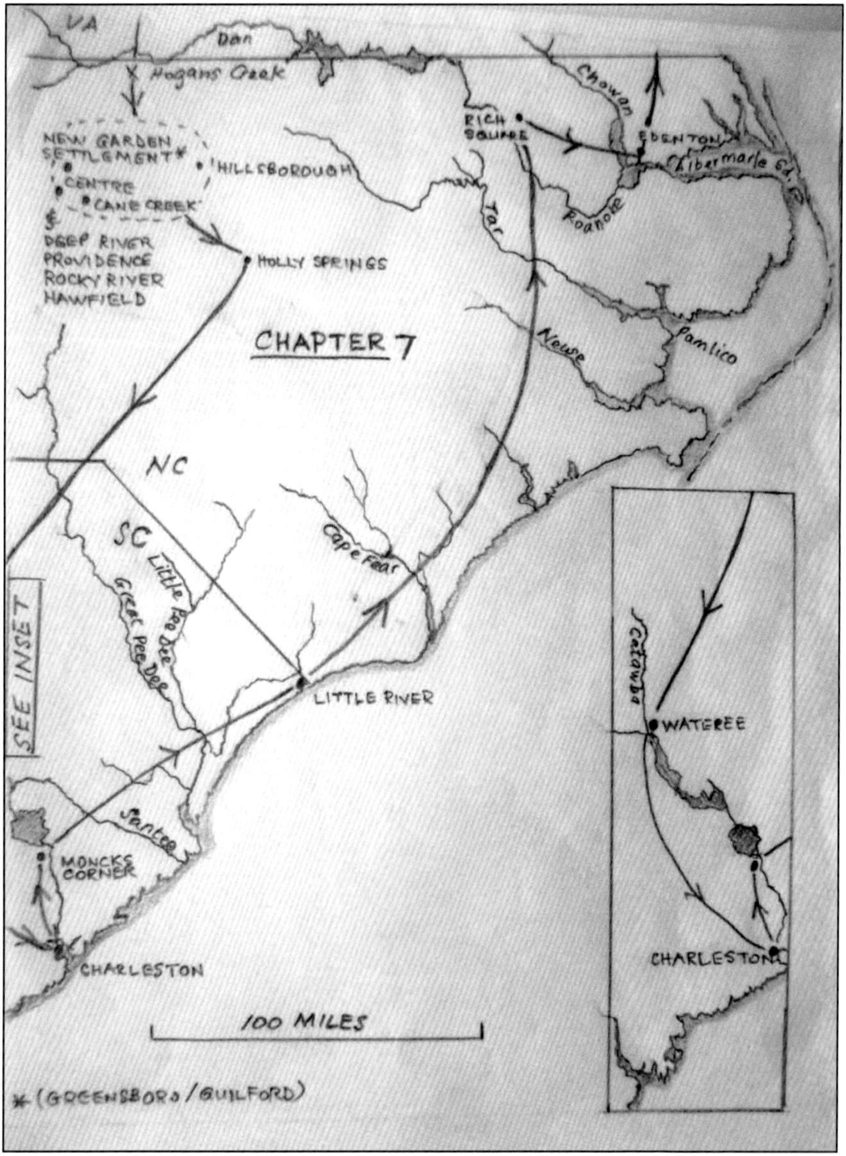
VA
Dan
Hogans Creek
Chowan
RICH SQUARE
EDENTON
Albermarle Sd.
NEW GARDEN SETTLEMENT*
HILLSBOROUGH
CENTRE
CANE CREEK
&
DEEP RIVER
PROVIDENCE
ROCKY RIVER
HAWFIELD
Tar
Roanoke
HOLLY SPRINGS
CHAPTER 7
Neuse
Pamlico
NC
SC
Little Pee Dee
Great Pee Dee
Cape Fear
SEE INSET
LITTLE RIVER
Santee
MONCKS CORNER
CHARLESTON
100 MILES
* (GREENSBORO/GUILFORD)
Catawba
WATEREE
CHARLESTON

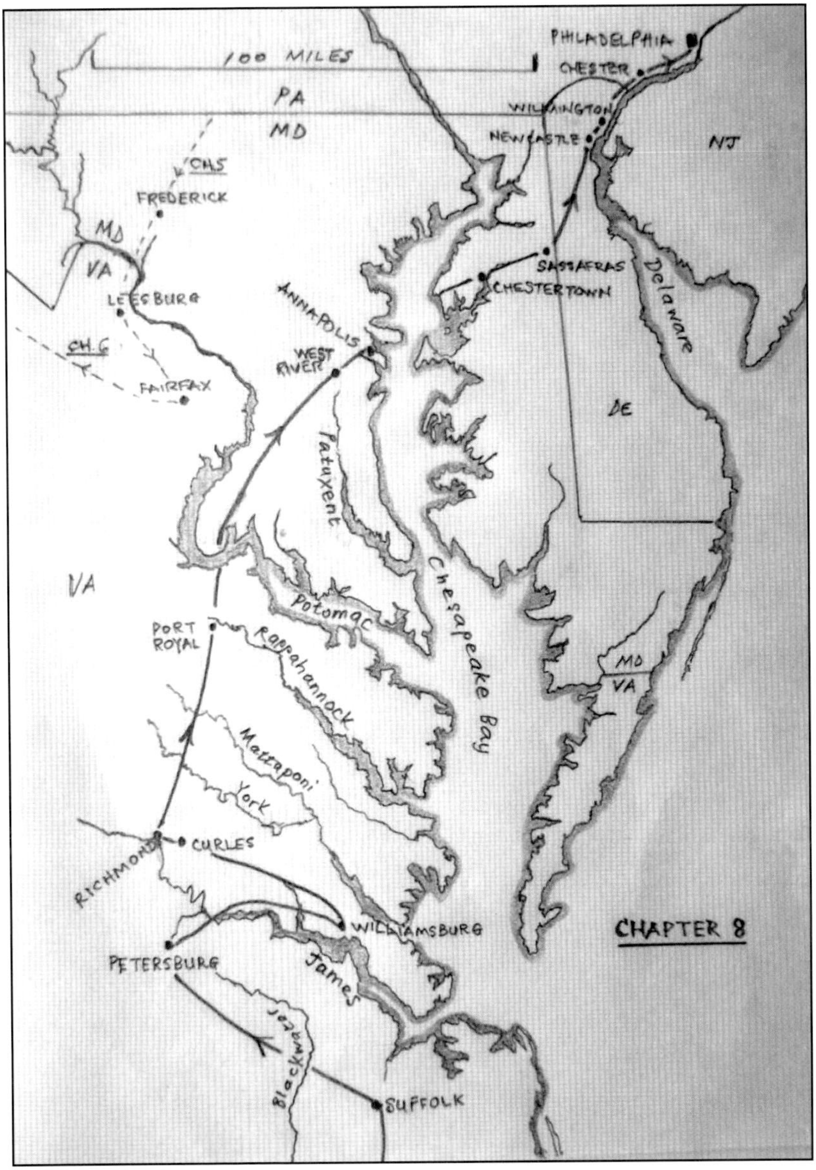
100 MILES
PA
MD
PHILADELPHIA
CHESTER
WILMINGTON
NEWCASTLE
NJ
CH.5
FREDERICK
MD
VA
SASSAFRAS
CHESTERTOWN
Delaware
LEESBURG
ANNAPOLIS
CH.6
WEST RIVER
FAIRFAX
DE
Patuxent
VA
Chesapeake Bay
Potomac
PORT ROYAL
Rappahannock
MD
VA
Mattaponi
York
RICHMOND
CURLES
WILLIAMSBURG
CHAPTER 8
PETERSBURG
James
Blackwater
SUFFOLK

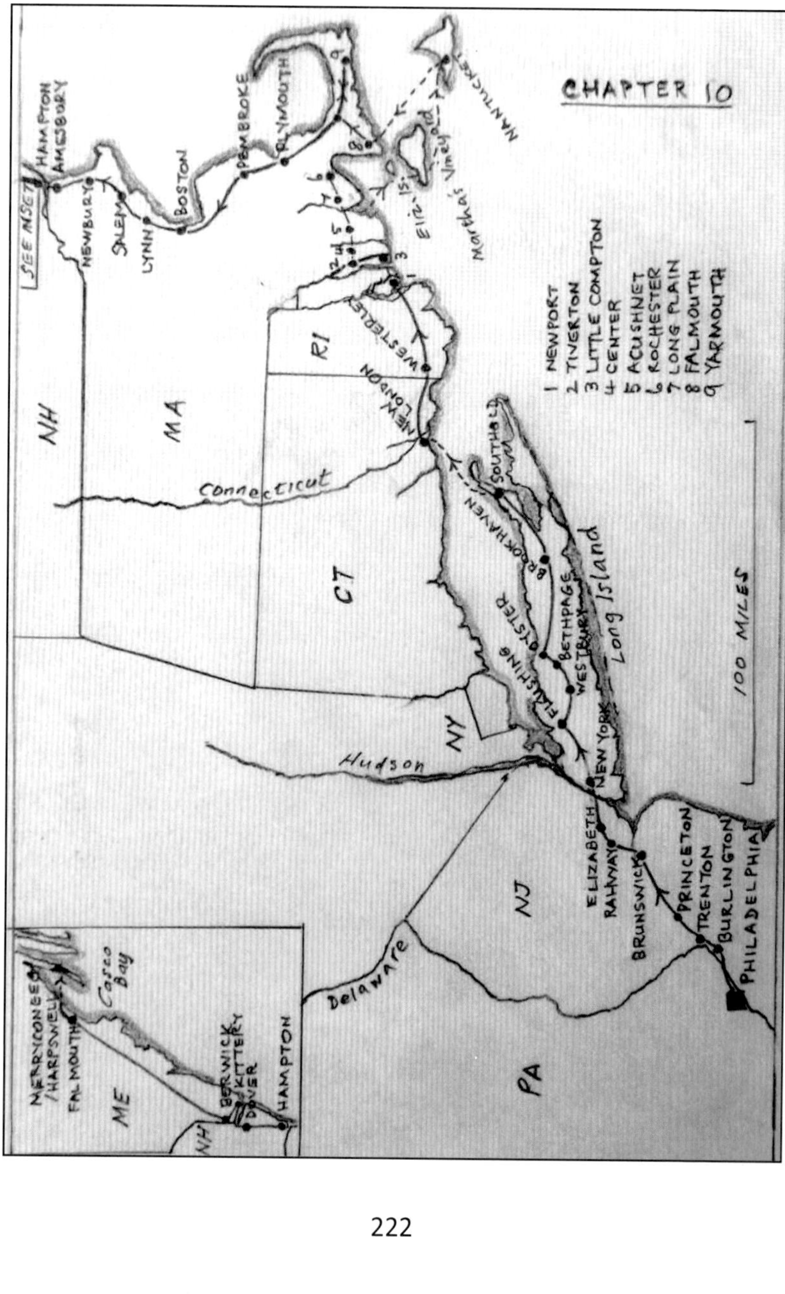
CHAPTER 10
1 NEWPORT
2 TIVERTON
3 LITTLE COMPTON
4 CENTER
5 ACUSHNET
6 ROCHESTER
7 LONG PLAIN
8 FALMOUTH
9 YARMOUTH
100 MILES
SEE INSET
HAMPTON
AMESBURY
NEWBURY
SALEM
LYNN
BOSTON
PEMBROKE
PLYMOUTH
NANTUCKET
Martha's Vineyard
Eliz. Is.
NH
MA
RI
CT
NY
NJ
PA
WESTERLY
NEW LONDON
Connecticut
SOUTHOLD
BROOKHAVEN
OYSTER
BETHPAGE
WESTBURY
FLUSHING
Long Island
NEW YORK
Hudson
ELIZABETH
RAHWAY
BRUNSWICK
PRINCETON
TRENTON
BURLINGTON
PHILADELPHIA
Delaware
ME
MERRYCONEEG
/HARPSWELL
FALMOUTH
Casco Bay
BERWICK
KITTERY
DOVER
HAMPTON

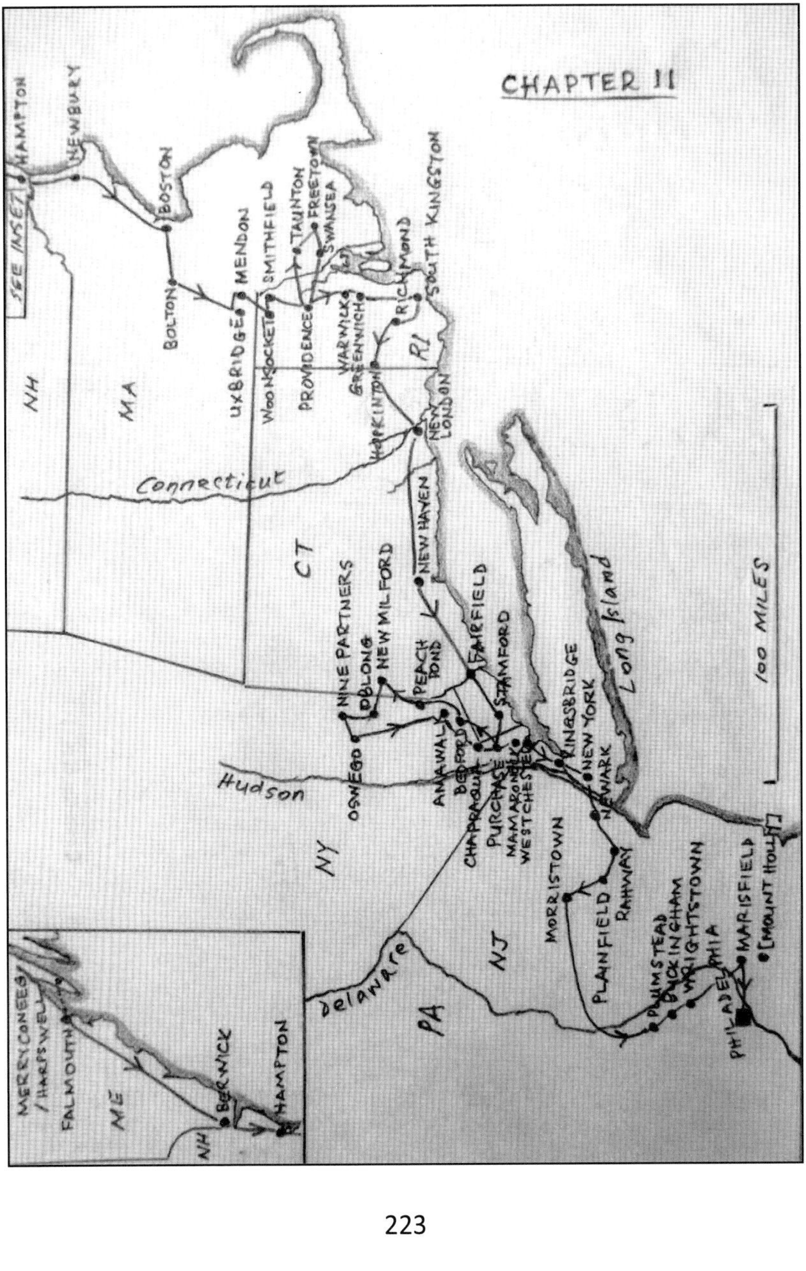
CHAPTER II
SEE INSET
HAMPTON
NEWBURY
BOSTON
NH
MA
BOLTON
MENDON
UXBRIDGE
WOONSOCKET
SMITHFIELD
TAUNTON
FREETOWN
SWANSEA
PROVIDENCE
WARWICK
GREENWICH
RICHMOND
SOUTH KINGSTON
RI
HOPKINTON
NEW LONDON
Connecticut
CT
NEW HAVEN
NINE PARTNERS
OBLONG
NEW MILFORD
PEACH POND
FAIRFIELD
STAMFORD
Long Island
KINGSBRIDGE
NEW YORK
NEWARK
100 MILES
Hudson
OSWEGO
AMAWALK
BEDFORD
CHAPPAQUA
PURCHASE
MAMARONECK
WESTCHESTER
NY
MORRISTOWN
PLAINFIELD
RAHWAY
NJ
Delaware
PA
PLUMSTEAD
BUCKINGHAM
WRIGHTSTOWN
PHILADELPHIA
MARISFIELD
[MOUNT HOLLY]
MERRYCONEEG / HARPSWELL
FALMOUTH
ME
BERWICK
HAMPTON
NH

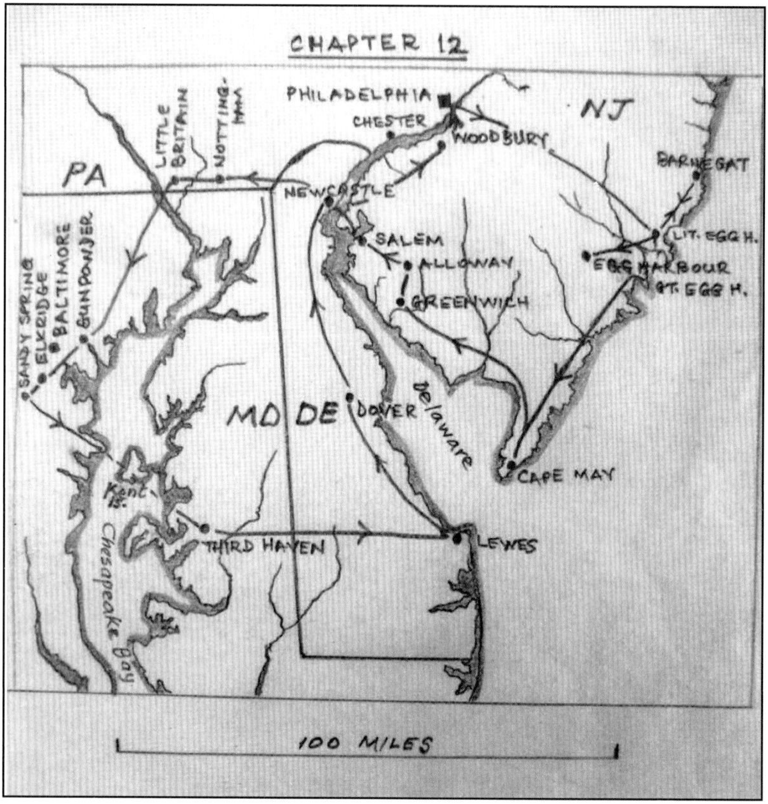


*Maps pp.217-224 (and photograph p.7) by Geoffrey Braithwaite*